D1482533

The Movies as History

The Movies as History

Visions of the Twentieth Century

EDITED BY DAVID ELLWOOD

LIBRARY
CALDWELL COMMUNITY COLLEGE
HUDSON, NC

DISCARDED

SUTTON PUBLISHING

HISTORY TODAY

These articles were first published in *History Today* between 1995 and 2000.
This selection with a new Introduction first published in 2000 by
Sutton Publishing Limited · Phoenix Mill
Thrupp · Stroud · Gloucestershire · GL5 2BU

Copyright © *History Today*, 2000

00-01 IN 16.89

All rights reserved. No part of this publication may be reproduced, stored in a retrieval system, or transmitted, in any form, or by any means, electronic, mechanical, photocopying, recording or otherwise, without the prior permission of the publisher and copyright holder.

British Library Cataloguing in Publication Data
A catalogue record for this book is available from the British Library

ISBN 0 7509 2331 8   00-01

Published with the support of the International Association for Media and History

*Iam*hist
The International Association for
Media and History

http:/www.leeds.ac.uk/ics/iamhist

Videos of all films discussed in this book can be obtained from filmworld.co.uk quoting *History Today* when ordering

Typeset in 10.5/15 Photina
Typesetting and origination by
Sutton Publishing Limited
Printed in Great Britain by
Redwood Books, Trowbridge, Wiltshire.

CONTENTS

Part Four: Films of Romance and Fantasy

LIST OF ILLUSTRATIONS

NOTES ON CONTRIBUTORS

Anthony Aldgate is Reader in Film and History at the Open University

David Culbert is Professor of History at Louisiana State University and Editor of the *Historical Journal of Film, Radio and Television*

Nicholas Cull is Professor of American Studies and Director of the Centre for American Studies at the University of Leicester

Modris Eksteins is Professor of History at the University of Toronto

David Ellwood is Associate Professor of Politics at the University of Bologna

Stephen Gundle is Senior Lecturer in Italian at Royal Holloway, the University of London

Sue Harper is Reader in Film History at the University of Portsmouth

Susan Hayward is Chair of French at the University of Exeter

Peter Krämer is Lecturer in Film Studies at the University of East Anglia

Dan Leab is Professor of History at Seton Hall University

Brian Neve is Lecturer in Politics at the University of Bath

David Nicholls is an independent scholar based in Leeds

Michael Paris is Senior Lecturer in Modern History at the University of Central Lancashire

Jeffrey Richards is Professor of Cultural History at the University of Lancaster

Graham Roberts is Lecturer in Communication Arts at the Institute of Communication, the University of Leeds

Pierre Sorlin was formerly Professor of Sociology of Audiovisual Media at the Université de la Sorbonne Nouvelle, Paris

Peter Stead was formerly Senior Lecturer in History at the University of Wales, Swansea

Sarah Street is a Senior Lecturer in the Department of Drama, Theatre, Film, Television at the University of Bristol

Michael Sturma is Senior Lecturer in History at Murdoch University, Perth, Western Australia

Philip Taylor is Professor of International Communications and Director of the Institute of Communication Studies at the University of Leeds

Brian Winston is Professor of Communication, Design and Media at the University of Westminster

INTRODUCTION

Some films make history, some try to rewrite it, some invent it from scratch. This book is about films as sources of history. The titles chosen are products of different societies at special moments of their recent evolution. Their images and sounds vividly portray the features and the details of those societies. They show their appearance, habits and rituals, their cities and countryside, morals and manners, work and ways of dealing with conflicts.

These movies also have a lot to say about the story of film-making. The stories told here highlight how it was done, who it was done by and who for. They demonstrate how films set out to entertain, enlighten, educate and at times change minds; what brought them success with audiences.

The twenty-one films selected by the contributors to this book show the cinema–society connection at work in a wide variety of historical settings. What the productions have in common is a distinctive capacity to communicate in images, plot, characterisation, music and style, an interpretation of the people and the times which made them. What differentiates them is not just moment and country of origin, but the means they use to convey their messages. Here we have propaganda films, war movies, a semi-documentary, a musical, light comedies, science-fiction and horror fantasies, the film version of a famed historical novel and a variety of feature dramas. There are black-and-white titles and the fruits of glorious Technicolor, the works of single geniuses and blockbusters from great studios. Propaganda made to mobilise masses and classics of artistic achievement sit alongside fun products for an evening's amusement. Action movies for male audiences accompany romantic comedies aimed directly at the huge female part of the cinema-going public.

Almost all the commercial films chosen were in their day – mainly the epoch between 1920 and 1960 when cinema was the dominant form of mass entertainment and enlightenment – big box-office and critical successes, at home and abroad. In this way their historical significance is confirmed and heightened. They had struck chords and found responses in imaginations up and down their societies, even across borders. Two of the later films chosen – *The Exorcist* (1973) and *Star Wars* (1977) – even succeeded in preserving their mass-market appeal over time, reappearing in the original or sequel forms in the late 1990s. In contrast, the official films selected are here because they have gained over the years a status as uniquely appropriate expressions of the ideologies and national sentiments they set out to convey, still seen with affection and recognition in television revisitations, learned discussions and history courses.

Each of the titles in the collection is open to a range of historical readings. Those inclined to see movies as historical remains or artefacts will want to know about each film's production history: how it was conceived, organised and financed, the people and approaches used to shoot and edit it. They will then trace its fate in the chain of marketing and distribution. Above all they will want to know how audiences received it, starting with official backers, going on to critics and festival-goers (when they were significant), and finally, above all, the mass of cinema patrons. These are the starting points for discussions on how a film text relates to its time context, and vice versa. For as the leading European specialist Pierre Sorlin has pointed out, films represent socially produced images, offering in their own terms fictional answers to urgent questions raised by a situation. Or as Peter Krämer puts it in his article here, movies such as *Star Wars* achieve their enormous success not because of any 'message' but 'from the multiplicity of meanings that can be extracted from them, and from the multiple uses they can be put to'.

Viewers who prefer to consider their chosen films as events will ask what it meant to pick out a particular subject or story at a particular moment, and how its treatment – including choices about what was presentable on screen and what was not – provides evidence of the bigger historical processes going on at that time (social, political, moral or whatever). And perhaps changed them: how many unpredicted shifts in attitudes, values, habits, fashions have been attributed to the arrival of key movies? For example, the Americanised features of so much European youth culture owe their origins to the arrival of *The Wild One* with Marlon Brando in 1954, and *Rock Around the Clock* in 1956, both of which set off riots across Britain and the Continent on their arrival. But today Paul McCartney insists that it was the now-neglected pop musical *The Girl Can't Help It* (1956), featuring Little Richard, the Platters, Fats Domino and others, which truly inspired his new generation of rockers. So, as the British producer David Puttnam has written, 'movies are more than fun, and more than big business'. Because they have 'shaped attitudes, created conventions of style and behaviour, reinforced or undermined the wider values of society . . . they are power'.

Hopefully the films in this collection will stimulate readers to find out more about the distinctive societies and film traditions that made them. Even titles with quite similar themes or plots can demonstrate totally different choices in cinematic styles: staging, lighting, locations, costumes, rhythms, visual and spoken languages, sound-tracks and all the rest (the classic example is Kurosawa's 1954 production *The Seven Samurai* and its 1960 Hollywood remake *The Magnificent Seven*). What experts call 'production values' refer not just to the amount of money invested in sets, costumes and key people. The phrase also embraces the relationship between studio and location shooting, the variety of scenes, the richness of the musical treatment, the imaginative and aesthetic effort employed. In time the ways all these factors have combined in their various settings have added up to a series of conventions, which means that anyone used to cinema-going knows by habit what is meant by 'British comedy', 'classic French art film', 'spaghetti western', 'Hollywood block-buster' and so on.

Although these are just some of the most obvious categories, it remains true that the working of creative and productive power in the cinema has tended to reinforce national styles over the long run, in spite of the increase of cross-border or intercontinental co-productions. The celebrated French director Jean-Luc Godard has gone as far as making a distinction between those societies which, in his view, have generated an authentic and original film culture – essentially the US, Russia, France, Italy, India and Japan – and the rest, with their bits and pieces of a film industry. The difference can be important because a true cinema culture is more likely to produce works with a universal significance that endures, while the influence of all the others is more likely to be limited to their national setting. A historical approach that relates the evolution of the single cinematic tradition to the other performing arts, the popular culture, the workings of modernisation in the society which expresses it – taken together with all these elements can show how a national experience has evolved, and what it shares and does not share with the main features of all our cinema history and social history.

The sections that follow are divided thematically and then chronologically. Throughout, each of the articles tells the story of a film and how that film's creation and reception provide evidence of some force of history at work. As the dominant genre relating film, society and history, the impact of war inevitably has to come first in the list of categories presented. So the selection of films studied has been chosen from among those that reflect most effectively the way twentieth-century wars have been represented and understood. Wars create myths of many kinds, sometimes unwittingly, sometimes deliberately. Twentieth-century wars added films very quickly to the stock of military and patriotic legend, and so successful was this effort that the collective memory of the era's major wars has become inseparable from the films those conflicts created. This is the message of the titles in this section, which range from a pioneering 1927 American production on the heroic fliers of the First World War, all the way through to the high-tech fantasy of the 1970s–90s *Star Wars* series.

The items selected for inclusion in the section on propaganda also relate to the big conflicts of this century. The 1927 Soviet production *The Great Way* celebrated the aftermath of the First World War in Russia in the triumph of Bolshevism and the Workers' and Peasants' Revolution. Leni Riefensthal's *Triumph of the Will* (1935) takes on much of its significance because of the forceful visual eloquence it brought to depicting the ideology, the Volk, and the man (Adolf Hitler) who would unleash the Second World War. When the Americans finally entered that conflict the US government and its film industry allies set in motion a vast effort of persuasion to convince every citizen of the stakes and their place in the effort. One of the results was *This Is the Army*, Hollywood's 'most seen, most profitable' effort in the whole of the Second World War. Finally, in a very different key, *I Was a Communist For the FBI* (1951) presents a commercialised form of propaganda produced by a now bereft industry in the worst years of the Cold War. Inviting a comparative reading of totalitarian output with the products of democractic societies, the essays also remind us that film propaganda is easier to study than commercial fiction for the simple reason that it usually comes accompanied by a large paper trail in propaganda ministry archives.

The story of *Citizen Kane*, the opening title in the section on films of social commentary, reveals that even studio-produced entertainment films were often seen as influential means of persuasion and propaganda. But only if the vision of a director or key actor coincided with the public mores of an epoch to produce a lasting impact. Between them Elia Kazan and Marlon Brando determined how *On the Waterfront* (1954) would 'resonate with its time', just as the new star Alberto Sordi and the director Steno brought glory to the theme of Americanisation and its pitfalls in the Italian comedy classic

Un americano a Roma of the same year. It was the combination of the Boulting Brothers and Peter Sellers that turned a loosely structured and unlikely plot into that unforgettable commentary on British industrial relations, *I'm All Right Jack* of 1959, while only Fellini and Mastroianni could have created the imagery and the philosophy of *La Dolce Vita* (1960), a highly characterised reflection on the multiple alienations produced by the new consumer society advancing in those years. Lewis Gilbert's 1966 hit *Alfie* made Michael Caine a star, such was the effectiveness of his portrayal of changing attitudes to youth and sex. Topical and successful films like these demonstrate as explicitly as possible the value of cinema fiction as a primary historical source.

In the opening contribution to the section on films of romance and fantasy, *Madonna of the Seven Moons* (1944) shows how an escapist tale of feminine recklessness gives access not to the realities of how people lived in a particular historical period, 'but to some of its imaginative habits'. These are reflected too in the artistic taste and sensibility of highly creative directors such as Jean Cocteau. His *La Belle et la Bête* (1946) not only went against the dominant trend of social realism produced by the end of the war, it also exalted a non-conventional form of female equality, and even sought to challenge the onrush of Hollywood products that swept into Europe along with the liberation.

In the Italy of the early 1960s disquiet about change and modernisation was sublimated in Luciano Visconti's classic *The Leopard* (1963), which was removed to mid-nineteenth-century Sicily. There the local aristocracy appeared anxious only to discover how few concessions it was necessary to make to ensure that all might remain the same. Reading the film through the lens of art history also reveals the many different visual levels great cinema employs to convey its meaning. Moving away from Europe, the 1950s 're-arrangement of American anxieties' about race lies behind the complex tale of racial and cultural tensions involved in the exhilarating musical spectacle of *South Pacific* (1958), set again in a previous time – the Second World War. In postmodern form the question of displaced anxieties can be seen at work in *Indochine* (1991), a self-conscious reflection on a historical period yet more remote but still remembered and discussed: Vietnam in the formative years of its struggle for independence (1928–32). By using a romantic key to explore post-colonial awareness, the film offers a possible means of reconciling today's French identity with the ambiguous legacy of empire. In total contrast *The Exorcist* (1973) brought its sense of anguish directly to the screen, with a horrific rendering of the presumed evils of its American age – inter-generational conflict, family breakdown, feminism, inhuman science.

The articles in this collection were first published in the 'Film in Context' series in *History Today*. I should like to thank Gordon Marsden, the magazine's editor in 1995, for starting the series and its present editor, Peter Furtado, for his support in bringing it to a new audience. For this edition the articles have been reordered and expertly re-edited by Charlotte Crow, with the special assistance of Jerry Kuehl. Recognition must also go to the Executive Council of the International Association for Media and History, which has partly sponsored the project. Among the contributors are many IAMHIST members. Like the original series, these articles aim to bring a new awareness of movies to everyone who reads or writes history, and a new historical sense to those who love cinema. And because they are classics – each in its own distinctive way – all the films chosen should provide memorable and happy viewing.

David Ellwood

Part One
WAR STORIES

1

WINGS

Michael Paris

In the immediate aftermath of the Armistice in 1918, films dealing directly with the Great War disappeared from American cinema screens. As one cinema history points out:

> Public taste underwent a violent change. Overnight everyone suddenly sickened of the patriotic war pictures which had been turned out wholesale: miles of film had to be scrapped, other pictures taken out of production. There was a general shift . . . to the light fare more suited to a victorious mood.

Not until 1925 was popular interest rekindled. In that year, the box office returns from *The Big Parade*, King Vidor's saga of US soldiers on the Western Front, clearly demonstrated that the war was once again an acceptable subject. However, unlike the romanticised, patriotic features made during the conflict, *The Big Parade* and the films it inspired reflected the prevailing mood of the times by focusing on the folly, waste and suffering of war. The war films of the second half of the 1920s were also distinguished from their predecessors by their massive scale – lavish, expensive productions employing hundreds of extras and providing audiences not only with a condemnation of war, but also with spectacular reconstructions of the horrors of the trenches.

It was in this climate of renewed interest that a chance meeting in early 1926 between John Monk Saunders, a young, ex-Army Air Service pursuit pilot, and Jesse Lasky, head of Paramount Studios, resulted in the creation of one of the most exciting of all the Great War films of the silent era, William Wellman's *Wings*.

Monk Saunders, attempting to pursue a career as a screenwriter, persuaded Lasky that a film dealing with the training and combat experiences of fighter pilots would prove even more successful than *The Big Parade*. Monk Saunders clearly intended to exploit the idealised images of the air fighters that had been created as part of the propaganda drive during the war, and take advantage of the current public fascination with aviation. Lasky, fired by the writer's enthusiasm, decided to take the gamble and commissioned Monk Saunders to produce the film and act as 'advisor' during the shooting. On the recommendation of B.P. Schulberg, Paramount's head of production, William Wellman, a young and relatively inexperienced film-maker, was appointed director.

Hollywood studios had already been attempting to exploit public interest in flying and had released a number of cheaply-produced aviation dramas. Several had even capitalised on the casting of real-life airmen: *Romance of the Air* (1919), for example, starred the American combat pilot Bert Hall, while the 1925 production of *Sky Raider* featured the French ace Charles Nungesser. However, aviation films were notoriously difficult to make; technically challenging, susceptible to weather conditions and requiring a substantial budget to hire aeroplanes, pilots and special equipment. Previous examples often betrayed slipshod production values and failed to make the most of the inherent excitement of the subject. In a period when war films had been generally unpopular, few studios could risk the financial outlay on a feature that attempted to deal seriously with war flying on a large scale.

In the case of *Wings*, however, to minimise the cost of what was intended to be a major project, Monk Saunders suggested enlisting the assistance of the War Department. In an unprecedented decision, the Department agreed to co-operate and allowed government land at Camp Stanley, Texas, to be used for location shooting – while the Army Air Service provided manpower and equipment. Major Oscar Estes was appointed liaison officer between the Department and the studio, and General George Connor took a personal interest in the production.

At a time when Air Service development was limited by budgetary constraints and rivalry with other forces, it might seem surprising that substantial and costly assistance was provided for Paramount's commercial enterprise. However, in July 1926, while the film was in its planning stages, Congress passed the Air Corps Act; legislation which not only changed the name of the Air Service and implied a greater degree of autonomy for the airmen, but also initiated a five-year expansion programme for military aviation. The Air Corps clearly saw *Wings* as a positive propaganda vehicle which would enhance the reputation of the air service and stimulate recruitment.

Filming began in the late summer of 1926 near San Antonio, Texas, and the production was completed late the following spring. The film, finally scripted by Hope Loring and Louis D. Lighten, opens in small-town America where two young men, Jack Powell (Charles Rogers) and David Armstrong (Richard Arlen), dream of becoming pilots. Both are in love with the same girl, the sophisticated Sylvia Lewis (Jobyna Ralston). Jack is idolised by Mary Preston (Clara Bow), the girl next door, but is too infatuated with Sylvia to notice. Suddenly America is at war and Jack and David at last get the opportunity to train for the Air Service, 'only for the bravest of the brave – a path of glory mounting to the stars', we are told. As they say goodbye to their families and friends, a misunderstanding leads Jack to believe that Sylvia is in love with him. In fact she feels only sorrow at his leaving for the war; it is David who has really stolen her heart. Sylvia confides in David about Jack and they decide not to tell him that he has mistaken her affections. The two young men depart for military training – the 'first step on the road to glory'.

Initially Jack dislikes David, seeing him as a rival for Sylvia. However, he changes his mind during a boxing match when, although outclassed by Jack, David proves his courage by refusing to give up. Respect turns to admiration, and by the time the two enter flying school they are the best of friends. The dangers of aviation are first demonstrated when another young pilot (Gary Cooper) is killed while attempting his first solo. Nevertheless, Jack and David become skilled pilots and are posted to the 39th Aero Squadron in France – 'the nest of the War Eagles'.

Before they are sent on their first patrol the men are warned to watch out for the German ace, Count von Kellerman, and his 'flying circus'. Needless to say, Kellerman soon attacks the US squadron and the two fledglings experience their first taste of the war in the air. In a splendidly filmed sequence, the sky becomes a bitterly contested battlefield as aircraft of both sides wheel and dive, a number exploding or crashing into flames. 'But', the captions tell us, 'there was chivalry among these knights of the air', for when Kellerman fires on David and the American pilot's guns jam, the German salutes his enemy and spares his life.

Jack and David eventually become veterans and are decorated by the French for their bravery, earning time out in Paris where 'soldiers of all races [take] a furlough from death'. Recalled from their leave to take part in the Battle of St Mihiel, they await orders 'to again face death, riding in the clouds'. In this anxious state a quarrel leaves Jack feeling betrayed by his friend. Suddenly they are ordered to attack German observation balloons before the Allied offensive begins. While Jack destroys the target, David protects him from German fighters and is shot down behind enemy lines. He manages to evade his captors, however, and hides out near an airfield.

The offensive is launched and Jack, believing that David has been killed, is now desperate for revenge, attacking enemy troops and supply convoys. Over the battlefield he sees a lone German aircraft and dives in to open fire. Puzzled by the German's reluctance to retaliate, he nevertheless damages the machine and forces it to crash land. What he does not know is that David has stolen the enemy fighter and is trying to return to base. David, of course, recognises Jack's plane but is unable to signal to his friend. Fatally wounded, he is forced down and pulled from the wreckage by French soldiers. Jack lands beside the smashed fighter to collect a souvenir and is horrified to discover that the pilot is not only an American, but his friend. Taking his injured comrade in his arms he begs forgiveness. David, with his dying breath, tells Jack that he understands and that nothing has meant more to him than their friendship.

Jack later discovers his mistake about Sylvia when he goes through David's papers before returning to the US. Welcomed as a hero in his hometown, his first call is on his friend's parents to tell them the truth about their son's death. They, wonderfully forgiving, blame the war and look upon Jack as their surrogate son. Finally, meeting Mary again, Jack realises that it is she he really loves.

The story, overly melodramatic and quite unconvincing, is clearly of secondary importance, a means of linking the exciting action sequences – the air battle with the flying circus, the attack on German observation balloons, the final aerial duel and the dramatic re-enactment of the Battle of St Mihiel (the US Army's first independent operation of September 1918), for which the army created a five-acre facsimile of the battlefield and provided tanks and over 5,000 infantrymen as extras. To cover these spectacular scenes, Wellman used a number of cameras – twenty-one for the St Mihiel battle scene alone – while Harry Perry, the cinematographer, pioneered what were to become standard techniques for aerial filming. Not content to film the action from another plane, Perry and Wellman wanted close-ups of the leading characters. Perry's technicians welded camera mounts over the engines and behind the rear cockpits. This allowed the principal actors to be shown, apparently flying their own single-cockpit pursuit planes. In reality, the planes had two cockpits, with the camera able to concentrate on the actor whatever the direction of shooting by filming over the head of the real pilot who could be seated in either the front or back seat. Other cameras were mounted on the wings and undercarriage of the aircraft.

The battle of St Mihiel – as re-enacted in Texas for *Wings*. Wellman's pioneering direction included twenty-one cameras, some mounted precariously on and around the cockpits of planes, and enlisted the US Army to provide tanks and 5,000 infantrymen as extras. (BFI Stills, Posters and Designs)

To give the impression of speed and movement, Wellman filmed the aerial scenes against a background of clouds: on one occasion, he waited for four weeks for the right weather conditions to shoot a particular sequence. Wellman, seeking authenticity, managed to acquire several aircraft of wartime vintage, but most of those used were clearly disguised army machines. The flying was mainly performed by army pilots, but Arlen and Rogers themselves flew in some of the less dangerous scenes, while the spectacular stunts were performed by the pilot Dick Grace.

Wings opened at the Criterion Theatre in New York on 12 August 1927. The foyer was decorated with seventeen huge paintings of wartime pilot heroes in what was called 'The Aviator's Hall of Fame', and the film was dedicated to 'Those young warriors of the sky whose wings are folded about them forever . . .' Wellman's carefully constructed epic of air warfare was an instant commercial success. Nor could Paramount have chosen a more opportune moment to release the film, coming, as it did, just three months after Charles Lindbergh had captured the public imagination and focused attention on aviation with his epic cross-Atlantic flight. The studio made the most of this interest, reinforcing the links by quoting in the opening captions part of Lindbergh's speech of 12 June 1927, on his return to America. Referring to the recent war, the aviator commented, 'In that time, feats were performed and deeds accomplished which were far greater than any peace accomplishments of aviation.' In such a climate, and with such an endorsement, *Wings* could hardly fail.

The film clearly depicts war as a terrible and traumatic experience, yet in tandem with this general condemnation it presents a considerably romanticised image of the pilots – 'young eagles' of the air – brave and noble, determined to fight a 'clean' war, face-to-face with the enemy and bound by the rules of chivalric combat. The young pilots are the very embodiment of the national spirit at war, heroic, bound by their sense of duty and camaraderie, patriotic but never mindless flag-wavers. The review in the *New York Times* was typical of how the film was received:

> This feature gives one an unforgettable idea of the existence of daring air fighters – how they were called upon at all hours of the day and night to soar into the skies and give battle to enemy planes; their light-hearted eagerness to enter the fray and also their reckless conduct once they set foot on earth for a time in the dazzling life of the French capital.

In 1928, the film's success was acknowledged by the industry when, during the first Academy Award ceremony, it was acclaimed 'Best Picture of the Year'. The publishers Grosset and Dunlap quickly brought out a hard-backed novelisation of the script illustrated with stills from the film – one of the first occasions when an outside agency sought to cash in on the success of a movie.

Wings has rightly been called the last of the great silent epics, but it was also to wield considerable influence over later, more technically advanced films. It was the direct inspiration for the millionaire businessman Howard Hughes's monumental production *Hell's Angels* and the ex-aviator Howard Hawks's more restrained *Dawn Patrol*, the two other great aviation films of the period (both made in 1930), which were themselves to exercise considerable influence over an emerging sub-genre of air war movies.

An aviation and cinema enthusiast, Hughes had already produced several films when he saw *Wings*. Although impressed with Wellman's work, he believed he could do better and told an acquaintance that he wanted to make a film that would 'glorify and perpetuate the exploits of the Allied and German airmen of the world war'. While *Hell's Angels* was in production, Howard Hawks, a friend of Hughes, was at work on *Dawn Patrol*, which like *Wings*, was based on a story suggested by John Monk Saunders. However, unlike the earlier films, Hawks intended to concentrate less on spectacle and more on realism. The film attracted little of the ballyhoo surrounding *Hell's Angels*, and appears a restrained and honest attempt to explore the experiences and camaraderie of combat pilots on the Western Front. Both were tremendous box office hits, although the critical response to Hughes's extravaganza was less than enthusiastic.

The three films have often been seen as a trilogy; *Hell's Angels* and *Dawn Patrol* reinforcing the ideas and images first seen in *Wings*. However, their commercial success inevitably attracted imitations and within months of the release of *Wings* the first derivative films began to emerge. First National produced *Hard-Boiled Haggarty*, based on a story by Elliott White Springs, another ex-aviator and a prolific writer. Paramount countered with *Now We're In the Air*, a comedy with Wallace Beery that made use of aerial sequences from *Wings*, and Warners released *Dog of the Regiment* with Ross Lederman and Rin Tin Tin. Audiences were no doubt disappointed to discover that the flying ace was played by Lederman and not the dog. But the trusty animal does at least help the hero to escape from behind enemy lines after he is shot down. The last production of 1927 was Universal's *Lone Eagle* which focused on an American volunteer in the Royal Flying Corps who is accused of cowardice.

Public interest in air war movies continued throughout the 1930s, with other releases including *Legion of the Condemned* (1928) and *Young Eagles* (1930), both directed by Wellman, *Cock of the Air*, *Sky Devils* (both 1932), *Crimson Romance*, *Eagle and the Hawk* and *Ace of Aces* (all 1933); *Hell in the Heavens* (1934) and *Suzy* (1936). Virtually all the later films used plot variations and aerial footage from one or other of the three major productions. The popularity of the sub-genre gradually began to wane after 1934, but even with the approach of another major conflict, the theme of the first great air war did not disappear from the cinema screen altogether. William Wellman's 1938 story of the conquest of the air, *Men With Wings*, had a central sequence set during the First World War, while *The Story of Vernon and Irene Castle*, a 1939 biography of the famous pre-1914 dance team, ends with Vernon (Fred Astaire) joining the RFC in 1914 and flying in combat on the Western Front.

In an age of political cynicism, and widespread pacifism, it is interesting to speculate on why these films were so successful with audiences. At a basic level, the Hollywood image of the war in the air was good cinema: exciting, dramatic and drawing upon established cinematic notions of the romantic hero. These ingredients sold films and it would be foolish to forget that film-makers were primarily concerned with earning profits and not with the accurate reconstruction of the past. Yet the popular conception of the heroic aviator fitted remarkably well into an existing stereotype, one which served the needs of society. The airmen could be seen, perhaps, as the last of the great frontiersmen, the 'rugged individualists' who dared venture into the unknown and pit themselves against both man and nature. The air fighter was indeed a warrior, but one who observed the traditional rules of combat, was prepared to give his life for a comrade and who mourned the fallen enemy – reassuring values in an age where the mass slaughter of the Western Front still cast a long shadow.

While it is possible to find them, examples of chivalric behaviour during the real air war were rare. It is difficult to find nobility or romance in a conflict

The real thing: personnel of the US 11th Bombardment Squadron at Maulan, France, in 1918. (Courtesy of Bruce Robertson)

where most of Richthofen's victories were against slow reconnaissance machines and where the British ace Mick Mannock was motivated by an intense hatred of all things German and enjoyed watching his victims go down in flames. Hollywood's reconstruction of the battles of the skies was clearly idealised and influenced more by romantic tradition than by reality. It might be assumed that this particularised view was due to ignorance – not uncommon when Hollywood went historical – but it is important to remember that these films were largely created by the aviators themselves. It was the airmen who shaped their own cinematic image. Monk Saunders had served in the American Air Service and Wellman was chosen to direct *Wings* on the basis of his own flying experience with the Lafayette Flying Corps in France. Howard Hawks had flown as a combat pilot during the war, as had Elliott White Springs, who wrote many of the derivative features; while Howard Hughes and the actors Arlen and Rogers were aviation enthusiasts (Arlen had also served in the Canadian RFC from 1917) well aware of the realities of war flying.

In his analysis of how the memory of the world wars has been shaped, George L. Mosse has invoked what he calls the 'myth of the war experience' – a means of constructing a memory designed to 'legitimise war by displacing its reality'. For the public, a romantic and chivalric view of the air fighters masked the terrifying realities of their potential to destroy. For the film-maker/aviators this mythic interpretation became a reality – to make their own experience less painful. Their films simply reflected this constructed experience.

What is clear is that *Wings*, *Hell's Angels* and the other reconstructions of the war over the Western Front established the parameters, style and content of air war movies that have remained almost constant from 1927 through the Second World War and Korea, and which can still be seen in such recent features as *Top Gun* (1986), *Supercarrier* (1988), *Flight of the Intruder* (1990) and *Into the Sun* (1991). The nature and technology of warfare has dramatically changed since the First World War, but because of *Wings* and the 'Hollywood airmen', the chivalrous and romantic image of the air fighter remains.

2

ALL QUIET ON THE WESTERN FRONT

Modris Eksteins

'I hate it', the *Sunday Times* critic Sydney Carroll told his readers after seeing *All Quiet on the Western Front* in June 1930. 'It made me shudder with horror. It brought the war back to me as nothing has ever done before since 1918.' But then he added that he admired the film too, for the same reason: its realism, 'its unshrinking crudity, . . . as colossal as the world-war itself'. And finally, with a flourish, Carroll called *All Quiet* 'the greatest of all war films'.

That ambivalent reaction to Lewis Milestone's award-winning classic is one that many have shared, both at the time and since. Some seventy years later, the battle sequences still exude an extraordinary energy, and indeed a verisimilitude that has led to their inclusion over the years in many a documentary about the First World War. The one massive attack and retreat sequence, where the battle line sways to and fro, amid explosions, smoke, barbed wire and horror, only to return to its original position, remains breathtaking.

The scenes that put that action into a context – like the debate over the origins and meaning of the war itself – are, however, a different matter. Here there was controversy from the start, and even today undergraduates groan at some of the dialogue and overacting. These groans may confirm that late twentieth-century youth has been brought up on a diet of irony and cynicism, but they may also suggest that some of the ideas and sentiments expressed in Hollywood's 1930 version of the German author Erich Maria Remarque's famous war novel are a little too ingenuous.

Remarque's novel, published by Ullstein in January 1929, a decade after the end of the war, became a stunning success overnight, the first genuine international best-seller. As sales in Germany rocketed, Ullstein was forced to use six printing and ten bookbinding firms to keep abreast of demand. By the end of the year some twenty translations had appeared and sales world-wide were in the millions.

With this tale about a class of schoolmates who had gone off to war, full of youthful enthusiasm, only to be destroyed, one by one, cruelly and methodically, Remarque had struck a nerve. After a decade of trying not so much to make sense of the war as to repress the pain of sacrifice and loss, the public in the principal belligerent states was only too willing, finally, to allow emotion to well up and utter a cry of anguish for a lost generation – for the youth that had been destroyed by the war, and for the talent, energy and hope that had been lost. By the tenth anniversary some were prepared to go even further and to say that the war, with all its nihilistic fury, had been in vain.

Remarque's novel unleashed a passionate debate. *All Quiet* was, of course, only part, though the most sensational part, of a huge wave of war material – novels, memoirs, drama, film – that flooded the West at the end of the 1920s and the beginning of the next decade. In Britain, R.C. Sheriff, Robert Graves, Siegfried Sassoon and Vera Brittain were part of this wave, as was, in a broader sense, Sellar and Yeatman's famous spoof on British history, *1066 and All That*, which Methuen first published in 1930 and which contained the celebrated assertion that with the Great War history had come to a '.' The most successful artists in this 'war boom' questioned the purpose of the war and the tenability of the values – revolving around honour, duty and sacrifice – that had fuelled it.

Success or notoriety of any sort naturally piqued Hollywood's interest, then as now. Carl Laemmle, a Swabian who at the age of seventeen had gone off to America to seek his fortune and who, after a start in the nickelodeon and then the cinema business, had launched Universal Pictures, journeyed to Europe in the summer of 1929 and purchased the film rights to Remarque's novel.

Hollywood, unlike the European literary world, had not been averse to the theme of war in the twenties, so war movies were not uncommon. But a story as depressingly negative as Remarque's, in which the existential doubt was thick and pervasive, and whose 'heroes', moreover, were enemy soldiers, would certainly be unusual as a Hollywood production. Laemmle clearly had moments of personal doubt; rumours even circulated that he wished to impose a happy ending on the film.

In a remarkable statement of paternal confidence, he put his 21-year-old son, Carl Jr, in charge of production. Given the subject of the planned film, Universal's position in the industry and its reputation for producing films of mass appeal, that move raised plenty of eyebrows. Hollywood wits, alluding to R.C. Sheriff's *Journey's End*, spoke of *All Quiet* as heralding 'Junior's End'.

But Junior surprised the sceptics. Lewis Milestone was hired to direct; proven writers were engaged, including the eminent playwrights Maxwell Anderson and George Abbott; and Arthur Edeson was chosen to shoot the film. Milestone, like the elder Laemmle, born in Odessa, had come to America via Belgium in 1913. That *All Quiet* was to be a product, in significant part, of expatriates was not lost on its European critics. The actors cast as German schoolboys were all cherubic young Americans; the central character Paul Baumer was played by the virtually unknown Lew Ayres.

Filming began, with symbolic intent, on Armistice Day, 11 November 1929. But this was, of course, less than a fortnight after the great stock market crash on Wall Street. That the mood of the film should coincide with mounting fear and foreboding about the future of America, and the Western world as a whole, was completely unintended but perhaps not unwelcome. Interior scenes were shot at Universal's studios; the major battle scene was staged at the Irvine Ranch (adjacent today to the Irvine campus of the University of California).

Here, in typical Hollywood fashion, a world war was recreated. Trenches were dug, barbed wire was strung and the landscape pockmarked with shell holes. The effect was masterful. Genuine French and German uniforms were imported. In the filming of that famous battle sequence a huge crane was used to allow the camera to hover over the battlefield. The film was to cost well over $1 million. Two versions were completed, one silent, for those cinemas not yet wired for sound, and one talking. The initial sound release was almost two-and-a-half hours long.

Production concluded at the end of March, and the film premiered in Los Angeles and New York in late April, 1930, little more than a year after the publication of Remarque's novel. General release was in mid-May. Despite the rapidly deepening economic depression and a drop in cinema attendance (this trend would be reversed as the Depression continued), *All Quiet* played to consistently full houses, setting box-office records throughout America. It reached London's West End in June and played simultaneously at two first-run cinemas, the first time any film had been accorded such prominence. In late November it opened the newly built Ermitage cinema on the Champs Elysées in Paris.

In these Allied – and one should add, victorious – countries the critics were for the most part full of praise for the film, its simplicity and power. The German boy-soldiers were seen to represent all soldiers. Classes of school

Lewis Milestone directing a trench scene at the Irvine ranch location for the film, 1929.
(BFI Stills, Posters and Designs)

children in England were taken to see it. At one London performance in the late summer of 1930, when the news was shown after *All Quiet*, several items on Germany were spontaneously applauded by the audience.

In Germany, however, the reaction was altogether different. The defence ministry, under General Greener, was from the start opposed to the film and intent on having it banned, on the grounds that it cast aspersions on the German military. The army brass disliked a great deal in the film, but especially those scenes that portrayed German soldiers cowering in the face of enemy artillery, eating like ravenous dogs, and denying any purpose to the war. The wily and stunningly ugly Katczinsky, played by the veteran actor Louis Wolheim, was said to represent Hollywood's impression of the barbaric Hun.

Greener drew up a long list of foreign, primarily American, films which he described as *Hetzfilme* – propaganda films inciting negative feelings about Germany. *All Quiet* was merely the latest salve in this barrage of foreign hatred – which included such films as *The Big Parade* (1925), *What Price Glory?* (1926) and the re-release in 1927 of Chaplin's *Shoulder Arms* – a barrage no self-respecting German government could willingly permit without protest and countermeasure.

Interestingly, the German foreign office did not agree initially with this position and argued before the Berlin censorship board for the film's release. Banning the film, its representative said, would do more harm to Germany's image abroad than showing it. On the strength of this opinion, *All Quiet* was approved for screening, but, to appease the military, the censors insisted upon some significant cuts.

Thus even before its release in Germany opinions were divided on the film, as they had been on Remarque's novel. The nationalist right denounced what it regarded as a campaign of defamation – from within as well as without – against Germany's honour and integrity. Remarque, Laemmle and Milestone were simply part of the modern wave of negativism that replaced 'eternal verities' with smut, sex and latrine humour. Instead of being honoured with the Nobel Peace Prize, as some in America now urged, the threesome ought simply to be silenced. That was certainly the opinion within the Nazi Party, which just three months earlier had won mammoth gains in national elections, jumping from 12 to 107 seats in the Reichstag. The circle around Joseph Goebbels, the inventor of Nazi propaganda strategy, and his Berlin newspaper *Der Angriff* was particularly outspoken, pointing out that both Laemmle and Milestone were Jewish and insisting that *All Quiet* was, as a result, a Jewish creation.

For the first public performance of the film, on 5 December 1930, Goebbels and his supporters bought up a block of about 300 seats (about a third of the total) in the Mozartsaal of the Theater am Nollendorfplatz in Berlin's West End. Shortly after the start of the film the famous ruckus began – members of the crowd shouted abuse, white mice were released and stink bombs let off. The size of the demonstrating contingent and the stench were such that the performance had to be halted and the cinema cleared. Further demonstrations outside the cinema and general rowdiness accompanied subsequent performances until the police president of Berlin banned open-air demonstrations on 10 December.

On the same day, the German government, a fragile minority coalition wary of surging nationalist sentiment in the country, watched a private screening of

'If you know a better hole . . .': Lew Ayres as the young German alongside a dying French soldier. (BFI Stills, Posters and Designs)

All Quiet. The foreign minister, Curtius, who had not seen the film before, found it unacceptable and now insisted that his ministry no longer defend its showing. On 11 December, the Berlin film censorship board considered an appeal, launched by a number of state governments, of the previous judgement on the film. At this hearing, representatives of the defence, foreign and interior ministries all spoke against the film: the board decided to reverse the earlier decision and to ban *All Quiet* on the grounds that it harmed Germany's image.

The German moderate left was of course outraged at the decision. Carl von Ossietzky noted that the ban implied that Germans were now forbidden to say that war was evil and that peace was preferable to war. Foreign comment on the ban was not kind. 'That there is a revival of German militarist emotion has been clear for some time', noted the *Manchester Guardian*. 'That the force opposed to it is so weak is a startling and sinister revelation.'

Despite the ban, the Laemmles did not give up on their efforts to secure a re-release. The German market was much too important. In the summer of 1931, after the film had received Hollywood Academy Awards in 1930 for best film and best direction, the Laemmles offered to cut it further, to a length of about two hours from its two-and-a-half hour original form, and to show the abbreviated version worldwide. (This seems to be the version most readily available now.) German government officials and the Berlin censorship board accepted this offer and in September 1931 *All Quiet* re-opened, without disturbance, in Germany. However, the rest of the world hardly noticed – the damage to Germany's image had been done the first time around, not by the film but by the German response to it.

When Hitler came to power in January 1933, *All Quiet* was banned once again and Remarque's novel was burned as an 'un-German' account of the war in the symbolic book-burnings of 10 May. Not all foreign observers were appalled. G.K. Chesterton applauded 'this service to literature, the nearest that Germany will ever come to atoning for setting fire to the library of Louvain'. Chesterton found the whole temper of the war boom, which was now abating, to have been objectionable:

> The thesis thrust upon us was not really the obvious thesis that war is heart-rending and horrible; it was the thesis that there is nothing noble about defying horror or enduring the rending of the heart.

Germany was not the only country to proscribe *All Quiet*. Italy, Austria and initially New Zealand also did so. The New Zealand chief censor noted curtly:

'No entertainment. Packed with the nauseating side of war from start to finish.' It appears that almost everywhere the film was shown local censors insisted on cuts – usually, however, the references to bodily functions and mild sexual innuendo, rather than the scenes to which the Germans objected.

All Quiet has come to be regarded as the classic anti-war film. Given its technical brilliance and the speed at which it was produced, it was a remarkable accomplishment. The sentiments about war which the film expressed were widely held at the end of the 1920s. However, contrary to the publicity surrounding the film, they were not representative of the prevailing attitudes of soldiers during the war, when a sense of purpose among the fighting men, while perhaps dulled with time, never disappeared in the way Remarque suggested. And that was the crux of the debate. Remarque's novel and its film version purportedly told 'the truth about the war', or as London's *Sunday Chronicle* put it, 'the true story of the world's greatest nightmare'. But that was clearly not the case.

Both the novel and the film were products of the turbulent 1920s, of the disillusionment, frustration and anger of that decade, of its imploring hopes and often treacly sentimentality. But that said, one must also acknowledge that no other book or film has had as great a role in forging popular impressions of the Great War, and perhaps of modern war as a whole, as *All Quiet on the Western Front*. Novelists and film-makers, one is tempted to conclude, have played a more important role than historians in developing the twentieth century's historical imagination.

In 1979 a new three-hour version was made for television, directed by Delbert Mann and starring Richard Thomas and Ernest Borgnine. It received mixed reviews and there was general agreement that it lacked the brooding intensity of the original. But what about that original, before the censors started snipping and the Laemmles colluding? In 1983, after four years of painstaking efforts to reconstruct the 1930 film, Jurgen Labenski, an editor with the West German television network ZDF, unveiled a 139-minute version. While eleven minutes short of the 150 Milestone claimed he shot, this may now be the closest we will get to the original creation.

3

FIRES WERE STARTED

Jeffrey Richards

All countries live by and through myths, episodes from their history that are removed from their context, shorn of complications and qualification, stripped down to their essentials and endlessly repeated as manifestations of the nation's character, worth and values. The Second World War produced a succession of such myths, one of the most powerful being that of the Blitz. It is simply told. In September 1940, German aircraft began the systematic heavy bombing of London. From 7 September, for seventy-six consecutive nights (apart from 2 November, when bad weather frustrated the enemy), London was pounded by the Luftwaffe. Thereafter, raids were frequent until May 1941. Buckingham Palace and the House of Commons were hit. Death and destruction were extensive. It was the reaction of the population of London – one of heroic stoicism – which gave birth to the myth, and to the defiant 'London Can Take It' attitude that was emulated in other industrial centres and seaports to which the Germans later turned their attention.

Since the end of the war, historians, whose stock-in-trade is the debunking of myths, have examined the events of the Blitz in detail. Evidence has emerged that there was some looting and some panic. There was also unrest in the East End about shelter provision. But the general picture of a courageous, determined and good-humoured people surviving everything that the Luftwaffe could throw at them remains substantially intact. In the most extensive and thorough examination *The Myth of the Blitz* (1991), the historian Angus Calder confirms that the myth developed immediately and spontaneously and was based on direct observation of how Londoners behaved. The story was reported extensively in the press both in Britain and in the United States and the fully formed myth was taken up by the propaganda machine and promoted worldwide.

One of the media by which the myth of the Blitz was perpetuated was the British documentary film movement. Nurtured and promoted by John Grierson in the 1930s, the movement aimed to produce an authentic picture of the real life of the common people and to educate the nation for participatory democratic citizenship. It committed itself fully to the war effort. Under the aegis of the Ministry of Information, the GPO Film Unit, which had produced films promoting the virtues of the postal service, was transformed into the Crown Film Unit in 1940. The Ministry prescribed three principal themes for film-makers during wartime: 'Why we fight', 'How we fight' and 'The need for sacrifice if the war is to be won'.

Ian Dalrymple, head of the Crown Film Unit, explained in 1941:

We say in film to our own people 'This is what the boys in the services, or the girls in the factories, or the men and women in Civil Defence, or the patient citizens themselves are like, and what they are doing. They are playing their part in the spirit in which you see them in this film. Be of good heart and go and do likewise.' And we say to the world, 'Here in these films are the British people at war.' . . . It has seen the truth and it can make up its own mind.

The central theme of the documentary-makers, therefore, was 'the People's War' – of which the myth of the Blitz was a prime example. It was to be memorably celebrated in one of Crown Film Unit's most notable productions, *Fires Were Started* directed by Humphrey Jennings in 1942.

Cambridge intellectual, poet, painter, literary critic and film-maker, Jennings had scattered his talents in many directions. He had been an organiser of the International Surrealist Exhibition in London in 1936 and was a founder of Mass-Observation, set up in 1937 to gather, record and archive the opinions and experiences of ordinary people. But with the outbreak of war Jennings found his questing mind increasingly drawn to the war effort and its exploration in relation to the nature of England and the English. Documentary film, he discovered, provided the ideal medium for his purpose. In one way his films were intensely and deliberately personal, but in another, by addressing themselves to the nature of England, they were resoundingly public.

Working for the Crown Film Unit and producing mainly short films for non-theatrical distribution at home and overseas, Jennings' language and imagery captured the soul of the nation at war. *London Can Take It* (1940), co-directed with Harry Watt, depicted the capital standing up to the Blitz. Its key images were used and re-used in postwar television documentaries until they became etched on the collective consciousness as an indelible record of the events. *The Heart of Britain* (1941) examined the effects of the war on the provinces. *Listen to Britain* (1942), co-directed with Stewart McAllister, evoked the myriad sounds of the nation at war. *The Silent Village* (1943) movingly recreated the Lidice massacre in the Welsh village of Cwmgiedd. *A Diary for Timothy* (1944-45) interpreted the events of the last winter of the war for a new-born child. *Fires Were Started* was Jennings' only feature-length work. But all his films fulfilled exactly the three propaganda requirements laid down by the Ministry of Information. Together they shaped and defined the image of Britain at war that was to be circulated round the world and handed on to future generations.

Jennings' film style was crucially moulded by his two great pre-war influences: Surrealism and Mass-Observation. The aim of the Surrealists – to present 'a solidified dream-image' – was achieved by the technique of juxtaposing apparently incongruous elements in order to upset traditional modes of perception, thus liberating the imagination. Jennings and his regular editor, Stewart McAllister, consciously planted striking images in the films. For example, the shot of a terrified horse being led to safety through the smoke in *Fires Were Started* was not a casual piece of observation, but was scripted and designed in advance of the filming. Mass-Observation, as a precise anthropological study of everyday reality, also informed Jennings' approach to his subjects – the desire to record the lives of ordinary people accurately and truthfully.

Jennings' world-view was crystallised by the war, and in a sense his films stand alongside George Orwell's essays *The Lion and the Unicorn* and *The English People* in articulating a robust Socialist patriotism, a full-blooded love of England and the English. This love centred on three basic principles: admiration for the common people, an instinctive belief in individualism but within a wider community ('we like to think of ourselves as a family' Jennings said in a later film, *Family Portrait*) and a feeling for English culture. Several commentators have stressed the importance to Jennings of music. Music of all kinds was integral to his films, but it also influenced their structure. William Sansom recorded: '. . . His films were composed in the swelling-dying, theme and repeat-theme notation of a kind of musical composition'. *Fires Were Started* reveals a very definite three-movement structure, which helps to give it its classical shape.

The war proved a revelation to Jennings in that it showed him the real worth and strength of ordinary people. This comes across in his letters to his wife Cicely whom he had evacuated, with their children, to the United States. He wrote to her of the Blitz on 20 October 1940:

Heroic images: a Blitz scene from the film, imbued with the power of almost surreal imagery. (BFI Stills, Posters and Designs)

Some of the damage in London is pretty heart-breaking but what an effect it has had on the people! What warmth – what courage! What determination! People sternly encouraging each other by explaining that when you hear a bomb whistle it means it has missed you! People in the north singing in public shelters: 'One man went to mow, went to mow a meadow.' WVS girls serving hot drinks to fire-fighters during raids explaining that really they are 'terribly afraid all the time'. . . . Everybody absolutely determined: secretly delighted with the privilege of holding up Hitler. Certain of beating him; a certainty which no amount of bombing can weaken, only strengthen.

It was this indomitable spirit that Jennings celebrated and honoured in his films. *Fires Were Started* brought together many of his preoccupations and gave visual form to his feelings about England and the English. It stressed the heroism of ordinary men and women in the Blitz, carefully characterising them as distinctive individuals. It placed them securely within their cultural framework, with popular songs resonating throughout ('One man went to mow', 'Please don't talk about me when I'm gone', 'Out with my barrow and my moke all day', 'Ah, sweet mystery of life'). Their actions are underscored by the heroic symphonic music of William Alwyn.

The film was the result of a proposal to make a feature-length work about the fire service. Besides paying tribute to the heroism of the fire-fighters, it would also serve to fulfil a demand being made for propaganda to encourage teamwork. In the words of a memorandum from the Public Relations Committee of the Civil Defence:

> The simple idea that we would like to see brought to life is that the action of the people of Great Britain today provides the finest example of teamwork the world has ever seen . . . In time of war, we make the most of what we already possess and faith in the power derived from voluntary teamwork is immeasurably superior to that of a nation dragooned for war. But to make the most of our national genius and to mobilise quickly our inherent strength, we must through propaganda make the idea of teamwork more articulate, conscious and dynamic.

Jennings agreed to make the film and set about gathering detailed accounts of fire-fighting from Liverpool and London on which he based his script. The script (which can be seen in the Jennings papers at the British Film Institute) went through five drafts between October 1941 and January 1942 before a final, detailed scenario was completed. From the outset it was intended that one of the firemen would be killed, in line with the concern of the Ministry of Information to stress the need for sacrifice in winning the war. This is important in the light of claims made about Jennings' method of work. William Sansom, for instance, has commented that:

> . . . [there was] no script. A general scheme of course which we did not know about. The film was shot both on and off the cuff. Dialogue was always made up on the spot – and of course the more germane for that – and Jennings collected detail of all kinds on the way, on the day, on the spot.

According to Ian Dalrymple: 'There was never any script. That wasn't the way Humphrey worked.' Such statements have led to the belief that Jennings' films were improvised. They were not. He was certainly ready to improvise where necessary. He would incorporate interesting details encountered during filming, like the penny-whistle blower who appears in the introductory sequences. Jennings improvised the details of the sing-songs, though he had always intended that there should be one, and some dialogue improvisations were worked out with fireman Fred Griffiths on the set. But it is clear that the film was carefully scripted and structured before shooting began and even if Jennings kept the details in his head, they were thoroughly worked out.

Jennings selected real firemen from stations around London, who were seconded for the duration of filming. They were Fred Griffiths, a cockney taxi driver who had joined the AFS before the war; Philip Wilson-Dickson, previously in advertising; Loris Ray, a sculptor; T.P. Smith, a former waiter; John Barker, a Manchester businessman; Johnny Houghton, and Commanding Officer George Gravett, a regular with the London Fire Brigade. One of the officers in the control room is Ernest Lough who, as a pre-war boy soprano, had made a hit gramophone record singing 'Oh, for the Wings of a Dove'. The new man to the unit, Bill Barrett, was played by William Sansom. Sansom later drew on his firefighting experiences for a work of fiction, *Fireman Flower* (1944), and a factual account of the fire service, *Westminster At War* (1947, re-issued in 1990 under the more resonant title *The Blitz*). In this, he recalls the Blitz as 'a hotchpotch time of paradox, strain, pain, hard work, fidelity and often of laughter', all of which Jennings was to capture.

Filming took place between February and October 1942, with facilities provided by the Ministry of Home Security, the Home Office and the National Fire Service. Exteriors were shot on location – with the fire specially staged in a warehouse at St Katherine's Dock – while interiors were filmed at Pinewood Studios, headquarters of the Crown Film Unit. In a letter to Cicely, dated 12 April 1942, Jennings described filming in Stepney and Wapping:

The place and the people illuminating beyond everything . . . it has now become fourteen hours a day, living in Stepney the whole time, really have never worked so hard at anything or I think thrown myself into anything so completely. Whatever the results it is definitely an advance in film-making for me – really beginning to understand people and making friends with them and not just looking at them and lecturing or pitying them. Another general effect of the war.

The film that resulted from all this activity was initially known as *I Was a Fireman*. Though made in 1942, it looks back to 1940 to recreate one night in the Blitz. The opening title explains that the action takes place before August 1941 when the unified National Fire Service was created by a merger of various independent brigades of regular and auxiliary firemen. The Auxiliary Fire Service had been set up as a branch of civil defence in 1938 and the firemen in Jennings' film wear AFS insignia. In what was to become one of the key works in creating the mythic image of the London Blitz, those heroic figures silhouetted against the blazing inferno sweeping the dockside warehouse came to embody the epic of the ordinary men and women who calmly and courageously took up the defence of their city.

The action follows the experiences of Heavy Unit One, a single fire engine and its crew stationed at a dockland fire station. Like Jennings' other work, the film is carefully structured, falling into three distinct movements: the build-up, the fire, the aftermath. But unusually for Jennings, he adopts a conventional, linear narrative form. Within it, however, he inserts a number of typical Jennings images, all of them drawn from reality and observation. There is the one-legged man hobbling on crutches past the ruins, three large women wheeling a rickety pram through the confusion, a solitary tree in full blossom in the station yard, a graceful sailing barge gliding down the Thames, and a barrage balloon floating majestically above the river. The river is a recurrent image, flowing on serenely and timelessly, in peace and war. All these are images of life continuing amid the crisis, but they also help to give the film the feel of the 'solidified dream-image' of the Surrealists.

The pace of the first section is relaxed, concentrating on the depiction of routine. The crew members are introduced in turn, as the film cuts back and forth between each individual and the life of the streets and docks going on as usual – the picture of normality. The crew gathers at sub-station 14Y with a litany of 'good mornings': cheerful cockney taxi driver Johnny Daniels; jaunty tobacconist 'Jacko' with his permanent cigarette; Scottish intellectual Rumbold, nicknamed 'The Colonel'; chirpy B.A. Brown; pleasant Vallance and quiet Walters. They are introduced to a new man, advertising copywriter Bill Barrett, who is put in Johnny's hands to be shown the ropes. As the fire engine is cleaned, we hear the voices of the girls in the control room receiving the routine daily reports on the state of the fire-fighting equipment and appliances, a device which integrates those at headquarters with the work of the men on the ground. The crew perform their drill and then Johnny shows Barrett over their patch. The newcomer's role enables the audience to identify with Barrett, while, through him, the functions of the Auxiliary Fire Service are explained.

As night falls, the crew wait for the air raids to begin. The blackout is put up. The men chat and in the recreation room there is beer, snooker, darts and table-tennis. When Johnny discovers that Barrett can play the piano, he gets him to improvise a rumba and Johnny and B.A. do a comic sand dance until they are all sent off to get kitted up. As they return, Johnny gets Barrett to strike up with 'One man went to mow', which is taken up in turn by each fireman as he comes in. This is a conscious, but potent, artistic device to show the newcomer integrated into the group. The air raid siren sounds during the last verse of the song and with it the first movement of the film ends.

Events begin to move rapidly and the pace of the editing speeds up too. Guns and bombs are heard. Control begins to plot the locations of fires and order out appliances. Heavy Unit One is sent to a warehouse fire in Trinidad Street, which threatens a munitions ship moored nearby. The fire-fighting is intercut with shots of headquarters receiving and relaying information, a process that continues even when a falling bomb causes a shower of debris in the control room. The firewoman on the telephone simply dabs her cut forehead, apologises for the interruption and carries on. This demonstrates the real threat faced by all members of the service, whether on the ground or at headquarters. It also shows them facing danger with the same degree of dedication and composure.

To get a better angle of attack on the fire, Jacko, Rumbold and sub-officer Dykes go up on to the roof and direct their hose into the heart of the blaze. Dykes is injured and has to be lowered to the ground. Jacko carries on alone, flames licking around his feet, until he is overcome and falls to his death amid the blazing rubble. There is an enormous explosion from the warehouse, as if to signal the extent of the loss of a single heroic individual in the struggle. More appliances and hoses arrive from other forces and the fire is gradually subdued. Dawn breaks, the 'All Clear' sounds and the second movement ends.

The aftermath shows the results of the fire in the bleak, grey light of morning: smoke, rubble, water and men physically and mentally drained. Clearing up, Barrett finds Jacko's battered helmet. A mobile canteen arrives with a 'nice cup of tea' – that distinctively British symbol of normality. A workman coming on duty observes laconically 'Bad night'. 'Bad night', replies Johnny, 'You wanna go down the road. There's a boat down there, good as new. She ain't got a scratch on 'er, a sight for sore eyes.' This is the justification for their work, but a price has been paid.

The film ends with the funeral of Jacko, the coffin borne by his surviving comrades, the trees of the graveyard, leafless. But the grief and formality give

Jacko on duty immediately before his death. (BFI Stills, Posters and Designs)

way to a sense of triumph as the scene dissolves into the prow of the munitions ship moving safely out to sea. The fire comes to symbolise the war itself, beaten by organisation, teamwork and individual sacrifice: the film itself, the distillation of the qualities of the People's War.

According to William Sansom *Fires Were Started*, using real firemen, real locations and authentic episodes, was literally true: 'As a practising fireman I could say this: the film was true to life in every respect. Not a false note – if you make the usual allowances for the absence of foul language which was in everybody's mouth all the time.' But it transcends the mere photographing of reality. The placing of the camera, staging of the action and tempo of the editing do not merely record, they celebrate the men and their struggle. The crew are individually characterised by the consistent use of close-ups, while their activity shows them acting as a team, pitted against the elements – night, fire, water. With no sight and little mention of the enemy, the fire becomes almost an abstract symbol of struggle, highlighting the qualities that the nation needs at its moment of supreme crisis.

During the war there was an unofficial rota under which the principal commercial distributors took it in turn to handle the release of official films. It was the turn of General Film Distributors (GFD) to handle *I Was a Fireman*. But GFD chiefs Arthur Jarratt and C.M. Woolf refused to take the film as it stood. They wanted a change of title and cuts in the first reel to speed it up. Jennings resisted, but eventually an agreement was reached. Crown would cut the film from seventy-four minutes to sixty-five, and the title would be changed to *Fires Were Started*. In return, GDF promised a West End opening on 29 March 1943, with general release on 12 April.

Press reaction was almost uniformly ecstatic: 'inspiring and dramatic' (*Daily Mirror*); 'magnificent, stirring and often deeply moving' (*Star*); 'a vivid piece of British social wartime history that speaks for itself, (*Daily Herald*); 'a noble and convincing tribute to the firemen' (*Daily Mail*); 'Thrilling and admirably made' (*News Chronicle*); 'an impressive testament to the courage of a fine body of Spartans' (*Manchester Guardian*). It is the longer version of the film that is now in circulation but it has retained the title *Fires Were Started*.

The stature of the film has steadily grown over the years. The director Lindsay Anderson summed up the general opinion when he declared: 'No other British film made during the war, documentary or feature, achieved such a continuous and poignant truthfulness or treated the subject of men at war with such a sense of its incidental glories and its essential tragedy.'

As for the firemen, there was another dimension to their story that was publicised even at the time. It was in 1941 that AFS member Michael Wassey published his highly critical *Ordeal by Fire*, complaining bitterly of the lack of recognition of the AFS and of the lack of parity with the regular service, in terms of pay, compensation, status, conditions and promotional opportunities. But a year after Wassey's book, the AFS received its recognition and its tribute in Jennings' film, which inscribed in the national record for all time, the courageous reality at the heart of the myth. During the war, 50,000 emergency calls were answered by London firemen, 327 men and women of the London fire service were killed in action and over 3,000 injured. The crew of Heavy Unit One stood for all of them.

4

THE GREEN BERETS

Philip Taylor

At the end of December 1965, President Lyndon B. Johnson received a letter which began: 'Dear Mr President. When I was a little boy, my father always told me that if you want to get anything done see the top man – so I am addressing this letter to you.' The author was a 58-year-old John Wayne, the Hollywood legend (born Marion Michael Morrison) and by then veteran of around 140 films, most famously, westerns and war movies. Wayne went on to propose a patriotic feature about America's growing involvement in the Vietnam war. The eventual result, *The Green Berets* (1968), which Wayne both starred in and directed, was the most blatantly propagandist contemporaneous American film to be made about the conflict.

Not that there were many to choose from. Apart from a few documentary films about the war and a small number of later features like *The Angry Breed* (1969) and *The Stone Killer* (1973) – dealing with crazed Vietnam veterans going on the rampage on the home front – or *The Losers* (1971) – about motorcycle gangs recruited to rescue a US diplomat from the Communists – the reluctance of the American film industry to tackle Vietnam for a period of at least ten years (*c.* 1963 to 1973) is striking. All the more so compared to the battery of Vietnam films produced after the war, of which the best known are *The Deer Hunter* (1978), *Apocalypse Now!* (1978), *Rambo: First Blood, Part Two* (1985), *Platoon* (1986), *Full Metal Jacket* (1987), *Good Morning, Vietnam* (1987) and *Hamburger Hill* (1987). Even the North Vietnamese were more prolific in the number of films they produced on the war while it was still being waged, from *The Young Woman of Bai-Sao* (1963) to *The Girl from Hanoi* (1975).

Such films, like anything a wartime enemy says or shows, could easily be dismissed as propaganda. But in his letter to the President, Wayne wrote:

'The kind of picture that will help our cause in the world' – John Wayne in action as Colonel Mike Kirby in *The Green Berets*. (Batjac Productions/Courtesy Kobal)

Some day soon a[n American] motion picture *will* be made about Vietnam. Let's make sure it is the kind of picture that will help our cause throughout the world . . . We want to tell the story of our fighting men in Vietnam with reason, emotion, characterisation and action. We want to do it in a manner that will inspire a patriotic attitude on the part of fellow Americans – a feeling which we have always had in this country in the past during times of stress and trouble.

The problem, as Wayne recognised, was that Vietnam was not 'a popular war', all the more reason why he felt it 'extremely important that not only the people of the United States, but those all over the world should know why it is necessary for us to be there'. In fact, this viewpoint was to cause considerable controversy when the film was released in 1968 – at the height of the anti-Vietnam war demonstrations.

By December 1965, the number of US troops in Vietnam was approaching 200,000 and President Johnson greeted Wayne's project with enthusiasm. But there were some among his staff who expressed doubts about an association between the film star, well-known for his right-wing, Republican sympathies, and the Democratic administration of Johnson. Meanwhile, the Hollywood studio MGM – described by one Johnson official as 'our friends politically' – was also interested in making a Vietnam film, as was Columbia. However, Jack Valenti, a special advisor to the President, was of the opinion that 'Wayne's politics are wrong, but in so far as Vietnam is concerned, his views are right. If he made the picture he would be saying the things we want said. . .'. Accordingly, the Department of Defense was instructed to extend its co-operation to Wayne's film company, Batjac, and to the film's producer, Wayne's son, Michael:

> Not only do we want and need a feature motion picture on Vietnam but we believe here is an opportunity to direct and develop a project that will contain story elements that are favourable to the Department of Defense and to the overall effort as stated by the President.

By the spring of 1966, work began on the script based on Robin Moore's best-selling book *The Green Berets* about US Special Forces in Vietnam. James Lee Barrett, an ex-marine who had served in Vietnam and had scripted both *The Greatest Story Ever Told* and *Shenandoah* in 1965, was employed to incorporate certain themes, such as the losses which the brave and committed Vietnamese allies were incurring, and to make the point (in Wayne's words) 'that the Commie guerrillas are ruthless, having killed 20,000 civic leaders and their families during these years of slaughter'. Wayne also thought that the inclusion of scenes such as casualties receiving medical attention, the handing out of toys to children, 'and little things like soap', would prevent the film from becoming simply 'a message vehicle'. He was wrong.

Following visits to the Pentagon and to the Special Forces base at Fort Bragg, Wayne declared himself most impressed with what he had seen:

> We found the soldiery of such quality that, if people of the United States were apprised of it, it would renew their confidence in the ability, the decency and the dedication of our present-day American fighting men.

This may well have been true for the majority of law-abiding, patriotic American citizens, as reflected in numerous public opinion polls, but they were nonetheless a comparatively silent majority. Most of the noise against the war was being generated by a vocal – and, thanks to television, highly visible – group of anti-war protesters, students and other peace supporters. Wayne even took it upon himself to write to five US senators who publicly expressed doubts about the escalation of the war in Vietnam (Richard B. Russell, John Sherman Cooper, J.W. Fulbright, Clinton P. Anderson and George Murphy), reminding them of 'some public information', namely the mass killing of thousands of civilian leaders:

> Imagine the equivalent percentage of our leadership being murdered. That would be around 250,000 which would be enough to include every mayor, every governor, every senator and every member of the House of Representatives and their combined families.

This same point is made by one of the characters in *The Green Berets*, even using the exact same words, so Wayne must have had personal input into the scripting of the final film.

Wayne wanted the movie to address directly the controversy about why US troops were fighting in the war, and the film does this via the mouthpiece of a sceptical journalist (a device also adopted by postwar Vietnam films), in this instance George Beckworth (played by David Janssen). One of the opening scenes depicts Special Forces troops in training in a public relations exercise performed for the benefit of a group of journalists. When one of these asks why Americans are fighting in Vietnam, the master sergeant replies: 'Foreign policy decisions are not made by the military . . .' Beckworth interrupts to ask whether the sergeant agrees with this, to which the latter suspiciously retorts: 'Can I have your name, sir?' Tension between the military and the media is immediately apparent and further explanation is only forthcoming when a female journalist asks that the original question be answered. The more sensitive, feminine request is answered – significantly – by a token black soldier (played by Raymond St Jacques): 'As soldiers, Miss Sutton, we can understand the killing of the military. But the extermination of a civilian leadership, the intentional murder and torture of innocent women and children? . . . They need us, Miss Sutton, and they want us.'

As the soldier elaborates, the journalists (and the cinema audience) hear Wayne's public information message to the senators, together with a lesson in

American constitutional history and about worldwide Communist support for North Vietnam. The military clearly win the argument, but Beckworth remains sceptical and is only put in his place when Wayne's character, Colonel Mike Kirby, asks him whether he has ever been to South East Asia, to which he has to admit humbly he has not. (Wayne himself, of course, had visited as part of his research for the film).

Thereafter, the plot resembles a 'good guys versus bad guys' type of western. The troops leave for Vietnam (accompanied by Beckworth), arriving at their as yet unfinished base camp A107, nicknamed 'Dodge City'. The Vietcong or 'Charlie' are really Red Indians in the Hollywood stereotypical mode, capable of atrocities against 'innocent women and children'. Indeed Beckworth's conversion from his sceptical stance to one sympathetic to the cause – epitomised by his exchange of civilian safari suit for regulation military fatigues – is facilitated by seeing an example of Vietcong brutality (the body of a young girl who has been raped). This is depicted in stark contrast to American sensitivity towards the locals on whose behalf they are fighting to keep free. The reluctant adoption of a young Vietnamese boy 'Hamchuck' by one soldier named Peterson (Jim Hutton) personifies this theme, subsequently labelled 'host nation sensitivity' by the American military. An exchange between Colonel Kirby and Hamchuck, after Kirby breaks the news of Peterson's death to the boy, in the closing lines of the film is sentimentality of the finest order:

Hamchuck: 'What will I do now?'
Kirby: 'You let me worry about that. You're what this war is all about.'

Beyond the military nonsense, the entire message of the film is that one is unqualified to judge the rights and wrongs of war, unless one sees the realities for oneself – even though in *The Green Berets* the only 'realities' depicted are instances of Vietcong brutality. By implication, the film is saying 'don't believe everything you read in the newspapers': when it is against the war and the military effort, that is. Another exchange suggests a different pro-war perspective. After the film's central battle for control of Dodge City, Colonel Kirby asks Beckworth 'What are you going to say in that newspaper of yours?' 'If I say what I feel, I may be out of a job' the convert declares. 'We'll always give you one', says Kirby. 'I can do you more good with a typewriter', Beckworth replies.

That the power of the press should be given such weight in the film seems odd. Vietnam, after all, is remembered as America's first 'television war'. There

'Dodge City', the fictional base camp in a scene from the film. (BFI Stills, Posters and Designs)

remains, even today, a dubious perception that the nightly showing of television newscasts, of napalmed children and burning villages – all in glorious colour – undermined popular support for the war and for the US military, especially as these atrocious acts were being committed by 'us' and not 'them'. In *The Green Berets*, the Beckworth character may have represented the military's view of the media in general, but television is a different medium. If a picture can speak a thousand words, then moving pictures can speak millions. Television reporters were allowed relatively unfettered access to battle zones in this, the most uncensored war of the twentieth century. Although historical research has demonstrated that in fact neither the press nor TV were against the war, the contemporary perception was that they were. In turn, this has been used as a justification for subsequent military censorship in low-intensity conflicts involving the US, such as Grenada and Panama and, most spectacularly, during the Gulf War.

The release of *The Green Berets* in 1968 was accompanied by an advertising campaign which claimed: 'Their badge of honour was a green beret and it said they had lived it all.' But as for the depiction of military realities, one audience which included a number of marines was reported to have roared with laughter:

> This is the funniest movie we have seen in a long time. . . . At the end . . . John Wayne walks off into the sunset with a spunky little orphan. The grunts laugh and threaten to pee all over themselves. The sun is setting in the South China Sea – in the East – which makes the end of the movie as accurate as the rest of it.

Despite the troops' mirth, the growing ranks of anti-war civilians who saw it felt the film repugnant and many picketed the cinemas. Reviewer David Wilson wrote that 'propaganda as crude as this can only do damage to its cause', while critic Penelope Gilliat felt that it was a film 'best handled from a distance and with a pair of tongs'. There were rumours of congressional and senatorial investigations into the making of the movie and certainly the anti-war, liberal activist Allard Lowenstein made all sorts of accusations of government propaganda in the press. He was not that far wide of the mark, given that the first script was rejected by the Pentagon and had to be re-written in order for army co-operation to continue. Michael Wayne admitted to film historian Laurence Suid in 1975 that 'the re-writing of the script had been along the lines suggested by the Pentagon'.

Nevertheless, *The Green Berets* still proved a commercial success, grossing $8 million domestically. Why it did so well raises many questions. It may have been due to the publicity and hype surrounding the film, or down to John Wayne's enormous popularity. It may simply have been that the silent majority of American citizens who supported the US military, regardless of the rights and wrongs of a foreign policy dedicated to containing Communism, were watching a film that reinforced their patriotism. In deconstructing films as texts, historians too little recognise that the effect the medium can have on audience emotions can tell us more about ourselves than the film itself ever can. But in spite of its success, the fusion of denunciation and mockery surrounding *The Green Berets* probably contributed to Hollywood's subsequent reluctance to tackle the subject of the war again until after it was all over. The impact of America's 'first military defeat', not just on the veterans and their families, but in terms of wider US public confidence, prompted a necessary period of mourning before there could be a reappraisal of the Vietnam conflict, its causes and course.

In the cinema, this led to the release of films like *Coming Home* and *Missing in Action* after a gap of five years or so. But feature films rarely deal with history with integrity (*Schindler's List* being an obvious exception); through the process of reconstruction, they tend to re-write the past and apply contemporary values. By the time a former Hollywood actor was elected to the White House in 1980, the American film industry felt more confident about re-inventing, as well as its usual re-writing of history, so that in *First Blood, Part Two* (1985) Special Operations Vietnam veteran John Rambo could ask with more confidence, 'Do we get to win this time?'.

5

STAR WARS

Peter Krämer

When the special edition of George Lucas's film *Star Wars* was released in January 1997, the distributor's press book proclaimed: 'While *Star Wars* was a defining event for one generation, it has been embraced by new generations, assuring its place as a timeless epic of grand design and boundless fun.' This claim was confirmed by articles in *Time*, *Newsweek*, the *New Yorker* and the *New York Times* which stated that the film was 'part of the culture' and its 'lessons' about good and evil, humanity and technology, hubris and redemption were 'a very powerful force indeed'.

These publications noted that contemporary mass media are full of references to the film and that many words and phrases from it have entered into everyday language, but they mentioned Ronald Reagan's appropriation of the *Star Wars* term 'evil empire' only in passing and none of them pointed out that for several years in the mid-1980s the film's title had been identified with the former president's missile defence programme. When other publications did discuss this connection, they incorrectly assumed that it was Reagan himself who had linked the term 'Star Wars' to his defence programme. With popular memory so unreliable, and George Lucas's new *Star Wars* trilogy on everybody's mind after the massively hyped and hugely successful release of *Star Wars: Episode 1 – the Phantom Menace* in May 1999, it is interesting to look back at the origins of Reagan's defence programme and its association with the film.

In a televised speech of 23 March 1983, President Reagan asked the American public for its support of the defence budget he had submitted to Congress. To gain this, he explained the key principle of military strategy in the nuclear age ('deterrence of aggression through the promise of retaliation') and highlighted the dramatically increased military power of the Soviet Union. This power, he claimed, undermined the ability of the US to guarantee retaliation

Artist's impression of the American government's Strategic Defense Initiative (SDI) or Star Wars weaponry in action against an intercontinental ballistic missile attack over Norway. (Erik Viktor/Science Photo Library)

and thus to maintain deterrence: 'The Soviets . . . have enough accurate and powerful nuclear weapons to destroy virtually all of our missiles on the ground,' he declared. In response to this threat, Reagan called for a continuation of the 'major modernisation program' of conventional and nuclear forces that he had initiated after taking office in January 1981.

The President framed the main body of his speech with a futuristic vision. At the beginning he promised to reveal 'a decision which offers a new hope for our children in the twenty-first century', and at the end he outlined 'a mission to counter the awesome Soviet missile threat with measures that are defensive'. He asked:

What if free people could live secure in the knowledge that their security did not rest on the threat of instant US retaliation to deter a Soviet attack; that we could intercept and destroy strategic ballistic missiles before they reached our own soil or that of our allies?

Reagan acknowledged that 'this is a formidable technical task', but he was confident that 'the scientific community who gave us nuclear weapons' could now 'turn their great talents to the cause of mankind and world peace; to give us the means of rendering these nuclear weapons impotent and obsolete'. As an important first step, the President initiated 'a long-term research and development program to begin to achieve our ultimate goal of eliminating the threat posed by strategic nuclear missiles'.

Reagan's vision of missile defence turned this address into one of the most controversial and influential presidential speeches of the 1980s. Some political analysts argue that by dramatically raising the stakes in the military competition between the US and the Soviet Union, Reagan paved the way for the success of later arms reduction talks. However, when Senator Edward Kennedy first attached the 'Star Wars' label to the President's vision in comments made on the floor of the Senate the day after the speech, it was to accuse Reagan of 'misleading Red Scare tactics and reckless *Star Wars* schemes'. Kennedy's comments were meant to point out the fantastic nature of the missile defence programme and the real dangers of Reagan's escalation of the arms race into space. Yet, despite these critical intentions, the 'Star Wars' label was so evocative and ambivalent that it was immediately embraced by some of the President's supporters, and henceforth the programme, which did not acquire its official – and rather uninspiring – title of Strategic Defense Initiative (SDI) until the spring of 1984, was universally known as 'Star Wars'.

How did this convergence of politics and science fiction, reality and fantasy, Washington and Hollywood come about? In his psycho-biographical study *Ronald Reagan, the Movie*, Michael Rogin traces Reagan's vision of missile defence back to the 1940 Warner Brothers movie *Murder in the Air*. In this film, Reagan plays a Secret Service agent who prevents a foreign spy from stealing the plans for a powerful new defensive weapon. By being able to stop and destroy any attacking vehicle or missile, this weapon will, according to one of the film's characters, 'make America invincible in war and therefore be the greatest force for peace ever invented'. Rogin's central thesis is that the future president was 'made' in 1940s Hollywood. It is not only that Reagan extensively referred to movies in his later speeches, quoting in Congress, for example, Clint Eastwood's famous line 'Go ahead, make my day' from one of the *Dirty Harry* movies, with reference to his promised veto on tax increases, or stating in July 1985, after American hostages held in Lebanon had been released: 'Boy, I saw Rambo last night . . . Now I know what to do next time this happens.' More worryingly, according to Rogin, the President's identity and his conception of reality had been shaped by Hollywood films to such an extent that he was unable to step outside the fictions he had once inhabited.

In sharp contrast to this psychological critique, military historian Donald Baucom's exhaustive study *The Origins of SDI* shows that, far from being a Hollywood fantasy, Reagan's vision of missile defence was in line with an important strand in US strategic thinking. Soon after the German launch of the first V-2 ballistic missile against London in September 1944, the American military initiated a research and development programme to create defences against future missile attacks on the United States.

In subsequent decades, the notion of effective missile defence was gradually displaced by the principle of nuclear deterrence (appropriately known as MAD, for Mutually Assured Destruction). However, in the late 1970s, interest in strategic defence systems re-emerged in certain scientific, military and political circles which exerted a strong influence on Reagan, who was already opposed to the concept of offence-based nuclear deterrence and genuinely concerned about the vulnerability of the US in the event of a nuclear attack. During a visit to the North American Air Defense Command centre in the summer of 1979, Reagan was dismayed when confronted with a screen display of the simulated tracks of nuclear missiles moving towards targets in the US without the American military being able to stop them. He became interested in the development of a missile defence system, a project that gained some urgency early in his presidency, when he could not find an acceptable basing mode for the new MX intercontinental missiles, meant to guarantee retaliation after a Soviet attack.

Reagan was also affected by increasing religious opposition to the principle of nuclear deterrence. In October 1981, twenty Catholic bishops declared that it was immoral to possess nuclear weapons, and for May 1983 the National Conference of Catholic Bishops announced the publication of a pastoral letter on war and peace which was expected to reinforce this declaration. Then there was a broad-based nuclear-freeze movement which demanded an end to the testing, production and deployment of nuclear weapons, and culminated in the success of freeze proposals in several state referenda. Public support for Reagan's defence policy, in particular his massive military build-up, was eroding rapidly. Furthermore, following the 1981–2 recession and the attendant rise in unemployment, the President's popularity reached a low point. With a record budget deficit of $200 billion and inevitable cuts in social programmes, Reagan's budget for the fiscal year 1983–4, submitted on 31 January 1983, which included a 10 per cent increase in defence spending, met with strong opposition in Congress. This forced the President to postpone budget deliberations in Congress and to appeal directly to the American public in his speech of 23 March.

In the context of this crisis in his presidency, Reagan's remarks on missile defence made eminent political sense. In response to criticism of nuclear deterrence and military spending, he re-defined American defence strategy, offering hope for a non-nuclear future, which could be achieved only through enormous investments in military research. Reagan's vision was also a rhetorical masterstroke, worthy of the man known as the 'Great Communicator'. He gave an optimistic spin to what was otherwise an often quite negative speech about American decline and the increasing Soviet threat, setting up a heroic task for the American people and expressing confidence that, as before, they would rise to the occasion. The President also simplified complex political issues, bringing them down to the level of common sense, and by asking 'Would it not be better to save lives than to avenge them?', 'Is it not worth every investment necessary to free the world from the threat of nuclear war?'

Putting it this way, Reagan made it difficult for the American people to answer 'No' – and they didn't. Numerous opinion polls taken after the speech showed overwhelming support (around 70–80 per cent) for his missile defence programme. However, polls taken a few months before the speech had already indicated that while most Americans were unaware of the fact that the US had no defence against missile attacks, once they were told this, they were strongly in favour of developing a defence system. Thus Reagan only told the people what he knew they wanted to hear. And he did so at a time when the *Star Wars* films had popularised the notion of space-based weapons systems.

Following its release in May 1977, the original *Star Wars* movie quickly became the highest grossing film of all time in America. The film was accompanied by an unprecedented merchandising craze which would eventually earn billions of dollars, while its sequel *The Empire Strikes Back*, released in May 1980, became the country's second highest grossing box office triumph. This was followed by the successful launch of the *Star Wars* video in May 1982 and the film's first appearance on pay-TV in February 1983 which whetted public appetite for the forthcoming release of the second sequel, *Return of the Jedi* in May of that year. When Reagan addressed the nation on 23 March 1983, therefore, *Star Wars* was on everybody's mind.

In fact, the film seems to have been on Reagan's mind, too, as one of his most notorious speeches, given to the Annual Convention of the National

Association of Evangelicals on 8 March, suggests. In this speech, the President characterised Communism as a totalitarian ideology in which 'morality is entirely subordinate to the interests of class war', leaving no place for God or religion. Because of this, he declared the Soviet Union to be 'the focus of evil in the modern world'. Reagan urged his audience 'not to ignore the facts of history and the aggressive impulses of an evil empire, to simply call the arms race a giant misunderstanding and thereby remove yourself from the struggle between right and wrong and good and evil'. He argued that, 'while military strength is important, . . . the real crisis we face today is a spiritual one; at root, it is a test of moral will and faith'.

Reagan's controversial application of religious categories to the rivalry between the two superpowers was encapsulated in the phrase 'evil empire', which had been popularised by the *Star Wars* films. This link encouraged the press and the public to see his future speeches through the prism of *Star Wars*, which helps explain why, two weeks after this speech, people tried to make sense, or nonsense, of his announcement of a missile defence programme with reference to the movie. The fact that Reagan slipped an oblique reference to the film into his address, might have further encouraged such a response: when he referred to 'a new hope for our children in the twenty-first century', he quoted, probably inadvertently, the subtitle of the first *Star Wars* movie: 'A New Hope'.

The extreme popularity of a Hollywood film such as *Star Wars* derives not so much from any fixed message it may be said to convey, or any single response it aims to provoke, but from the multiplicity of meanings that can be extracted from it, and from the multiple uses it can be put to. Referring to the Soviet Union as an 'evil empire', or labelling Reagan's missile defence programme 'Star Wars' are two such uses, which may mobilise any of the meanings previously attached to the film or the term, and may also add new meanings to the existing repertory.

The pre-release market research for *Star Wars* is revealing in this respect. Researchers found that, when asked to give their response to the title and to judge a brief description of the film, potential movie-goers – with the exception of males under twenty-five – expressed their lack of interest in seeing it, because it was associated with the science fiction genre, combat and technology, aliens and robots, and was therefore expected to lack a human dimension. To overcome the resistance of older and female audiences, the advertising campaign that was developed from these tests emphasised the film's epic scope, its echoes of classic mythology, as well as the centrality of its human characters. The campaign characterised *Star Wars* as a science fiction fairy tale; hence the tag line: 'A long time ago in a galaxy far, far away. . . .' In this way, the film's appeal was broadened beyond the core audience of young males to reach all sections of the cinema-going public. Each of these audience sections was encouraged to see something different in *Star Wars*.

The introductory text which scrolls across the screen at the very beginning of the film already lends itself to a range of political interpretations:

> It is a period of civil war. Rebel spaceships, striking from a hidden base, have won their first victory against the evil Galactic Empire. During the battle, Rebel spies managed to steal secret plans to the Empire's ultimate weapon, the Death Star, an armored space station with enough power to destroy an entire planet.

A poll conducted in 1986 found that about half of all respondents saw the Empire, abstractly, as an embodiment of 'evil', whereas 24 per cent saw it as representing right-wing dictators and 12 per cent saw it as representing Communism. The real-life equivalents of the Rebels, as identified by respondents, ranged from the heroes of the American revolution and leftist revolutionaries in contemporary central America to right-wing, so-called 'freedom fighters'. When asked whether 'the movie is in favor of the conservative idea of "peace through military strength"', conservative respondents overwhelmingly said 'yes', whereas the majority of moderate and liberal respondents said 'no'. This poll suggests that *Star Wars* allowed everyone to extract from it precisely the political meaning they were most comfortable with.

It is no surprise, then, that people started using terms from *Star Wars* in political debates, often ignoring values and meanings explicitly attached to those terms in the film. Arguably, the film's story demonstrates the primacy of the spiritual power of 'the Force' over the technological power of space weapons, that is, the primacy of metaphysics over physics (which, in fact, was very much in line with Reagan's beliefs as expressed in his 'evil empire' speech). However, the film itself was celebrated as a great technological achievement, its special effects being put to their most impressive use in the space battle sequences. Drawing on the original associations of the film's title, therefore, people began to employ terms from the movie in discussions of technological and military issues.

One of the key proposals in the revival of strategic defence in the late 1970s was to set up space stations which were equipped with laser weapons able to

Darth Vader and the Evil
Empire provided an image of
the enemy that all Americans
could recognise. (Lucasfilm/
20th Century Fox/ Courtesy
Kobal)

shoot down missiles launched against the US. When this weapon system was
first proposed in an article in *Aviation Week* in October 1978, it was called
'battle station' – the very term used in *Star Wars* for the Evil Empire's Death
Star. Like the Death Star, the planned space stations were a kind of 'ultimate
weapon', and supporters of this research programme obviously felt that it
would profit from its association with the movie, despite the fact that this
association inverted the moral judgements of technology made in the film.
After all, the Death Star is an offensive weapon employed by the bad guys.

When the missile defence schemes of the US military gained wider
circulation in the early 1980s, commentators in the general press immediately
criticised them with reference to the film in articles entitled 'No Need for Star
Wars' or 'Make Way, Please, for Star Wars'. These articles prefigured the
rhetorical intervention made by Edward Kennedy: missile defence systems were

disqualified as a dangerous science fiction fantasy. In subsequent debates about the Strategic Defence Initiative, *Star Wars* references continued to be used effectively by Reagan's opponents to undermine his credibility as a politician and military strategist.

In various political cartoons, Reagan is associated with characters from the film, so as to indicate his inability to distinguish between Hollywood fantasy and political reality. The *San Diego Union* showed Reagan at his desk, making a televised speech on 'space-age defence', while surrounded by, as he says, 'a crack team of experts to advise us', including C3PO and R2D2 as well as ET. *The Boston Globe* portrayed him posing with a sword in a Darth Vader costume in front of his wife Nancy, telling her: 'And then I'd yell to Andropov: Lasers at dawn, you commie fink.' This cartoon did not only suggest that Reagan was living in a childish fantasy world, but also identified him with the force of evil in the Manichaean universe of the *Star Wars* movies. This further implied that, if it ever worked, Reagan's defence system would be used for offensive purposes, eventually leading to the destruction of the whole planet (which is what the Death Star is used for in *Star Wars*).

However, in line with the differing political readings of the original movie, *Star Wars* references could also be used to support the Strategic Defense Initiative. A cartoon in the *Indianapolis News* portrayed the Soviet missile defence programme as a huge Death Star dwarfing a tiny spaceship representing SDI, while the *Dayton Daily News* portrayed Andrei Gromyko as Darth Vader. Phyllis Schlafly welcomed the identification of SDI with *Star Wars*, because, like the movie, Reagan's vision was a 'drama of the battle between good and evil, and of the triumphs of good over evil through adventure, courage and confrontation'. These comments indicate the close connection between the two speeches Reagan had made in March 1983. In the minds of his supporters, the technological and strategic vision presented in the President's 'Star Wars' speech was ultimately justified by the moral vision he had outlined in the 'evil empire' address. Like the popularity of the movie, then, the cultural impact of Reagan's two-part vision derived from its successful combination of spectacular technology and profound spirituality.

While opponents of missile defence programmes had originally introduced the 'Star Wars' label in the early 1980s for the purpose of ridicule, by the mid-1980s it was generally acknowledged that the association of SDI with *Star Wars* worked in its favour. Reagan himself disliked the emphasis on large-scale war that the film reference brought to his initiative, yet he also acknowledged the compatibility of the film's spirituality and moral vision with his own world-view. In comments made in March 1985, he first rejected the 'Star Wars' label by saying that SDI 'isn't about war. It is about peace'. But then he added: 'If you will pardon my stealing a film line – the force is with us.'

The fact that the President stole this line, and numerous SDI supporters used references to the movie in their publicity and advertising campaigns, distressed *Star Wars* creator George Lucas, a typical Hollywood liberal, who had actually written the part of the Evil Emperor with Reagan's Republican predecessor Richard Nixon in mind. In 1985 Lucas brought a suit against two advocacy groups that campaigned for SDI, intending to forbid them from using the 'Star Wars' label. However, in November 1985 US District Judge Gerhard Gesell ruled that anyone could use the term 'Star Wars' in 'parody or descriptively to further a communication of their views on SDI'. As far as Lucas was concerned, the dark side of the Force seemed to have won. But it did not prevail. Just over eleven years later, the Strategic Defense Initiative was no longer a matter of intense public debate, and the surprisingly successful re-release of *Star Wars* took place without any unpleasant echoes of Reagan's programme. In a final ironic twist, in 1999 the much vilified figure of Darth Vader, who in the debate about SDI had been used by both sides to personify the political enemy (Gromyko or Reagan), was presented to the world as the real hero of George Lucas's space saga. The *Star Wars* prequel, *The Phantom Menace*, introduced him as slave boy Anakin Skywalker, future father of Luke, the hero of the first trilogy (Episodes 4 to 6). In Episodes 2 and 3 the boy will grow up to become a Jedi Knight and then turn to the dark side of the Force, thus becoming Luke's opponent Darth Vader, who nevertheless in the end will, of course, save him and the known universe from the Evil Emperor. Obviously, the politics of *Star Wars* continue to be very fluid indeed.

Part Two
PROPAGANDA CINEMA

6

THE GREAT WAY

Graham Roberts

The year 1927 was crucial in the history of the Soviet Union. As the country celebrated its tenth anniversary, power struggles over its future direction were taking place among the higher ranks of the Communist Party. Developments which would come to a head between November 1927 and the winter of 1929 would settle the nature of the Soviet state – and its leadership – for decades to come. The year 1927 was also important for Soviet cinema; when film-makers were expected to produce suitable offerings on screen to commemorate the anniversary of the Great October Revolution. The Bolsheviks clearly understood (perhaps even overestimated) the power of film. This was particularly true of Stalin who in 1924 had told the 13th Party Congress: 'The cinema is the greatest means of mass agitation. The task is to take it into our hands.'

The first film-maker to take up the challenge of celebrating the Revolution was Esfir Il'inichna Shub. Shub came to the city from the outskirts of Moscow as a student in 1919. Finding herself caught up in the artistic avant-garde, she soon gravitated towards cinema, seeing this, as she put it in her memoirs, as 'a method of expressing all that the Great October Revolution had brought . . . a new life was beginning. . . .' Shub decided to enter directly into the practical side of the industry. After a number of false starts and rejected applications, she landed a job in the film section of the Commissariat of the Enlightenment in 1922. Here she worked for the State Cinema Organisation, Goskino, re-editing and re-titling foreign films to render them ideologically sound for distribution. Tailoring the work of others to the needs of the Soviet regime was to have a profound effect on her own productions.

Shub proved herself a skilled editor and a trusted worker. Although she was not a member of the Communist Party, her memoirs recount that she was given the politically important and technically difficult job of creating two

Idealisation of the masses, emphasis on an economy on the move and a heavy-handed contrast between the old regime and new Soviet youthfulness were all expertly realised by the film's director Esfir Il'inichna Shub. (David King Collection)

documentary·films for the anniversaries of 1927 using material compiled from earlier newsreels. The first of these, *The Fall of the Romanov Dynasty* (*Padenie Dinastii Romanovykh*), was to chronicle the events which led to the end of the Tsarist regime, while the second, *The Great Way* (*Velikii put*), was to celebrate ten years of achievement in the world's first socialist state. The cinema establishment was keen to be involved in the project. Mark Tseitlin, a young newsreel editor who went on to teach at the State Film School after the war, was assigned as 'historical consultant'. Shub was also given a small team to help to collect the scattered, often insufficiently sourced, scraps of footage.

Once she had located and catalogued the available material, Shub had to reshape it to form two ideologically sound, coherent and artistic, complete films. Few of the sequences gathered were of any great length, but Shub actually turned this problem into one of the major strengths of the films. A key feature is the use of titles followed by illustration. Brief scenes are brought together or intercut with bold titles (written by Shub and Tseitlin) to create a direct, powerful, yet graceful, montage form. This meant that a wide range of material could be used effectively to emphasise a single, encompassing message. In a process that was very much in the Russian Marxist tradition, from Plekhanov, through Lenin to his successors, documentary footage was thus manipulated for a political cause – unselfconsciously and without apology.

During the seventy minutes of *The Fall of the Romanovs* Shub presents a dialectic which draws itself (and those watching) to an unavoidable conclusion: that the success of Bolshevism is inevitable. Such an effect cannot be produced by assembling a collection of archive work alone (however good); it is the work of an experienced and highly skilled *montageuse*. The film closes with a smiling, confident Lenin greeting well-wishers. Shub ends her narrative with this triumphant moment, reinforcing for the audience the sense of inevitability they must associate with Bolshevik victory.

When *The Fall* was released (to public and critical acclaim), Shub was already preparing for her second film *The Great Way*. The length and pacing of this film (nine – as opposed to seven – reels running for a total of eighty minutes), as well as its subject matter, give the impression of a huge historical pageant. Nonetheless, *The Great Way* is full of splendid detail and tinges of humour. The film opens with a surprise. The viewer is presented with a shot of the back of a Tsarist statue; a rider and the rump of a horse. The next shot is of broken statues; a striking image of the impotence of the Tsarist system, its symbols shattered. A small child – icon of the new – plays among the debris of the old regime. Interestingly, almost identical scenes were used in countless documentaries and news items made between 1989 and 1991, both inside and outside the country, during the collapse of the Soviet empire; a fact that suggests that Shub's film had been studied by (ex-) Soviet film-makers who recycled the image until it came to represent the 'end of the Soviet Union'.

Immediately after the shattered statues in *The Great Way*, we see a flag flying over the Kremlin. The text proclaims, 'On the stage of October stood the victorious masses.' We see street scenes from Petrograd in 1917 and a crowd milling about in front of the camera. (The crowd, seen as a backdrop in much of *The Fall*, is in this film significantly to the fore.) Shub briefly shows some shots of leaders of the capitalist world before we see the workers' international. 'Through their leaders the proletariat of all lands are solidly behind the workers' and peasants' revolution' reads the accompanying statement, which is illustrated by footage of German Communists performing a drill, followed by scenes filmed in 'Mexico' and 'China':

Under the Red Banner they vow. They vow together with the masses of the Soviet State under the Red Banner together with the workers of the Soviet Republic with our own leader Lenin.

Shub is constructing a clear historical argument. The Russian Revolution was a mass movement which required (Bolshevik) leadership. The Russian masses have appeal – and support – throughout the world. The audience can then be shown how the Soviet beacon of socialism was strengthened against the threat of international capitalism.

Reels two and three deal with the setting up of the new Soviet state and the internal and external threats which it faced. We are shown the Smolny Institute and informed that this was the headquarters of the Bolshevik Central Committee, as well as the Petrograd Soviet and the Military-Revolutionary Committee (which planned and co-ordinated the seizure of power). The footage is roughly shot and edited but also rather atmospheric as the camera is close to the frenetic action, which is mainly composed of drill parades. The initial impression is of spontaneous popular action – a message which would not have fitted in well with the developing leadership-centred orthodoxy of the late 1920s, and which became a cult in the 1930s.

In the next sequence we see the new leadership: Lenin, Lunarcharsky, Krylenko, Antonov-Ovseenko and Sverdlov. Stalin does not feature at all. This is historically accurate, but could only have placed Shub under suspicion at a later date. (She did not make the same mistake with her 1937 film *Land of the Soviets* where, short of footage, the titles glorify Stalin's role in the Revolution.) The camera lingers over an order from Lenin (dated 5 January) calling for peace. The next shots, showing soldiers fraternising, look bogus. The cameras are placed behind the 'German' trenches and the troops look like they are acting. At the end of the sequence they hold up a banner demanding 'All power to the Internationale'. In contrast to this we are shown the 'Peace Agreement' at Brest-Litovsk. However, the only film used to illustrate this meeting is some shaky footage of the Austrian delegation. The sequence ends with a still shot of the Kaiser signing the treaty.

Reel three begins with the statement 'The whole world was against the Proletarian Revolution with blockade and interventionist encirclement. 16 March – The Germans enter Kiev.' Fortunately for Shub and her historical consultants, the Germans had filmed themselves arrogantly strutting through the streets of the Ukrainian capital. They also filmed the 'Ukrainian Independent Nationalists' who could thus be portrayed as collaborators. Next we see the 'Japanese Liberators' in Vladivostok. They are greeted by peasants – ostentatiously praising God and carrying icons – and lots of priests. The caption reads: 'The monarchist flag flutters together with the flag of the Japanese Imperialists.'

'The first repercussion of October – revolution in Germany' opens the next reel. The (German) footage is ragged and disorganised but has real energy: 'November 1918 – Berlin in the days of revolution' – we see extensive damage to buildings, while people walk about in front of the camera, oblivious. The captions gloat about the fall of another dynasty, while a specially produced animation sequence showing the Imperial eagle falling and a graphic of the Brest-Litovsk treaty crossed out, is intercut. This section provides several examples of the techniques which were Shub's particular trademark. Firstly,

As Commissar of War, Trotsky (here being filmed in 1922) was one of the 'stars' of Shub's film, although his hunger for publicity eventually brought him down – just as the film was being released. (Hulton Getty)

her use of text from documents, newspapers or even writing from the plinths of statues, to anchor the accompanying images, and, secondly, her use of 'enemy' material to make political points beyond those intended by the original film-maker. Shub was expert at using non-Soviet film cuttings which she manipulated or re-titled to make pointed criticisms of the actions of industrialists, politicians and anti-Soviet forces in general. A good example is her presentation of the Paris peace conference ('of victors') which relies – for obvious reasons – on French footage. The main figures go about their business self-importantly, ignoring the camera, as the crowd moves about in the background. Shub underlines her point by juxtaposition. The most interesting section shows the French street parties – 'They celebrate' – which Shub contrasts with Soviet celebrations under the caption 'In a capitalist encirclement – The Soviet State becomes a beacon.' The Soviet celebrations are less gaudy than the French ones, but the people are more joyous and energetic. A Soviet audience would have noted that the Soviet citizens – who could indeed be themselves – are not merely watching the entertainment: they are *part* of it. Members of the leadership – including a broadly grinning Bukharin – are *among* the crowd.

A long sequence of titles reminds the audience of slogans promulgated by the Second Congress of the Communist International and statements from Lenin: 'Now begins a new era in world history.' There follows a funeral of 'Commissars defending Soviet power against the English'. An old woman mourns over one coffin. The crowd carries a banner: 'We vow to take the Communist Revolution to the whole world.' This powerful sequence would prove to be problematic. The issue of 'internationalism' was largely settled at the 14th Party Congress in April 1925 with the victory of Stalin (socialism in one country) over Trotsky (Permanent Revolution) – a personal triumph for Stalin. However, balancing the needs of the first socialist state with the cause of International Socialism and the nature of the relationship between the USSR and the West were issues which would be raised again and again within the Communist Party – during the Depression, the rise of National Socialism and the Spanish Civil War.

Reels five and six deal at length with the Russian civil war of 1918-21. The 'star' of this particular section is the (then) Commissar of War, Leon Trotsky. However, in January 1925, Trotsky, out-gunned by a combination of Stalin, Kamenev and Zinoviev, had lost this position. Within a year of the 14th Party Congress he was out of the ruling Politburo and Stalin was moving against his erstwhile colleagues. At precisely the time Shub was making *The Great Way*,

Trotsky's image was being removed from Eisenstein's 'anniversary' film, *October*, while the man himself was about to be condemned to internal exile as an 'enemy of the people'.

Reel seven announces that 'The victory of Communism will begin with improvement on the economic front. . . . Under the direction . . . of Lenin. . . .' With the leader's image brought to the fore, and having established an argument about future success, Shub can confidently deal with the potentially devastating event of January 1924. Ships are shown stranded in the ice and snow. A flag flutters in the wind. A newspaper headline flashes up the news: 'Lenin is dead.' We see the coffin carried by leading Bolsheviks. Footage showing Stalin at the funeral is featured, but only as part of a sequence showing Lenin's family and colleagues in attendance. A tattered flag (presumably red) blows in the wind. Another flag, rather better preserved, flies above the Kremlin. Crowds mass inside and outside the Hall of Columns. Gun salutes are fired in Moscow and the Arctic. The tattered red flag flutters again in the strong northern wind – a solemn and moving moment. But the audience must not be allowed to dwell on negative aspects. After lengthy coverage of the funeral the reel finishes with the caption 'Lenin is dead but his venture lives on.' The factory sirens sound and the work continues.

In this way Shub has paid her respects to the 'cult of Lenin', so important for the continuing solidarity of the Party – 'Lenin lives in the soul of every member of our Party . . .' – if not the whole state. The development of the cult was also crucial to Stalin's rise to power. Not seen as any kind of rival by the post-Lenin leadership, the Party Secretary had carefully utilised his (completely fallacious) image as Lenin's chief apostle. With a long-held and growing interest in cinema, Stalin would have been pleased with Shub's contribution, but may have been disappointed by his less-than-central role in her story.

Reel eight is another exercise in the use of 'enemy' material. It begins with a bold, single word title: 'THERE'. Wall Street fills the screen, a scene of frenetic activity: 'The uncrowned Kings of Capitalism' – illustrated by a grinning 'Rockerfeller' (*sic*) and Ford strutting at a parade. The sequence of footage showing the Paris stock exchange which follows is astonishing in its complexity and pace, especially in contrast to the preceding parade. Shots of the stone griffins of Notre Dame looking down on Paris are strikingly intercut with speeded-up footage of the traffic below. Shub moves on to one of her dialectical montages. 'Next Door' – are the slums of Paris. 'In the Colonies' – we see huts. The workers are described as 'slaves'. The following scenes show a strike in the United States. Clearly Shub intends the audience to make a connection between these workers of the world. The American footage focuses on police brutality. A shocking scene shows five large policemen attacking a lone woman. We are shown an archetypal 'capitalist' chatting to a police officer and then the text: 'They organise a reprisal.' The violence continues. The capitalist world – and its evils – needs to be connected to the Soviet Union. Shub does this with a caption: 'The Labouring Masses Will Remember. They Are Ready To Attack. We See. We Are Ready.' A formation of battleships is shown. Peep-holes open, periscopes rise, guns are levelled. Troops drill and tanks roll forward. The caption reads: 'The USSR. The first country in the world where workers and peasants are successfully building Socialism.'

The camera tours the city, concentrating on transport and traffic signals in particular. Workers 'escaping from repression' are shown arriving in Moscow. As they emerge from the train they are greeted with banners – in Russian and German – proclaiming 'Workers of the World Unite'. 'We are building factories and plants. We are building a new life getting women out of the kitchen.' We see factories and then some 'model housing'. A new factory kitchen is shown where both men and women are at work; the communal dining room is neat and tidy, small children smile at the camera. Next we see the first Soviet tractors. They are filmed driving past horse-drawn ploughs. Shub is illustrating the Party's efforts to modernise the countryside, but as the caption states: 'Every new tractor strengthens the link between the peasants and the workers.' We are in the age of *smychka* – the 'link' central to the New Economic Policy launched by Lenin in 1921 when he recognised the need for peasant support. This co-operative stance was still the Party line in 1927, but was about to be abandoned as Stalin convinced the Party, for his own political reasons, that Bukharin's arguments against the 'left' policy of exploiting the peasants were out of date. Kalinin – 'the All-Union elder' – visits the peasants for tea to introduce 'Electrification of the Countryside'. The titles remind us of the call of the Party Congress for an increase in machine production. We see more trains.

Next, under the banner of Komsomol, the Communist youth-wing, we see a group of teenagers, some younger children are standing in front of them: 'Hurrah For Change . . .' reads the caption. An old woman waves her handkerchief and faces cheer. This image dissolves into a well-ordered march past of children. The final moving image of the film shows a column of young Leninists marching off screen (and into the future) with the title:

They swear to finish their Fathers' work on this Great Way For Il'yich and the strengthening of the Soviet Union.

The film was released in Moscow on 6 November 1927, the eve of the Revolutionary celebrations. That same day Trotsky, together with his old rival, Zinoviev, launched one last desperate attempt to stop Stalin's inexorable rise to power. Their failure left Stalin with only one possible rival: Bukharin. But Bukharin had already lost his ideological struggle centred on a slow but steady move towards complete socialisation of the countryside. In December 1927, the 15th Party Congress – packed with Stalin's appointees – voted for the crash collectivisation of agriculture. In October 1928, the Politburo launched the first Five Year Plan (aiming, with supreme confidence, to fulfil the targets by December 1932). Autumn 1929 saw the start of the disaster of forced collectivisation. That November, the anniversary celebrations coincided with the defeat of 'right opposition' and Bukharin was expelled from the Politburo. By December, Stalin could celebrate his fiftieth birthday in total command of the Soviet system.

By the end of the 1920s, Shub's films had become problematic for the newly triumphant leadership. Stalin would undoubtedly have been pleased by the constant 'vows' that are made; his vow to continue Lenin's work had already entered Soviet mythology. But the Party – in spite of all the references in Shub's titles – does not feature prominently in the visual content of the film. When members of the leadership do appear, they are Lenin, Trotsky and Bukharin; not Stalin or his acolytes. Furthermore, the film takes a clearly internationalist perspective at a time when the non-internationalist implications of 'socialism in one country' were just becoming clear. The triumphant past and present are naturally celebrated, but this approach rather undermined the new 'general line' of impending crisis that required drastic policy changes.

In the period after the film's release, the Soviet film industry was to change dramatically from the one Shub had entered in the early 1920s. The extent of this shift, or strengthening of control, had not been signalled by the change of name of the central body from 'State' to 'Soviet' Cinema Organisation in the summer of 1924. By 1928, the film industry's political masters were impatient. The key to future development was 'proletarianisation', a process which would require closer control by the Communist Party. Shub was not a member. Increasingly, the criterion for advancement became political reliability rather than talent. Reliability came to be measured by the ability to produce films 'intelligible to the millions' (as a resolution passed at the Soviet Cinema workers conference of December 1928 put it).

The Great Way was well received following its release, particularly among Shub's contemporaries in the film industry. The positive response of

Mayakovskii and other critics of 'the left' was in stark contrast to the abuse they heaped upon Eisenstein's *October* and Pudovkin's *The End of St Petersburg*. However, the plaudits of other film-makers were not necessarily advantageous to Shub at a time when the Central Committee of the Party itself was calling for a 'strengthening of cadres'. She ceased to be so productive. *The Russia of Nicholas II and Lev Tostoii* (1928) was followed by *Today* (1930), but the latter film was delayed by an unwillingness of the cinema authorities to purchase foreign newsreel material. Shub then struggled for two years to produce her first documentary with soundtrack, *Komsomol: Chief of Electrification* (1932).

As her efforts to make films continued, those she made – perhaps too thought-provoking and demanding of audiences – were rarely shown. Her memoirs catalogue numerous ideas – ostensibly ideologically sound – for films which were never made, or which became projects for other (lesser) film-makers. By 1934 Shub was writing articles for magazines with headings like 'I Want to Work' (none of which were even published). When, in 1937, she was offered Stalin's commission to remake history (and indeed her own film), she gratefully accepted. In *Land of the Soviets* (*Strana Sovetov*) the roles of the Party and especially of Stalin were given a higher profile with the heavy-handed use of titles.

Worthy of much praise as a piece of film-making, *The Great Way*, must of course be treated with caution as evidence. As an unashamed propaganda project which deliberately manipulates historical material, it is a less-than-reliable account of Soviet history from 1917 to 1927. Nonetheless, it is an invaluable source of photographic material of the period. Beyond that, both the film and Shub's later career are clear reflections of the atmosphere in the Soviet Union during 1927 and as such they offer part of the explanation for what followed in 1929 and later.

7

TRIUMPH OF THE WILL

Brian Winston

In the canon of great films, the place of *Triumph of the Will*, a documentary about the sixth Nazi Party Congress of 1934 directed by Leni Riefenstahl, seems to be impregnable. For received opinion, the film is, in Susan Sontag's words, 'the most successfully, most purely propagandistic film ever made'. Yet this is more than a little curious, for the film lives, outside of neo-fascist circles, only as a species of awful warning against fascism. It is not regarded as a persuasive text – unlike say, the silent, Soviet film, *Battleship Potemkin*, which Nazi propaganda master Joseph Goebbels thought 'a marvellous film without equal in the cinema . . . anyone who had no firm political conviction could become a Bolshevik after seeing the film'. Even in the 1930s, few claims were made that *Triumph of the Will* would do the same for fascism. In fact, political scientist and film historian Richard Taylor states that 'the film was not used generally for propaganda purposes' in Germany at the time.

The response of most non-fascist viewers is probably best summed up by critic Lotte Eisner's 1952 judgement that: 'The film leaves one finally with an impression of insanity.' Images from *Triumph of the Will* are endlessly recycled in every anti-Nazi documentary precisely as evidence of the essential madness of those who appeared in, and paid for, the film. Surely this is strange for what is, supposedly, 'the most successfully, most purely propagandistic film ever made'.

The initial problems with the film in terms of propaganda are easily understood. The sixth annual National Socialist Party Congress was not quite the jubilant affair it ought to have been. Hitler had been Chancellor of Germany for over a year. In the election of March 1933, following the Reichstag fire, the Nazis had taken 44 per cent of the popular vote. But it was the destruction of the leadership of the SA (the *Sturmabteilung*, the storm troopers) in the episode known as the Röhm Putsch just a few weeks before the faithful gathered in Nuremberg for the Congress that threatened to spoil it.

The backbone of Nazi support came from the middle and lower-middle classes but nevertheless the Party, by its very use of the term 'socialist' in its title, also sought working-class support. Although the SA had its share of minor civil servants and schoolteachers, young working-class lads constituted a major recruiting ground for the organisation's brown-shirted street-fighters. Ernst Röhm, the SA leader, became the guardian of the populist rhetoric of the Party. In the aftermath of the 1933 election the SA needed to redefine its role, just as Hitler's successful strategy of seeking power through the ballot box was now leading him into accommodations with other elements of the German establishment. The SA would have been an embarrassment even if Röhm had not chosen to stress a populist, 'socialist' agenda. Demanding machine guns for his 2 million Brownshirts, he had declared: 'The SA is and will be the arbiter of Germany's fate.'

Encouraged by the German establishment, especially the army, and pressured by the French, Hitler, with Goebbels and members of the SS (the *Schutzstaffel* or Black Guards) and the Gestapo (the *Geheime Staatspolizei* – the secret state police) murdered Röhm and his entire command at Bad Wiessee during what became known as the 'Night of the Long Knives', 30 June 1934. Hitler's pretext, plausible enough, was that Röhm was planning a putsch against him; but, within weeks, he had to fly to Nuremberg to confront the mass of Röhm's SA at the sixth *Parteistag*. 'Men of the SA and the SS', he cried . . .

> a few months ago, a black shadow spread over the movement. And the SA has as little to do with this shadow as any other institution in the Party. They deceive themselves who think that even a single crack has appeared in the edifice of our united movement. . . . And if any one sins against the spirit of my SA this will break not the SA but only those who dare to sin against them. Only a madman or a deliberate liar could think that I, or anyone, would ever intend to dissolve what we have ourselves built up over many long years. No, comrades, we stand firmly by our Germany and we must stand firmly by this Germany.

What this speech lacked in eloquence and logic was more than compensated for by nerve. Hitler performed this 'big lie' before 97,000 SA men gathered together in the Luitpold Stadium, after more than 200 of their leaders had been murdered and while many thousands more lower-level cadres were still being purged. An American eye-witness noted:

Hitler and Riefenstahl during the making of *Triumph of the Will*. Despite the grandiloquence of scenes from the film, such as the mass banners march past, it is arguable that the whole adds up to less than the parts. (BFI Stills, Posters and Designs)

Hitler faced his SA storm troopers today for the first time since the bloody purge. There was considerable tension in the stadium and I noticed that Hitler's own bodyguard was drawn up in front of him separating him from the mass of Brownshirts.

But this rally was to be a perfect example of the *Führerprinzip*, the 'leadership principle', in action. Appearing in SA uniform at all times, Hitler used the Congress to insist on personal loyalty to himself even as he offered ceremonial and rhetorical crumbs of the populist sort favoured by Röhm. Any potential internal threat to the Party was removed. This, then, is the immediate and potent triumph of Hitler's will which necessarily becomes the central theme and organising principle of the filmed record of these events. Despite the blindness of cinema scholars, who would save *Triumph of the Will* for art by ignoring its politics, and the strenuous denials of Riefenstahl, who has a pressing need to disclaim any political understanding on her part, the film – especially in the selection of the speeches – deals with either the SA problem, the need for absolute loyalty to Hitler, or the Party's undying concern for the German worker and peasant.

Rather than as a propaganda classic, *Triumph of the Will* should be seen as a classically flawed effort of persuasion in that it had two contradictory aims. Albeit some considerable time after the event, it functioned as an internal Party message demonstrating, with the compelling supposed veracity of the moving photographic image, that the vast mass of the SA were, quite literally, with Hitler. It implicitly confirmed that the populist concerns of the SA remained central to the Party. But, by the same token, it did not work as a general propaganda message for the majority of Germans who, even after the intimidations of the March 1933 election, had not voted Nazi. On the contrary, by constantly referring to the problem with the SA (safely buried by the time of the film's release in late March 1935), *Triumph of the Will* highlighted the fact that the Party was perhaps not as monolithic as it appeared. By stressing the *Führerprinzip* and virtually deifying Hitler visually, it drew attention to the cult surrounding a political leader whom 56 per cent of voters had rejected.

Furthermore, in terms of the overall propaganda tactics of the Nazis, the film was aberrant. 'We National Socialists', Goebbels remarked in his initial briefing to the German film industry in 1933, 'do not place any particular value on our SA marching across the stage or screen. . . . The National Socialist government has never asked that SA films be made. On the contrary – we see danger in a surplus of them.' Goebbels developed a coherent propaganda strategy relying primarily on the news media – press, radio and cinema newsreels – for direct political message-making. The new technology of television was also in part encouraged and deployed for these purposes. A complex structure was put in place immediately the Nazis came to power in 1933, whereby a public distance was established between Goebbels' ministry and these organs of opinion. All artists and media workers, including print, broadcast and film journalists, were licensed through the *Reichskammer* system. The existing trade unions, artists' leagues and other organisations were either banned or transformed. Goebbels claimed that this 'concept of corporate professional groups' was going to be 'the great sociological concept of the twentieth century'. Membership was, of course, restricted. 'Alien' – that is Jewish and other undesirable elements – were excluded and could not work; but Goebbels required no further proof of loyalty, such as Party membership, from those included. Indeed, it was more useful to the regime if prominent public figures, the film star and director Leni Riefenstahl, for example, remained 'independent'.

Goebbels was also at pains to maintain the fiction of the independence of production companies such as the newsreel firms. Both UFA and Tobis, the leading newsreels, were taken over by a Nazi trust company in 1936 in what historian David Welch calls, 'almost complete secrecy'. It is not hard to see why Goebbels adopted such an approach. Although the implicit triumphalism of films celebrating the Party's uniformed ranks, or the *Führerprinzip*, might (except, perhaps, in the circumstances following a Röhm putsch) encourage the faithful, it was not necessarily going to win converts to the cause. Immediately after the 1933 election, as the new Reich Minister for Popular Education and Propaganda, Goebbels had told the film industry that the Nazis were 'not satisfied with having 52 per cent of the nation as supporters while terrorising the other 48 per cent. We want the people as the people, not only passively but actively'. But he did not require 'parade ground marching and the blowing of trumpets' as the means of getting them. And, the newsreels apart, the industry did not proffer such images – with the exception of *Triumph of the Will*. So why was it made? The answer is to be found in the opening frames of the film, in a title which declares: 'The document of the National Party Congress 1934, produced by Order of the Führer, created by Leni Riefenstahl.'

By her mid-twenties Riefenstahl was a star, specialising in the popular German genre of mountain pictures. The Nazi leaders were no less attracted by the glamour of show business than other politicians have been, before and since. Riefenstahl was friendly with them prior to 1933, sometimes taking her mother and father with her on social visits to Hitler. As a very famous, extremely beautiful and charismatic actress, she had a line to the Führer which was outside Goebbels' control. 'Produced by Order of the Führer' meant *not* produced by order of Goebbels. Hitler had previously personally commissioned Riefenstahl to contribute to the sequence of Party Congress films which had begun in 1927. She had produced *Victory of Faith*, a short account of the fifth *Parteistag* in 1933. He then asked her to film the sixth as well. Goebbels had two good reasons, outlined above, for objecting to this plan: it did not fit within his announced film policy and he was also against publicising the unavoidable aftermath of the Röhm affair in so relatively permanent a form as a documentary film. Moreover, apart from any feelings of personal animosity or sexism, he was concerned at the explicit threat to his power that Riefenstahl's special relationship with Hitler represented. However, the only effect of Goebbels' hostility was to provide Riefenstahl with the basis of her defence to subsequent charges of complicity with the regime. She cited Goebbels's animosity towards her over this project (and over her subsequent film of the 1936 Berlin Olympics) as evidence of her distance from the Nazis. Naive American officers over-seeing Riefenstahl's postwar denazification proceedings completely misunderstood the significance of this, just as they failed to appreciate the reason why she was not a member of the Party – another element of her defence.

Goebbels's hostility towards Riefenstahl and her project, however, was as nothing compared to Hitler's support. She was allowed to deploy extraordinary resources – some forty-nine cameramen (nineteen of them senior cinematographers), an airship and a plane to help make the film. She was given total co-operation from the Congress organisers, including the provision of special camera positions and the option of re-staging shots if anything went wrong. Albert Speer claimed she re-shot some speeches in Berlin because of sound problems, and I also believe from evidence within the film that some shots in the sequence of Hitler's arrival at the airport were not filmed at the time. Riefenstahl eventually had more than sixty hours of material from which she edited 107 minutes.

Despite received critical opinion, the end result is as unimpressive a piece of film-making as it is propaganda. The majority of Riefenstahl's cameramen were work-a-day newsreel operators who provided their usual level of coverage. In spite of their numbers, there are endless continuity jumps. For example, on Hitler's triumphal drive into Nuremberg the windscreen of his Mercedes assumes a number of different positions. There are even shots of Hitler himself which are out of focus. But the real problem with the film is that – shaped by Riefenstahl's Nazi sensibility – it is monotonous and repetitive, as march past follows march past and ceremonies succeed ceremonies. Take the last quarter of the film. The Ceremony of the Fallen, at which Hitler makes the 'shadow' speech quoted above, lasts 11 minutes and 17 seconds, more than half of which is taken up with marching. It is followed by 18 minutes and 4 seconds of a great march past. This in turn is followed by the closing sequence which contains, as well as a lengthy march past of banners, Hitler's fifth speech of the film. So why is it so highly regarded? Why did it win the Gold Medal at the Venice Film Festival in 1935, and, more surprisingly, the Grand Prix at the Paris Film Festival in 1937? Why have film critics (assuming they are not themselves Nazi

Art or propaganda? The opening night of *Triumph of the Will* in Berlin. (BFI Stills, Posters and Designs)

or neo-fascist) continued to claim that *Triumph of the Will*, in the words of film-buff Glenn Infield, is 'one of the technical and artistic masterpieces of film history, a truly great film', when it is palpably no such thing?

The answer lies with Albert Speer. It is in fact the glamour of the spectacle that Speer created for the 1934 Party Congress that has blinded us to the extremely limited value added to the event by Riefenstahl. Given more or less professional film coverage of a stadium filled with 100,000 anonymous, uniformed men in perfect formation, it would be hard to produce an unimpressive image. And that is all that Riefenstahl does. The power of *Triumph of the Will* is not one conjured up by the director. It is rather the raw power of the original event which even a modestly talented film-maker could not obscure.

Riefenstahl's postwar reputation in the English-speaking world dates from October 1971 when she allowed herself to be interviewed by an American cineaste Gordon Hitchens. Safe behind the veils of time, she rehearsed what was to become a familiar litany. She knew nothing of the Röhm business, not least because she was location hunting in Spain at the time for her feature film, *Tiefland*. Goebbels hated her. She was never given a prize by the Nazis. She knew nothing about atrocities or anything else. She never did anything of which she is ashamed. She was not political. She was never a member of the Party. All of this is either false, extremely unlikely or, at best, tendentious. Riefenstahl was, for instance, given the Nazi national film prize in 1935. She used Romany extras taken from a holding camp for *Tiefland* (which she eventually began shooting in 1941) and, according to the Holocaust chronicler Nina Gladitz, they were then returned to the camp system and ultimately to Auschwitz. Nevertheless, unquestioning critics and journalists have endlessly repeated Riefenstahl's tale and in the process have transformed her into 'an authentic genius', 'ignorant of the outside world', 'an artist of an immensely naive political nature'. Moreover, her reputation has also been unexpectedly boosted as a result of the rise of the women's movement. For example, Susan Sontag has stated that Riefenstahl is 'the one woman who made films that everybody acknowledges to be first rate'.

Triumph of the Will was firmly declared to be 'art' rather than 'propaganda' – although, paradoxically, it was still a propaganda masterpiece. Within what has become a veritable Riefenstahl industry, some of these critics do have the grace to concede, in the words of Richard Barsam, that the film sustains 'a vicious ideology'. But the 'art versus politics' division allows for this. Nowhere is the distinction between form and content more insistently made than in favourable appraisals of *Triumph of the Will*. The film has also gained from being little seen, certainly in its original form. There are re-cut shortened versions in circulation which omit the speeches and the smaller-scale ceremonials to highlight Speer's brilliant spectacles. Riefenstahl's authorial claims to such versions are tenuous.

The authority for making the art/politics distinction is Hitler himself who said in an interview of 1934: 'It makes me sick when people make art under the guise of politics. Either art or politics.' Goebbels, of course, agreed. He was already classifying films as valuable politically, artistically or culturally. *Triumph of the Will* ('produced by Order of the Führer') was classed (inevitably) as '*Staatspolitisch besonders wertvoll*' – 'Politically especially valuable'. It could have been '*Staatspolitisch wertvoll und kunstlerisch besonders wertvoll*' – 'Politically and artistically especially valuable' – but it was not. If Goebbels understood this, why can't we? The time is long past for the glamour of Speer's spectacle to be dispelled and for this film to be classified historically where it really belongs – not in the artistic canon of great cinema works, but in the archive as vivid evidence of the manic dimension of twentieth-century totalitarianism.

8

THIS IS THE ARMY

David Culbert

Between 1940 and 1945, the most watched, most profitable movie to come out of Hollywood was Warner Brothers' *This Is the Army*. Irving Berlin's musical extravaganza about a wartime stage show, set within a slender romantic narrative, and based on actual stage shows from the First and Second World Wars, included a cast of hundreds of soldiers released from front-line duty.

Directed by Michael Curtiz, Berlin adapted *This Is the Army* from his 1942 Broadway hit of the same name. As a rapturous *New York Times* critic noted at the time of the film's release, in July 1943, 'There is something so peculiarly and indigenously American about Mr Berlin's fabulous hit that no other country could ever create a show quite like it. . . . Being a democracy's sort of show, it likes to kid the Army.'

More successful than the phenomenal RKO hit of 1946, *The Best Years of Our Lives* and ranking second only to *Gone with the Wind* (1939), *This Is the Army* was the most profitable film in the entire history of Warner Brothers (the total revenue was $10,445,000). Berlin had decided to donate all the profits from his wartime hits to the Army Emergency Relief Fund for deserving wives and parents of servicemen. Inspired by his generosity, many of those who appeared in *This Is the Army* performed for free. Having agreed to make the film, Warner Brothers initially planned to keep half of any profits, but in a 'patriotic' gesture later decided to donate the lot. However, the film seemingly made more money than the studio wanted insiders to know, a curious state of affairs since every studio gloried in word-of-mouth publicity accompanying giant box-office successes. Perhaps some at Warners were ashamed that quite so much money (in the region of $9 million) was to be given to charity.

Why should we be so interested in how much money the film made? Its success suggests that it spoke directly to American audiences, which in turn

Hundreds were relaesed from front-line duty for Berlin's film, *This Is the Army*, which earned Warner Brothers its biggest profit. (Warner Bros/Courtesy Kobal)

says something about the way average Americans thought about the purpose and meaning of the war. With its optimism, muted ideological message and escapism (it literally gives the viewer a song and dance), *This Is the Army* provides an example of the 'unwitting testimony' that historian Arthur Marwick cites as a reason for considering film in terms of historical context. Context of another sort was provided by *Variety*, trade organ of the entertainment industry, which arranged to have Al Jolson review the film. Jolson was the entertainer who introduced Hollywood screen musicals in 1927 with his singing of 'Mammy' in *The Jazz Singer*, the very first talkie. *Variety*'s front-page headline was a calculated piece of crassness: ' "Army" a Terrific Lump-Raiser, in Cash and Throats, Says Jolson'.

In 1943, exhibitors understood only the context of box-office receipts. What about the rest of us? Why has *This Is the Army* been ignored by those who write about American films of the Second World War — the heyday of mass cinema attendance? Why has it been ignored as an outstanding example of a Hollywood musical? The answer lies in the concerns of a later day. In his 1993 volume, *Projections of War: Hollywood, American Culture and World War II*, Thomas Doherty's discussion of the film is sarcastic: 'a choral multitude of grim-faced soldiers sing out bloody murder and point bayonets at the camera. . . . The studio allowed that the performance was "not symbolic of the humane manner in which the United States has waged war". . . .' In short, Doherty implies, since *This Is the Army* promotes war, it must be morally deficient. But who thinks that a Hollywood musical is the proper vehicle for inculcating the virtues of militarism?

More extreme is the moral outrage of historians Gregory Koppes and Gregory Black, whose 1987 survey of propaganda and censorship in Second World War Hollywood films has found many readers. To them, *This Is the Army* is a perfect vehicle for indicting American censors, propagandists, studio executives and wartime viewers, all in one fell swoop:

> Hollywood resuscitated one of the worst showbusiness stereotypes – the minstrel show – in Warner Brothers' *This Is the Army*. . . . Here was the black man not as worker, father, or solid citizen, but as lover, playboy and flashy dresser – and the war as fashion show. . . . The blacks break into the inevitable tap dance and, turning on their stereotypical rhythm, put the whites to shame. But there is no integration in this picture. *This Is the Army* is as segregated as the real army of democracy.

So what, then, is the film really all about? Shot in lavish Technicolor, with an onstage cast of hundreds, and much of the action performed before a vast theatre audience, it opens with the title 'New York 1917'; we see James Montgomery Flagg's poster, 'I Want You for the US Army Enlist Now'. A popular female vocalist, Gertrude Niesen, sings a rousing patriotic Berlin number, 'Your Country and My Country', from the back of a truck, to promote recruitment. The actor George Murphy, unsuccessfully 'aged' with some grey in his hair, plays Jerry Jones, a Broadway producer of a wartime show. We see him backstage after a performance, receiving his induction papers.

Cut to Camp Upton, Long Island, where a tough drill sergeant awakens recruits, suitably horrified to find that their day begins at 5.30 a.m. The sergeant hates happy songs, to him a camp show is anathema; wiser heads prevail: the kindly commanding officer says that morale is helped by a song or a smile and approves the idea of a soldier production, which Jerry Jones organises. An inept bugler plays the reveille, whose famous tune Berlin incorporated into his great First World War hit, 'Oh How I Hate to Get Up in the Morning'. The song makes a wonderful folksy connection between civilian and soldier, in a refrain that touches every young person in an industrial society. In the film, Berlin himself sings the song at the very end:

> Oh, how I hate to get up in the morning,/Oh, how I'd love to remain in bed; For the hardest blow of all, is to hear the bugler call:/You've got to get up, you've got to get up, you've got to get up in the morning!/Oh! Boy the minute the battle is over,/Oh! Boy the minute the foe is dead;/I'll put my uniform away, and move to Philadelphia,/And spend the rest of my life in bed.

Jerry Jones's soldier show is so successful that it moves to Broadway, where it becomes a solid commercial hit. On the final night, the entire cast marches out through the audience to board a troop carrier for France. This part of the film is based on real events. In August 1918, Berlin had staged a soldier show entitled *Yip! Yip! Yaphank*, which had moved to Broadway, and ended up making $80,000 for the Army Emergency Relief Fund. On the final evening, the cast had marched out through the Broadway theatre audience before boarding a ship for France. Berlin was fifty-three when he volunteered to make a new soldier show for a new war. This, the stage version of *This Is the Army*, opened on 4 July 1942, with new songs plus some from the First World War.

In the film, stock Technicolor shots suggest the no-man's-land desolation of Lewis Milestone's *All Quiet on the Western Front* (1930). The word 'Armistice' on the screen signals an end to hostilities, as soldiers sing of the 'war to end all wars', and the Americans, in a Paris bistro, toast the idea that there will never be another. Cut to a map of Poland in flames (only from the German side; in 1943 no ally of Stalin's would make a map showing the simultaneous Soviet invasion of Poland). A radio announcer introduces a studio audience to 'the star of our program, Miss Kate Smith', who sings a new song, 'God Bless America'.

This so-called second national anthem had been introduced by Miss Smith on Armistice Day, 1938, and had become an enormous hit. Irving Berlin had originally written it in 1917, but fearing the song too sentimental, did not publish it until twenty years later when Depression America welcomed its simple verities, to say nothing of its fine tune: 'God Bless America Land that I

Ronald Reagan as Johnny Jones and Joan Leslie as Eileen Dibble provide the film's romantic interest. (Warner Bros/Courtesy Kobal)

love/Stand beside her and guide her through the night with a light from above/From the mountains to the prairies, to the oceans white with foam/God Bless America, my home sweet home.'

'God Bless America' is *This Is the Army*'s sermon, a religious sanctification of America's purpose in war and peace. In a twentieth-century American solution, organised religion was thus made marketable in the capable hands of America's greatest popular songwriter, who kept the message simple, while providing a memorable tune.

The bulky figure of Kate Smith, who donated her entire fee to Army Emergency Relief, presented a challenge for a visual medium which of necessity had to show her in close-up. Backed by a large studio orchestra and chorus, she sings her signature number with conviction. The arrangement features lots of brass triplet figures, and, in the second verse, cuts away to reaction shots of Americans across the country listening to her voice on their radios. Anyone who wants to appreciate the virtuosity of commercial Hollywood film-making, would do well to study the camera movement in this cameo appearance.

Cut to the Japanese attack on Pearl Harbor. There being no extant colour footage of this, it had to be replicated in Technicolor, using studio miniatures. The scene changes to a New York City music shop. The movie romance takes place between a uniformed Ronald Reagan (playing George Murphy's son, Johnny Jones, though in reality he was only seven years younger than his 'father') and Joan Leslie, who plays Eileen Dibble, a young woman who sells sheet music in her father's music shop, and wants to get married. When Johnny tells poor Eileen that marriage is 'not for us just now', his words are not well received.

This scene is interrupted by a wisecracking skit from the show that is right out of vaudeville. The earnest sentiment – no marriage before the war is over – is leavened with something the audience can appreciate. The on-stage private explains that he joined the Army for three reasons: he wants to help, he is patriotic, and 'third – they nailed me'.

Cut to Camp Upton. When Johnny, who has been assigned to organise the new show, is asked by Eileen what he thinks of Army life he replies with just one word: 'swell'. She returns her engagement ring. Reagan's character decides that the new show must include one number for old-timers from the First World War show, as in fact happened with Berlin's stage version of *This Is the Army*. A sales pitch voice-over accompanies shots of hundreds of dancers, jugglers, performers and entertainers of all sorts and conditions, suddenly ordered from highly active duty in every hazardous clime. They are told that their training at Camp Upton will be exactly as if they were at the front, and that they will return to active duty once the show closes.

One of these, black heavyweight boxing champion, Joe Louis (who plays himself as a sergeant, appearing in uniform throughout), is engaged in an exhibition match for the entertainment of recruits when he is ordered to Camp Upton. For this war, black entertainers and sports heroes are part of the entertainment team. Louis, as might not be remembered by all of today's viewers, was wildly popular at the time for having knocked out Nazi Germany's Max Schmeling in 1938, showing what a democratic society ready to embrace sports heroes could do one-on-one against an Aryan nation's very best.

Cut to one of Berlin's greatest Second World War songs, 'This is the Army, Mr Jones', with its insistence that you might once have enjoyed breakfast in bed, 'but you won't have it anymore'. As with 'Oh How I Hate to Get Up in the Morning', the song takes its theme from a military fact of life; the lyrics promise that elite favouritism is a thing of the past, as all join forces in a common endeavour. What that endeavour might be, in keeping with popular perceptions of a non-ideological, 'good' war, is never mentioned. Sacrificing the chance to be served breakfast in bed seems a modest contribution to the war effort and viewers are encouraged to imagine that no citizen is being asked to do much more than this.

Berlin the showman provides a break from all the marching and wisecracks, with a sentimental camp-fire scene on stage, in which James Burell, an Irish tenor of considerable attainment, sings of getting tired so he can sleep and dream of being close to his girlfriend. His camp-fire mates include the world's largest chorus of outstanding first tenors and second basses, all happy to be singing away their military duty doing what they know best.

The following scene needs to be studied carefully, especially by those who would equate a minstrel show with racism. The performance of the song 'Mandy' includes a large chorus of white soldier-performers in blackface, accompanied by other white troops cross-dressed as 'Mandies' in bandannas. Part of the number includes the refrain of Stephen Foster's 'Sewanee River'. Fancy choreography, including the highly practised tap dancing of Ralph Magelssen, adds up to a most impressive number. (All the dances of the production were staged by Leroy Prinz, one of Hollywood's most accomplished choreographers.)

George Murphy as the older Jones rebuts critics who might dislike this scene, when he says backstage (but on-camera): 'Who says that a minstrel song is too old-fashioned? It works as well as it did before.' One Mandy, backstage, takes 'her' bandanna off, revealing her white, male face. This touch dispels doubt in any viewer's mind that this is a black revue number, or that it makes use of black women in demeaning costumes associated with Negro servitude. These visual 'tips' suggest how sensitive the film-makers were to the wartime debate about changing attitudes towards race and class.

Next we get material taken directly out of the vaudeville musical tradition. The 'drag' number, the required staple of all-male soldier skits, features burly men in full skirts, each with hairy legs (only thick black hair will do) and combat boots. The men, all seasoned hoofers, wear straw boaters. Tough Sergeant McGee, played by the jovial character actor Alan Hale, who hates camp shows and loves to assign punishment through kitchen patrol duty (peeling potatoes, of course), is seen being forced by his commanding officer to put on a skirt in order to fill in for a sick colleague in the drag act. He receives an appreciative laugh when he picks up his 'gent' using one hairy arm.

The next number features black entertainers, in front of a stylised backdrop that vaguely suggests three figures attired in zoot suits. 'That's What the Well-Dressed Man in Harlem Will Wear' runs the title line. Joe Louis appears stage left, pummelling a punching bag, creating an extraordinary polyrhythm with the music performed for the other on-stage virtuosos. One of these is James Cross, a black performer who toured with Berlin's stage version of *This Is the Army* until November 1945.

In another number, the US Navy gets its due recognition, with hundreds on stage in a set intended to be the deck of a battleship. The heavy guns are spiked with stars; at the end the guns fire. Cut to the stage door canteen, with a montage of cities where the camp show actually went in wartime. Sgt Joe Louis appears in the montage sequence with no suggestion that he was forced to travel apart from other members of the troupe – in reality the entire American military was rigidly segregated throughout the Second World War.

The film concludes with the soldiers giving a command performance for the President in Washington, DC. We see Warner Brothers' stock Roosevelt lookalike in a long view of his private theatre box. The presentation of the President in this scene attracted the ire of leading author and film critic, James Agee, who noted in a short review that 'Warner Brothers' cuddly, reverential treatment of President Roosevelt . . . is subject to charges certainly of indecent exposure and, quite possibly, of alienation of affections.' Hollywood certainly felt that when it came to depicting FDR as commander-in-chief, they had to lay it on thick.

Roosevelt witnesses the part of the show where women volunteers in red-and-white striped aprons (hence the name, candy-stripers) serve soldiers on leave. We see Sgt Louis in close-up; the camera pans the same crowded room to focus on a Bronx-type smoking a large cigar. We have apparently just witnessed white women serving a black man in an integrated setting. But before this visual challenge to rigid segregation has had time to register in the viewer's mind, there is another shock in store: the women in aprons are revealed to have hairy male legs.

The show also acknowledges the Air Corps (which did not become a separate service arm until 1944). As the popular singer Robert Shanley croons a sentimental ballad for 'the one I love on the ground', a map shows Guadalcanal Island, in the Pacific, and the American Eagles take off, suggested on stage by the movement of stylised plane engines. A poignant moment follows. Irving Berlin himself, in his First World War uniform, sings 'Oh How I Hate to Get Up in the Morning', in the number given over to the old-timers. The show – and the film – end with a grand finale. Robert Shanley and a marching chorus dressed in fatigues fill the stage singing 'This Time is the Last Time', drawing their bayonets in a dramatic final gesture, before moving into the closing number 'Dressed Up to Win'.

The film's success rested more than anything else on the abundance of Irving Berlin songs. The enormously popular Broadway show on which it was based had continued as a military road show, travelling to every theatre of war, before closing in Honolulu on 22 October 1945, months after the war ended. In a reunion held in New York City in June 1997, black and white members of the troupe recalled how Berlin was a pioneer in insisting that the performers travel as an integrated unit, black and white eating and rooming together. This might surprise those who insist that *This Is the Army* is nothing but a reflection of wartime segregation and institutionalised racism. Orlando Johnson, a black singer recruited for 'What the Well-Dressed Man in Harlem Will Wear', recalled his experience in glowing terms: 'I am still on a cloud.' Bill Smith, a dancer at Harlem's Cotton Club who 'tapped his way from gigs with Cab Calloway and Duke Ellington into the Harlem number', remembered Berlin as a man who volunteered to travel with the troupe all over the world for almost three years. According to Smith: 'It was the greatest group in the world. The old man was fantastic.'

Berlin was patriotic; he worshipped the institution of the United States Army. He gave away his services to entertain the troops. So great was his generosity that in 1944, it cost him his business partnership with the man who had controlled his song royalties for two decades. Berlin's wartime ubiquity, and his ability to speak to the needs of the home front as well as those of the battlefield, is perhaps best observed in 'White Christmas', a song which does not appear in *This Is the Army*, but which was the basis of *Holiday Inn* (1942), a second major Hollywood success featuring his songs, which ran in cinemas while his Broadway revue toured base camps across America. In a piece published to coincide with Berlin's hundredth birthday in 1988, musicologist Josh Rubins explained why the song is so effective: 'White Christmas captures, with remarkable economy and restraint, the thick mixture of moods stirred up by the Christmas and New Year holidays: nostalgia, anxiety, tenderness, depression. . .'. The song perhaps typifies how the average American soldier thought of his own home, and his own enforced wartime separation.

We must remember the connection between 'God Bless America' and 'White Christmas' — two simple declarations of faith, platitudinous to the sophisticated, but a marriage of text and tune which struck a chord with millions of Americans in wartime, both soldiers and civilians. If Norman Rockwell's *Saturday Evening Post* covers depicting the Four Freedoms visually symbolised those official war aims to the average soldier and citizen, Berlin's two songs made those same too-simple pledges melodious, with a hymn about the costs of separation, and another invoking God's blessing on America.

What better way to escape the reality of separations imposed on a major percentage of the entire American population, than by transferring the problem to a series of song-and-dance numbers? The familiar conventions of the musical allude harmlessly to military life, desensitising a war in which Americans were injured or even killed. *This Is the Army* defines what Americans thought to be their own peculiar virtues: lack of sophistication combined with technological wizardry; a salesmanship perhaps overstated, but connected to an understated, almost simple-minded, ideological commitment. In this respect, the film should be the first place to look for an insight into how Americans understood the nature of their nation's participation in the battles of the Second World War.

9

I WAS A COMMUNIST FOR THE FBI

Dan Leab

The icy moment marking the start of the Cold War after 1945 remains a matter of vigorous debate. Yet, whatever the many controversies surrounding the outbreak of this 'war' and US responsibility for it, there can be no doubt that by the late 1940s the Cold War was being waged fiercely at home and abroad by the Truman administration. Anti-Communist hysteria marred American life. Among the forces heightening the social paranoia were self-appointed vigilante groups such as the American Legion and the Catholic War Veterans, parts of the media, including powerful reactionary press lords and journalists, and various federal and state legislative investigating committees, most notably the Un-American Activities Committee of the House of Representatives (HUAC).

The 'Red Scare' hit Pittsburgh hard. Historian David Caute has aptly described the hub of life in western Pennsylvania as 'the violent epicentre of the anti-Communist eruption in postwar America'. The city had a minuscule formal Communist presence – in 1950 the Communist Party (CP) could claim only 2,875 members out of the entire Pennsylvania population of 10 million, according to J. Edgar Hoover, director of the Federal Bureau of Investigation (FBI). For Hoover, head of the agency then characterised as 'the nation's first line of defence against the Red menace', as well as for other federal, state and local officials, these numbers were deceptive: behind 'traitorous Communists' were all too many 'fellow travellers and sympathisers . . . ready to do the Communists' bidding', as he put it. Under Hoover's almost obsessive direction, the FBI closely tracked Party members and individuals assumed to be sympathetic to Communist causes. The FBI and its predecessors had undertaken such monitoring with various degrees of intensity since the formation of an American Communist Party in the aftermath of the First

World War. Their methods included detailed scrutiny of CP functions and publications, electronic surveillance, surreptitious, often illegal, break-ins and widespread use of undercover operators (designated 'confidential informants'). During the late 1940s and the 1950s these informants surfaced as needed to testify at the Smith Act prosecutions of CP leaders and before Congressional committees investigating subversion.

Among the most sensational of such witnesses was Herbert Philbrick, who appeared at the first of the Smith Act trials in 1949. His memoir of service to the FBI, and as a mid-level Communist functionary, became the basis for a highly melodramatic, long-running, syndicated TV series, *I Led Three Lives* ('Citizen', 'Communist', 'Counterspy'). Philbrick also testified before HUAC, with which the FBI intimately co-operated. It briefed Committee staff, provided supposedly confidential files, and made available a flow of friendly witnesses, who, according to historian Kenneth O'Reilly, 'were the lifeblood' of the Committee. In February 1950, another FBI informant appeared before HUAC. The FBI had not steered Matt Cvetic·to the Committee, but, to the shock of both his comrades and non-Communist associates in western Pennsylvania, this minor CP functionary turned out to have been an FBI informant for nearly a decade.

Born in Pittsburgh to immigrant Slovenian parents in 1909, Cvetic had had little more than a high-school education. In 1937, after more than a decade of patchy employment (which included operating one of his father's gas stations), he had found a long-term job as a placement interviewer at the Pittsburgh branch of Pennsylvania's Employment Service (later the US Employment Service). His marriage of 1929 failed largely due to his shenanigans with other women, and he long neglected the twin sons born to him in 1932. As even a friendly Pittsburgh reporter once declared, Cvetic had 'a hard time' staying away from 'booze and babes'. Sometime in the early 1940s (probably 1941) Cvetic became a confidential informant for the FBI. Who initiated the relationship remains unclear, as does much about it. He did manage to ingratiate himself quickly with various Communist groups and in 1943 accepted an invitation to join the Party. Over the next seven years, he claimed to have supplied the FBI with 'over 30,000 pages of exhibits, letters, press releases, pamphlets and other propaganda publications' as well as 'the names of about 1,000 Communist Party members'. Despite his subsequent grand claims, however, Cvetic remained only a lower-echelon Party functionary. An anti-Communist supervisor apparently forced his resignation from the Employment Service in 1945. Following this, he worked for various CP organisations and 'front' groups but, by 1949, despite later statements about being an 'independent insurance agent', he seemed to make his livelihood from the $85-a-week expense money the FBI paid him, at that time a considerable (and untaxed) sum.

'Patriotism' may have led Cvetic to the FBI as he claimed, and initially the Bureau, which lacked Balkan-language speakers, found him a 'valuable source'. But, increasingly, his demands for more expenses, his alcoholism, his fits of depression and his indiscretions (especially with lady friends he tried to impress with his FBI connection) led to Bureau dissatisfaction with him. In late 1949 the FBI terminated his role as an informant – a decision that became known only a generation later. Cvetic's HUAC appearance in 1950 resulted from a deal he made with an anti-Communist Pittsburgh lawyer and a Hearst newspaperman in that city. He testified for six days on 'the Communist presence in western Pennsylvania' – naming over 290 men and women; describing in detail allegedly subversive activities of various Communist leaders, especially Steve Nelson, a veteran Party official who became district organiser for western Pennsylvania in 1948. Much of Cvetic's testimony focused on various Communist-controlled unions such as the United Electrical Workers. He presented himself as sincere, patriotic, dedicated – so committed to his undercover work that he had allowed it to ruin his family life.

Cvetic's HUAC testimony fitted the mood of the day and garnered favourable attention across the country. In March 1950 his associates sold his story to the then extremely popular weekly, the *Saturday Evening Post*. Cvetic collaborated with an associate editor, William Thornton ('Pete') Martin, a productive, lively writer known for his celebrity articles. In mid-July the first instalment of a three-part series 'as told to Pete Martin' appeared in the paper. 'I Posed as a Communist for the FBI' presented a self-sacrificing, patriotically motivated, deeply concerned Cvetic, and an ugly picture of American Communism as 'a secret conspiratorial movement operating in the interest of a foreign power (i.e. the Soviet Union)'. Subsequently, in court, Cvetic was forced to admit that, at best, the series was 'substantially true'.

Film companies had expressed interest in Cvetic even before the *Post* articles. But the interest seems to have been limited and in August 1950 Warner Brothers bought the rights to his story for $12,500. This was cheap even in 1950, especially in comparison with the $75,000 Twentieth Century Fox paid in 1947 for Soviet defector Igor Gouzenko's story. On announcing acquisition of the rights to Cvetic's story Warners declared that it intended to make 'a quality film . . . in the tradition of *Confessions of a Nazi Spy*', a serious, well-received 1939 production from their studio that was among Hollywood's earliest overtly anti-Nazi movies. Jack Warner, the head of production, boasted about the forthcoming film and declared that Cvetic deserved 'a decoration for . . . heroism'. In Hollywood, then as now, a direct relationship existed between the cost of acquisition and the amount spent on filming. Notwithstanding the studio's pronouncements, the Cvetic film was meant to be a low-budget production. Obviously, the studio hoped to cash in on the contemporary anti-Red hysteria. Dollars, not ideology, served as the motivating force.

It has been argued that the studios committed themselves to produce anti-Communist movies, 'to atone for the sins disclosed before' HUAC. Such is the conventional wisdom, as leading critic Nora Sayre puts it in her elegant, but flawed, study of American Cold War movies; the studios made anti-Communist films 'to demonstrate Hollywood was not unpatriotic'. Certainly an element of coercion did exist: the industry could not afford to ignore the urging of

Frank Lovejoy as Matt Cvetic in a still from the film. (BFI Stills, Posters and Designs)

politicians like HUAC member Richard Nixon, who declared that Hollywood
had 'a positive duty' to make anti-Communist movies. Yet, it seems to me,
economics more than politics governed the production of anti-Communist
films. As scholar Tino Balio points out, the general prosperity of post-Second
World War America led to 'a shift in expenditure patterns . . . and movies were
. . . caught in the squeeze'.

In 1947, even before the impact of television, US cinemas sold 3 million
fewer seats than in 1946. Between 1950 and 1956 audience figures dropped
by over 25 per cent. Hollywood, as one producer bemoaned, had become 'an
island of despair in a sea of prosperity'. Corporate profit margins shrank as the
average cost of making a film doubled between 1940 and 1950. In 1948, after
years of litigation, a Supreme Court decision forced the studios to divorce
exhibition from production. The producers could no longer count on their films
being shown and the studios lost what scholar Garth Jowett accurately
describes as 'the most profitable part of the motion picture business'. For
Warners, its cinemas represented 62 per cent of the company's corporate
profits.

It was against this background of distress, uncertainty and paranoia that the
studios fought to regain and retain a mass audience. In response they mounted
traditional Hollywood offerings on a grander scale ('Make Them Big; Show
Them Big; Sell Them Big'). The industry concentrated substantial resources on
blockbuster movies, made increasing use of colour, and introduced widescreen
processes and gimmicks such as 3-D films. Hollywood also determined (once
again) to make movies 'ripped from the pages of today's headlines'. Many of
these dealt with 'the Red menace'.

What the writer, John Izod, has characterised as the movie moguls' 'fearful
obsequiousness' certainly led to the establishment of the blacklist and may
have initiated the anti-Communist film cycle. But the quest for profits drove it.
In 1947 when HUAC began its hearings, many in the film industry shared
conservative actor Adolph Menjou's belief, as outlined in his testimony, that
anti-Communist films 'would be an enormous success'. In early 1948 *Variety*
reported that on screen anti-Communist plots had become 'the hottest topic'.
Years later one cynical Hollywood veteran, himself a victim of Red-baiting,
maintained that if studio bosses had thought that pro-Communist films would
attract audiences, the industry in its desperation would have produced them:
'instead of Andy Hardy, . . . "Young Joe Stalin" . . . that Stalin kid, he sure is
stubborn . . .; Lee Trotsky's always got his nose in a book, but Joey gets things
done'.

Even though box-office returns showed that anti-Communist films did not attract big audiences, such productions continued to be made. Whatever may have motivated the more important studios, the lesser ones certainly did not act for ideological reasons. Throughout the early 1950s, second- and third-class performers such as hillbilly star Judy Canova, Roy Rogers ('King of the Cowboys') and erstwhile Tarzan, Johnny Weismuller, appeared in films fighting subversion and villains named Ivan and Boris. The veteran independent producer Edward Small, known for his cheaply made films that earned large returns, proved less successful with *Walk a Crooked Mile* (1948), in which the FBI *and* Scotland Yard work together to break up a Soviet spy ring. At a time when *Life* magazine warned of 'waves of Red bombers' descending on the American heartland via the North Pole and Canada, serials such as the 1953 *Canadian Mounties vs Atomic Invaders* and the 1952, low-budget *Red Snow* played unsuccessfully on such fears.

The race to produce the first anti-Communist movie was won by Twentieth Century Fox. In May 1948 it released *The Iron Curtain*, a grim, dull film that dealt with Igor Gouzenko, a young Russian code clerk at the Soviet Embassy in Ottawa, who had defected in September 1945 with a bundle of documents. These, as a recent history summarises, showed that Canada, 'an ally of the Soviet Union', had been 'operating an extensive espionage apparatus . . . using personnel provided by the Canadian Communist Party. . .'. Even a generation later, Canadian statesman Lester Pearson found this situation 'almost incredible'.

The Iron Curtain, along with most of these movies, has long-since disappeared from view. *I Was a Communist for the FBI* has not. Its title is better than the film itself which, though not the worst of the anti-Communist genre, is far from the best, while its treatment of Matt Cvetic is a fascinating index to the mores of the time. The choice of production personnel indicated that the Cvetic story would not be an 'A' production. Bryan Foy, the producer assigned to the project, had a reputation stretching back to the 1920s for churning out melodramas cheaply and quickly – so much so that one wit dubbed him 'Keeper of the B's'. Foy tapped an old working partner, Crane Wilbur, to fashion Cvetic's story for the screen. Wilbur had a multifaceted career as a director and actor as well as a writer, but melodrama was his forte. Bordon Chase, who replaced Wilbur for a while, had pronounced political views, but was assigned to the Cvetic story because of his capacity for writing action-orientated screenplays. Gordon Douglas, chosen to direct, was an efficient technician who for over a decade had directed various genres without particular distinction.

The final choice to play Cvetic was Frank Lovejoy, a solid but undistinguished former radio actor.

Wilbur finished his work in September 1950. His version of Cvetic's story added a 'sincere' romance as well as gangster-film elements, such as two CP-ordered murders disguised as suicides. It also parroted Cvetic's fabrications about his sacrifices, his problems with his family and his views on Steve Nelson and other CP leaders. Bordon Chase's various efforts reeked of simple-minded anti-Communism and melodramatic contrivance, which led a Warners executive to admonish the screenwriter to be more restrained. The difficulty of delineating the Steve Nelson character epitomises the script problems faced by Wilbur and Chase. Studio executives could not decide how to portray Nelson. In one draft he clearly gives orders – be it for espionage, murder or merely cutting off long-winded speeches at a meeting – without any reference to superiors. In another version, Nelson has become a senior underling, powerful in Pittsburgh but fearful of Party chiefs in New York City and Moscow.

Filming began on 6 January 1951, with less than half the script completed. Principal photography continued until 21 February, running sixteen days over a projected three-and-a-half-week shooting schedule. Throughout filming Wilbur turned out new and revised pages, heightening the melodramatic aspects. The studio tinkered with the film almost until the day of its premiere in Pittsburgh on 19 April 1951. On 14 April, just hours before the release prints were to be shipped, adverse reactions at press previews caused the studio hurriedly to arrange for the processing laboratory to cut the following lines about the Soviet Union: 'Their state capitalism is a fascist horror far worse than anything Hitler ever intended for the world. That great liar of all times did speak the truth when he warned that to the East there was an enemy even more dangerous than he.' Such absurdities dominated the script that Wilbur cobbled together from the *Post* articles, his own earlier efforts and those of Chase. Not all the script's Red-baiting got filmed however. Part of a scene eliminated during production, for example, included one of the Party goons remarking to Cvetic 'our system makes Murder Incorporated look like an amateur set-up'.

Many Cold War clichés nevertheless found their way into the final film. Lovejoy sermonises directly at the audience in the depiction of Cvetic's HUAC testimony, in words that go far beyond anything the real Cvetic actually said: the screen Cvetic declares the American Communist Party 'is actually a vast spy system founded . . . by the Soviets, . . . composed of American traitors whose only purpose is to deliver the people of the United States into the hands

The film embellished the Cvetic story with anti-Communist clichés such as a Communist thug attacking a union official with a lead pipe wrapped in a Yiddish newspaper – stressing the fear of Jewish conspiracy with the far left. (BFI Stills, Posters and Designs)

of Russia as a colony of slaves'. The Steve Nelson character, now called James Blandon, informs his associates that 'sometimes a Communist must turn his coat for the good of the cause. Didn't Comrade Stalin join with Hitler in '39?'

The film embellished Cvetic's story and caricatured the history of the Communist Party. Cvetic's romantic interest is a schoolteacher who, realising she has been duped by the Party, declares she will name names. Blandon, in supposedly true CP fashion, orders her liquidation and an FBI agent sent to protect her is murdered. Cvetic saves her through a shoot-out with Communist heavies. Party thugs imported by Blandon use lead pipes wrapped in Yiddish newspapers to beat and silence union officers (including a Cvetic brother) who are trying to end a CP-induced wildcat strike at a Pittsburgh mill: the newspapers are part of the Communist plan to foment strife in the US. Blandon publicly preaches 'Negro rights' but privately calls blacks 'niggers' and works to exacerbate racial tensions (an FBI agent in the film, referring to deaths in the 1943 Detroit race riots, explains that 'those poor fellows never knew their death warrants had been signed in Moscow').

Warner Brothers contributed mightily to the furthering of Cvetic's image as a fearless, self-sacrificing folk hero, knowledgeably fighting the Red menace. He is shown facing ostracism from early on: 'Hey, stay away from my kid, he doesn't need your help. Baseball's an American game.' His family is hostile: 'You stinking Red! Get out of this house and don't ever come back.' The FBI needs him: 'thanks to Matt Cvetic', it obtains Blandon's plans to cripple Pittsburgh industry. Cvetic praises God for being allowed to testify before HUAC and to 'crawl out of my rat hole and live like a man again'.

The film received uneven reviews. The *Motion Picture Herald*, an important trade journal whose militantly anti-Communist editor had gushed over Cvetic, judged it 'a major advance in the screen's fight against Communism'. Influential Hearst gossip columnist, Louella Parsons, reviewing the movie for the adamantly anti-Communist publisher, called the production 'not just another' but 'the strongest exposé of dread Communism to date'. Various Hearst newspapers reviewed the film enthusiastically, but the media centred in New York City responded much more sceptically. Even vociferously anti-Communist *Time* magazine found it 'crude, over-amplified, mechanical', while the *New Yorker* slammed it. Warner executives may have foreseen the more critical reviews; the company's publicity campaign anticipated much of the negative response. However, the studio did not anticipate Hoover's lack of co-operation, caused by his distress over Cvetic's lifestyle and claims to have been an 'FBI counterspy'. Hoover would do nothing openly to cast doubt on someone like Cvetic whom the public linked with the FBI, but Warners felt an unusual lack of FBI co-operation at every level. Years later a Pittsburgh studio publicist recalled his amazement that he 'wouldn't get any assistance' from the usually willing local FBI.

Jack Warner did not tout *I Was a Communist for the FBI* as one of the studio's 'big pictures', but he nevertheless worked hard to sell it, later asserting that the movie 'had chalked up a highly successful box office record'. Although the exact figures remain unknown, one estimate has the film grossing double its production costs. In the years following its release, the real Cvetic earned a comfortable living on the lecture trail, warning about 'the Communist menace'. He also appeared as a 'professional witness' before Congressional committees, at deportation hearings and in court proceedings (most notably at the Pennsylvania sedition trials of Steve Nelson). In 1954 Cvetic narrowly lost a primary election to become the Republican candidate for a Pittsburgh congressional district. Suffering from alcoholism and an uneven mental state (he underwent shock treatment in 1955), Cvetic was formally 'disapproved' as a witness by the Justice Department after a 1955 court ruling that found his testimony 'evasive' and 'conflicting'. As his career petered out, he moved to California, became involved with Radical Right groups and was a John Birch Society recruiter when he suffered a heart attack in 1962 and died while taking a driving exam in Los Angeles. Cvetic lived a deceitful, generally unattractive life. The fact that he is still remembered, unlike so many other professional anti-Communists, has to do with the continued televising of *I Was a Communist for the FBI*. No matter how far removed from reality, the film gives him life.

That this meretricious, crude, fanciful, highly propagandistic film was nominated for an Oscar as the best full-length documentary of 1951 is some indication of the paranoid mood of the US at that time. Since then the title has become a comedic paradigm used in a variety of ways: a recent manifestation being a *New York Times* article which sarcastically closed with the words 'I was an Iraqi for the CIA.'

Part Three
SOCIAL COMMENTARY
ON SCREEN

10

CITIZEN KANE

Sarah Street

The production history of *Citizen Kane* reads like a film script. A boy genius is granted his wish to produce a film in Hollywood, hire his theatrical friends and use the best technicians available, unfettered by the constraints of the studio system. When Orson Welles signed his contract in July 1939 with RKO, one of Hollywood's major film studios, he was given final cut: complete control over what eventually appeared on screen, provided the film did not exceed a modest budget of $500,000.

This unusually generous contract was part of RKO's strategy to attract new talent and confer artistic respectability on a film industry which had experienced a turbulent decade with the Depression and the arrival of the 'talkies'. An enterprising producer, George Schaefer, secured a promising deal: the services of a controversial but charismatic radio personality and theatre producer who brought with him a cast of characters who were also new to film. Novelty and promise were the key ingredients of an arrangement that tested the limits of Hollywood's tolerance of aesthetic experiment, political bravado and sheer hype.

Now regarded as a film classic, it is ironic that *Citizen Kane* was not widely seen until 1956 when RKO sold its film library to television and *Citizen Kane* received an airing on the small screen and also, theatrically, just when Welles was returning to Broadway in *King Lear*. Its initial distribution was suppressed because it was commonly assumed that the film's central character, Charles Foster Kane (played by Welles himself), was a veiled critical portrait of newspaper magnate William Randolph Hearst. Hearst's success in 'killing' Kane, in 1941, tells us much about the power of the press in that period and how far a rich and powerful man would go to suppress criticism. It also reveals that cinema, the most popular form of mass entertainment, was widely recognised as an influential medium of persuasion and propaganda.

Media mania: Orson Welles as the eponymous tycoon lording it over his fictional newspaper *The Inquirer* in a scene from *Citizen Kane*. (Sight & Sound)

A second irony of the film's early history is that Welles did not go to Hollywood in the first instance to make *Citizen Kane*. His first project, a filmed version of Joseph Conrad's novella *Heart of Darkness*, was never produced because it exceeded its budget at the pre-production stage. It was only as a last-minute attempt to do something useful with his generous contract that Welles developed the *Kane* idea – in collaboration with the experienced screenwriter Herman Mankiewicz. However, since Welles was fascinated by contemporary politics it was likely that any film he made would involve themes reflecting this interest. The timing of the production and release of *Citizen Kane* gave it a sense of urgency: war had broken out while the film was still being written, and it is essential to regard it as a product of this critical situation.

Welles's politics are extremely important for a full understanding of *Citizen Kane* in its contemporary context, and partly explain Hearst's dramatic reaction against the film. In the 1930s, Welles was a fervent supporter of President Roosevelt's New Deal: the collection of interventionist economic and social policies enacted to combat the Depression involving public works schemes and social security measures. By the time he went to Hollywood, Welles had already produced plays financed by the Federal Theatre, a branch of the New Deal's cultural policy which was a relief measure to provide employment in the theatre. Having spent time in Europe (he was deeply attracted to European culture), Welles was also an anti-fascist who urged American intervention in the Second World War. Hearst, on the other hand, campaigned against the New Deal and was a firm isolationist.

Although not explicitly named as the model for Charles Foster Kane, Hearst bore close enough resemblance to the fictional character to invite comparison even before the film was complete. As an ex-newspaperman turned screenwriter, Mankiewicz had first-hand knowledge of Hearst and along with other writers had visited him in his vast mansion, San Simeon. Ostensibly *Citizen Kane* is about a reporter's search for the meaning of a dying newspaper magnate's last words, 'Rosebud'. This quest triggers five flashback sequences (the film is loosely set in the present in which it was made) when the reporter, Thompson (William Alland), investigates. He visits the archive of Kane's guardian, Thatcher (George Coulouris), and interviews four key people: Kane's business manager Bernstein (Everett Sloane); his friend Leland (Joseph Cotten); his second wife Susan (Dorothy Comingore); and his butler Raymond (Paul Stewart). The flashback structure allows us to glimpse key moments throughout Kane's life, from childhood to old age. We learn that he inherited a fortune by chance; was separated from his mother at an early age to be educated to use that fortune; started a newspaper, *The Inquirer*, which spawned an empire; embarked on a disastrous political career; lost his two wives; and ended his days in a pathetic condition in self-imposed exile at his baroque palace, Xanadu.

Before the flashbacks, however, we are given a brief, but comprehensive, series of 'snapshots' of Kane by means of a newsreel that has clearly been modelled in style on *Time* magazine's popular newsreel of the era, *The March of Time*. In an arresting blast of sound and image we are presented with segments from the life of a man whose exploits have been full of contradictions and are riddled with inconsistencies. A montage of newspaper headlines reporting his death describe Kane in startlingly different terms: while one refers to him as 'an outstanding American', another labels him 'US Fascist No. 1'. We see him as a man of the people, but also keeping company with Hitler.

As the story unfolds, the parallels between Hearst and Kane are obvious: both controlled newspaper empires; both frequently distorted the truth for a good story in the tradition of 'yellow journalism'; both supported the war with Spain in 1898; both dabbled in politics and both ended their lives cocooned in their palatial homes surrounded by precious art objects. Although Hearst did not, like Kane, force his wife into an unsuccessful opera career, he did exercise control over the film roles of his mistress, Marion Davies. Davies, whom Hearst never married, was a gifted comic actress but because most of her films were financed by Hearst she was forced to play romantic heroines to which her talents were unsuited. Welles used jigsaw puzzles – Marion Davies's liking for them was well-known – as a means of conveying Susan's boredom in Xanadu. With these and other glaring similarities it is not surprising that the first reviewers of *Citizen Kane* were struck by its contemporary significance. Tangye Lean, for example, described the film as 'coming from the studio of a postwar world rebuilding itself on the basis of new values' (*Horizon*, November 1941), while Otis Ferguson writing in *New Republic* said it was 'a film, an event and a topic of the times'.

Criticism of Hearst stemmed from Welles's New Deal liberalism and his desire for America to intervene in the Second World War; both these standpoints were opposed by Hearst's 'yellow press'. In this respect the film is a direct attack on Hearst's political beliefs, business activities and journalistic style. It is no coincidence that *Citizen Kane* was produced exactly at the height of the isolationist versus interventionist debate in America: the film was released six months before Pearl Harbor. The portrayal of Kane as obsessed and isolated, surrounded in Xanadu at the end of his life by *objets d'art* from all over Europe, stands for blinkered American isolationists, keen to absorb European culture but at the same time determined to steer clear of political involvement to assist Europe's plight against Fascism and the Nazi threat. By depicting Kane's political failure and subsequent exile in Xanadu, Welles was indirectly commenting on the contemporary European crisis.

At another level one also gets a sense that in *Citizen Kane* Wells is criticising fundamental contradictions within monopolistic journalism and political rhetoric. These contradictions were evident in Hearst's business practices and political ambitions. Kane represents the era of pre-New Deal attitudes, the 'old order', when newspapermen wielded enormous power. The film reveals that that power was founded on distortion and hypocrisy. One of *The Inquirer*'s campaigns is against monopolistic business trusts, but it is only the character Leland who sees that Kane's newspaper empire is guilty of a similar kind of encroachment. When Kane's growing empire poaches staff from a rival paper, *The Chronicle*, we know that the reporters will adapt their style to fit the ideological remit of the *The Inquirer*. In his political role, Kane claims to represent 'the people' but he is fundamentally opposed to trade union organisation. Ironically, his political career is destroyed by press exposure of his affair with Susan Alexander. Kane proves that he can make an untalented singer into an opera star by falsifying the reviews. In this way Welles uses one medium, film, to expose the evident hypocrisy of another, the press.

In the late 1930s, film was but one of the mass media which were beginning to exert a great influence over public opinion. As well as cinema, radio was extremely effective and popular: Roosevelt's 'fireside chats' had taken political propaganda literally into the homestead. Indeed radio provided Welles's first encounter with notoriety with Mercury's infamous *The War of the Worlds* broadcast in 1938, which persuaded millions of Americans that Martians were attacking Earth. Welles's experience with this broadcast and the panic it created prepared him in some ways for the furore over *Citizen Kane*. He was acquainted with controversy and fully aware of the different forms of power to be found in the press, radio and film. But whereas *Citizen Kane* suggests that the old order of newspaper journalism was flawed and outdated, it is ironic that Hearst's reprisals demonstrated that the 'yellow press' still wielded considerable influence.

In the film, Welles is also commenting more generally on the historical enterprise in the sense that the reporter is researching a man's past by examining particular sources familiar to all historians: memoirs and interviews. Indeed Thompson's investigation could be a cautionary tale about the need to scrutinise sources: in the process, we learn more about Kane's associates and his ex-wife than we do about the man himself. In spite of the rigour of cinematographer Greg Toland's deep-focus photography (everything in the frame is of equal definition), the film medium has proved no more successful in revealing the 'truth' of Kane's life than the press. The impossibility of the 'truth' is reinforced by the fact that we end up knowing little more about Kane than we already knew from the mock newsreel. The revelation that 'Rosebud' is Kane's childhood sled (with all it symbolises in terms of lost innocence and the shock of being separated from his mother) answers some questions, but by no means all. The mass media are thus presented cynically by Welles, as being incredibly powerful but not always capable of rendering the truth.

Welles directing on the set of *Citizen Kane*: its path-breaking techniques and aesthetic experimentation did not save it from being canned because of the wrath of Hearst. (BFI Stills, Posters and Designs)

More than anything else, the Hearst controversy overshadowed discussion of the artistic qualities of *Citizen Kane*. Although its brilliance was noted by many reviewers ('close to being the most sensational film ever made in Hollywood', claimed Bosley Crowther in the *New York Times* in May 1941), the most damaging aspect of Hearst's revenge was his success in persuading cinemas not to show the film and his refusal to give RKO any publicity in his papers. The fact that the studios were worried about Hearst's threatened anti-movie reprisals is testament to their reliance on the press in terms of advertising new film releases. The movie moguls were also afraid, perhaps, that Hearst papers would expose salacious gossip about them on their society pages. George Schaefer remained loyal to Welles throughout the Hearst controversy, at one point refusing an offer of money by a studio boss to destroy the negative and prints. However, such difficulties finally forced RKO to withdraw the film from distribution and it was not reissued until the 1950s. The generation of film-goers for whom *Citizen Kane* was produced was unable to see it.

But, had the film not been prevented from receiving nationwide distribution in 1941, it is arguable whether it would have been a box-office success. Contemporary audiences may have found its themes too bleak and its 'hero' too de-centred; the flashback structure was unusual and possibly alienating. More typically, Hollywood films subscribed to 'unwritten' rules of structural coherence; goal-orientated heroes who triumphed against obstacles; unobtrusive camera and editing techniques and an obligatory happy ending. *Citizen Kane* had none of these and so it is unlikely that outside the 'art house' market the film would have done well. In the few locations where it played, business was poor. Although critics praised its artistic merits the film won only one Academy Award (it was nominated for nine) and this was for the screenplay.

Citizen Kane's second and far more sustained 'lease of life' began in the late 1950s, the result of a critical reappraisal by critics such as Andrew Sarris of Hollywood directors who had managed to create interesting and innovative works of film art within the constraints imposed by the studio system. The studio 'factory' was seen to have produced its *auteurs* against the grain of artistic standardisation and economic regulation. Having suffered from studio interference in the films he made after *Citizen Kane*, Welles was the perfect candidate for re-evaluation. This linked in later with (initially grudging) appreciation of the technical achievements of Welles's collaborators, primarily Greg Toland and Herman Mankiewicz. Mankiewicz was resurrected as an important contributor to the script by critic Pauline Kael with her 'Raising Kane' article in the *New Yorker* in 1971 (the 'Rosebud' hook was his idea whereas Welles insisted on the line 'I don't think that any word explains a man's life').

Gradually *Citizen Kane* has crept into the canon of 'great film classics', a model of cinematic achievement and an obtrusive display of what cinema can do best: visual spectacle. RKO technicians had used special effects to create startling images of cameras apparently swooping through windows; models were filmed to create the illusion of large buildings, while Toland's deep-focus photography gave the film its distinctive crisp style. As interest in the application of psychoanalysis to film studies has grown, theorists have stressed the significance of Kane's Oedipal crisis and taken seriously what Welles dismissed as the 'dollarbook Freud' element of the plot. The film has meant many things to many people and continues to engage film scholars and impress new generations.

Although due credit to his collaborators has been stressed, Welles's overall vision for *Citizen Kane* and his clear conception of the film's visual style are incontestable. These are the key elements in assuring its longevity as a classic. Also important to the film's appeal is its refusal to reveal all: by means of its investigative structure and enigmatic resolution, Welles has ironically pointed out a universal truth. The historian's task is complex and demanding – a single word does not explain a man's life, nor does a newspaper headline, a radio report or a densely composed film frame. All are sources which must be treated with the utmost scrutiny but which, taken together, can reveal significant 'truths' about elements of the past, which are often not what we want to learn. In this sense *Citizen Kane* is likely to continue to fascinate audiences for many years.

11

ON THE WATERFRONT

Brian Neve

A pantheon of the finest examples of 1950s American film-making might feature John Ford's *The Searchers* or Alfred Hitchcock's *Rear Window*, while the top box-office successes of the decade include *White Christmas*, *Cinerama Holiday* and *The Ten Commandments*. Yet if one had to pick a single film as an emblem of that era, and to illustrate the cinema's unique power to resonate with a sense of its time, Elia Kazan's *On the Waterfront* would be a strong contender.

While the image of Marlon Brando in the film has become an icon of the 1950s, *On the Waterfront* relates most strongly to the postwar decade that preceded its release in 1954. Context is provided by three inter-related circles of events. The first of these is the ideological and cultural conflict that dominated the late 1940s and early 1950s, and which was fought out in Hollywood as well as Washington; the second concerns the changing political economy of the American film industry, and finally there is the history of the New York waterfront itself.

The dramatic shift in dominant concerns that followed the end of the Second World War – caused not least, by the breaking up of the wartime alliance and the beginning of the Cold War – led to the formation of a new, right-wing Republican agenda which blamed successive Democratic administrations for what was seen as a reverse in America's interests. Soviet dominance in Eastern Europe and its testing of an atomic bomb in 1949, together with the victory of Communist China in the same year, all served to focus attention on the new totalitarian enemy. The House Committee on Un-American Activities (HUAC) first explained these reverses by pointing at enemies within, most notably in its successful charges brought against the former state department official, Alger Hiss. The Committee also pointed a finger at Hollywood, and by the early

1950s the studios were actively participating in the Red scare by means of a blacklist that identified for exclusion writers and artists who were not fully prepared to cooperate with the FBI and HUAC.

Joseph McCarthy, the senator who came to personify the anti-Communist 'investigations' of this period, did much to stoke the flames of domestic paranoia with his repeated claims of State Department betrayal. McCarthy helped to scare liberals away from a populist stance and to convince them of the need for elites to guide the process of democracy. The Popular Front alliance between liberals and radicals that had had such a cultural impact in the late 1930s and during the war was now splintered and disabled. Whittaker Chambers, the man who had first accused Hiss, published his influential book

Marlon Brando as Terry Malloy, the docker whose revolt against corrupt union leadership forms the central plot of *On the Waterfront*. (Columbia/Courtesy Kobal)

Witness in 1952, and by 1954, when McCarthy's sudden decline began with his censure by the Senate, the informer – or friendly witness – had become a contemporary hero.

The blacklist was only the most important of a number of shocks to affect Hollywood in the years after the war. From its peak in 1946, cinema attendance began a rapid decline that was to last until the late 1950s, while anti-trust action began a process by which the major studios divested themselves of their holdings of movie theatres. A brief wave of social realism came to an end as producers increasingly avoided films with themes likely to attract the unwelcome attention of politicians or American Legion pickets. The doubling of GNP in the postwar decade both changed the agenda and provided alternatives to cinema-going, the most important of which, in the 1950s, was the fast-growing television industry.

Defensive studio bosses turned away from social themes as they sought to recapture audiences, seizing upon new techniques such as 3-D and Cinemascope. The epics and musicals (now mostly in colour) that underscored the cinema's advantage over the small screen, proved gradually more successful in this respect, along with a slow recognition of the importance of the young as a key target for movie marketing. *On the Waterfront*, with its social theme and location shooting, and in particular its close observation of working-class life, was far from typical of its time.

The historical background on which the film draws is that of the New York and New Jersey waterfront in the late 1940s and early 1950s. Against this backdrop, the International Longshoreman's Association (ILA) – which was eventually expelled from the American Federation of Labor (AFL) in 1954 – New York politicians and the stevedore and shipping companies were involved in a web of corruption and intrigue which attracted widespread interest. Rank-and-file discontent with the system and with the ILA leadership increased as violence, loan-sharking and corrupt hiring practices – including the 'shape up', which gave 'shaping' bosses daily power to recruit casual labour, often in return for kickbacks – were publicised by journalists. Also pressing for reform were the so-called 'waterfront priests', notably Father John Corridan, who had campaigned on behalf of rebel longshoremen since arriving at the Xavier Labor School in the Hell's Kitchen district of New York in 1946.

Hearings into organised crime conducted by Senator Estes Kefauver paid particular attention to the New York waterfront and drew national attention to the issue when they were televised in 1951. In response to public concern, Governor Dewey of New York established a Waterfront Crime Commission which began its own hearings in late 1952; its report, issued the next year, called for changes, including an end to the shape up. (Despite a number of reforms, the ILA narrowly survived as the main bargaining agent, winning a ballot for recognition against a rival AFL union in 1953.)

It was to this subject and its attendant social problems that Elia Kazan turned in the early 1950s, first with Arthur Miller and then with Budd Schulberg. Kazan, an Anatolian Greek who had been brought to New York at the age of four, had come of age in the political and cultural movements of the Depression. He first gained recognition for his acting ability as the 'proletarian thunderbolt' in Clifford Odets's agitprop drama *Waiting for Lefty*; his hostility towards what he saw as the privileges of middle-class America also led him to membership of the American Communist Party in 1934 for nearly two years. An eager disciple of the leaders of the Group Theatre, Kazan later applied his knowledge of, and commitment to, Stanislavsky's theories to the Actors Studio, which he co-founded in 1947.

In the late 1940s, Kazan became a successful east- and west-coast director, working both on large budget, social issue movies and smaller budget, semi-documentary films at Twentieth Century Fox, while directing the key works of Arthur Miller (*All My Sons* and *Death of a Salesman*) and Tennessee Williams (*A Streetcar Named Desire*) on Broadway. His cinematic ambitions increased as he planned a series of more independent productions, including the film version of *Streetcar*, working on scripts with John Steinbeck (*Viva Zapata*) and Miller.

Arthur Miller's script, *The Hook*, was based on a pre-war case of rank-and-file action against six local members of the Brooklyn ILA, which had long been controlled by notorious criminals, including members of the Anastasia family. When Kazan and Miller proposed the script to Columbia Pictures in 1951 there were political objections which may have contributed to Miller's withdrawal from the project. Meanwhile, the novelist Budd Schulberg, who had been a Communist Party member from 1937 to 1940, had begun researching his own waterfront script, in particular by talking extensively to Father Corridan and a number of rebel longshoremen including Tony Mike deVincenzo, who had testified to the New York Crime Commission and declared himself 'proud to be a rat'. When Kazan contacted Schulberg, the writer worked up a script which was offered to, and rejected by, all the major studios. Production proceeded only with the support of the independent producer Sam Spiegel, whose previous films included *The African Queen* (1951). Filming began finally on location in Hoboken in the bitter winter of 1953.

Prior to this, both Kazan and Schulberg had been involved in appearances before HUAC, which had begun a second series of hearings in 1951. The Committee, working with FBI information, called before it individuals who had a Communist Party record and some fellow travellers. In the late 1940s witnesses who had refused to answer questions on the basis of the first amendment to the Constitution had served periods of up to a year in prison (they became known as the 'Hollywood Ten'). In the new hearings, witnesses who declined to answer questions about their political pasts needed to plead the fifth amendment, but such action led to their being blacklisted in the film, television and radio industries. Kazan, who had previously stated that he would refuse to testify, 'named names' before the Committee in April 1952, to the shock of his friends and admirers (he named those fellow members of a Communist Party cell in the Group Theatre). Budd Schulberg had similarly appeared as a 'co-operative witness' in 1951.

Whereas Kazan has sometimes been ambivalent about his action, Schulberg has consistently justified his testimony, arguing that he was a 'premature anti-Stalinist', and referring to the fate of Soviet writers that he had met while attending a writers' congress in Moscow in 1934. While self-interest was clearly a key motive for Kazan's volte-face – which he has admitted – there was an argument at the time that Communism presented an internal threat, and that secrecy served its purposes. (In addition, 25,000 Americans died in Korea in the period 1950 to 1953). At some point in the early 1950s Kazan joined the American Committee for Cultural Freedom (ACCF), which had been formed in 1951 to represent the views of anti-Communist liberals.

The completed film opened in New York in July 1954 to popular and critical acclaim; it was to receive eight Oscars at the 1955 Academy Awards ceremony, including one for Best Picture. *On the Waterfront* presents the labour conflict and corruption of the time in terms of the experiences of docker Terry Malloy (Marlon Brando), who begins to have doubts about his life from the moment he is forced by his brother Charley (Rod Steiger) and by Johnny Friendly (Lee J. Cobb), the leading officials of the local union, to set up someone to be murdered. The victim, Joey Doyle, has been talking to the Crime Commission, and with this opening scene the film introduces the notion that such testimony is considered to be informing, 'ratting on your friends', by the workers and by the union bosses in particular.

What is presented as Malloy's moral awakening is encouraged first by the murdered man's sister Edie Doyle (Eva Marie Saint) and then by Father Barry (Karl Malden), the 'waterfront priest'. Terry's dilemma remains the pivot of the

Moral awakening: the famous taxi scene between Terry Malloy and his brother Charley (Rod Steiger). (BFI Stills, Posters and Designs)

film, in part because of the emphasis of the script, which fits Hollywood's preference for individual heroes, but also because of the power and originality of Brando's performance. Only with the murder of Charley, following a taxi ride during which he fails to get Terry to agree to 'dummy up' (i.e. not to testify to the Commission), does the tension drop. Now Malloy's testimony can be seen as revenge for his brother's death, and after Terry gives evidence to the Commission against the union leaders he goes down to the dock to personally confront Johnny Friendly and claim his 'rights'.

Some writers have seen *On the Waterfront* as little more than a vehicle for Schulberg and Kazan to justify their own 'informing', and have stressed the role of the Catholic priest in manipulating Terry's 'conscience'. Yet the film is more complex and genuinely powerful than this view would imply. First there is the location shooting in mid-winter Hoboken, using real longshoremen as extras, as well as a number of authentic boxing 'heavies'. Then there is the strong sense, at least in the first hour, of ordinary life, captured in a way that recalls the style of Italian neo-realism as much as traditional Hollywood. On the tenement roof where Terry looks after his own pigeons and those of the murdered Doyle, we get a strong sense of his private life, and of a vulnerability and sensitivity behind the macho posturing of the world of work.

Terry Malloy is given a psychological depth which helps explain his behaviour. In the famous taxi-cab scene Terry complains to his brother that he 'could've been a contender' and could have had class, had not Charley and Johnny ended his chances of attempting to gain a title by forcing him to throw fights for 'the short-end money'. The crime investigator, visiting Terry on his roof, also reminds him of his boxing career and his sense of unfulfilled talent and ambition. Brando's anguished performance is perhaps the most striking example of the Method approach that related the motivations in the script to real memories and resentments in the actor's life, therefore bringing these feelings to the screen. Many of the cast were recruited from the Actors Studio and a number of other scenes, including the long take of Terry and Edie Doyle first talking in a playground, are classic examples of a naturalistic acting style and emotional realism. (Terry's use of the phrase 'You go to Hell' to Father Barry required a bending of the Production Code rules by censor Joseph Breen.)

Brando's mix of toughness and sensitivity, and his dramatic rebellion against the prevailing norms of his peers and elders, arguably connects the film to those starring that other Method icon of the period, James Dean. Kazan directed Dean in *East of Eden*, while his friend Nicholas Ray – from a similar 1930s milieu of social theatre and radical politics – directed *Rebel Without a Cause* in 1955. (Brando, aged thirty in 1954, was at least fifteen years younger than the top male box-office stars of the 1950s, including John Wayne, Gary Cooper and James Stewart.) While the Kazan-Brando film looks backward to the 1930s in its working-class locale, however, the Ray-Dean movie is more characteristic of the new Hollywood emphasis on the problems that affluence was bringing the middle classes.

Hollywood's responsibilities in the war years had led some to look forward to less escapist, more adult American movies. Certainly the socially conscious writers and directors who came to the film capital from the East Coast hoped for a more decentralised process of film-making, as the old authoritarian studios lost their power. But except for the most successful directors, and for a number of 'B' movies, such hopes were generally unrealised. Yet *On the Waterfront* did set a standard for a more cooperative film-making tradition based in New York; Sam Spiegel strictly organised the production, but the circumstances allowed the creative personnel more autonomy than was normal under studio supervision. The film also sounded different because of Leonard Bernstein's only film score, which used discordance to flag up the scenes on the roof, and the understated, 'unHollywood' romance between Terry and Edie, even if it also accentuated the melodrama of the finale. Similarly, the distinctive visual qualities, from day-time smoky vistas across the Hudson to striking night blacks, owed much to the cinematography of Boris Kaufman, who had worked decades earlier with Jean Vigo.

The characters generally avoid stereotype. Karl Malden drew some of his portrayal of Father Barry from the real-life Catholic priest, while the part of Edie Doyle – structurally important in pushing Terry towards what is defined as his 'public responsibility' – is not the one-dimensional presentation that characterised so many female roles of the day. Edie's desire to investigate her brother's death is the catalyst for the action, and the observation of her emerging relationship with Terry allows her – perhaps until the final scenes – a believable independence.

The way Terry is shunned by the boy from his old roof-top gang, following his appearance before the Crime Commission, reflects Kazan's own experiences following his testimony to HUAC. Kazan's desire to justify his actions pushed him, in the film, to change the context of informing: Terry Malloy testifies to murder, while Kazan named fellow members of the Communist Party cell that he belonged to sixteen years before, and left acrimoniously. When Terry approaches the union shack and tells Friendly that he is 'glad what I done to you', there is clearly a sense that this is echoing Kazan's feelings about the Communist Party.

Terry's final walk to work, following his fight with Johnny Friendly, was seen by the British film director Lindsay Anderson as fascistic; involving a sudden transfer of loyalty to a new leader by the watching, apathetic crowd. Although the 'walk', with its hints of religious symbolism, overstates the sense that there has been real change on the waterfront, Malloy hardly behaves as a leader, while Friendly is seen shouting that he will be back, and the men are shown to be little more than cautiously admiring of Terry's exhibition of his old boxing skills.

In short, the film shows little of the collective action that was an element of the real events, concentrating as it does – characteristically, for the time – on issues of personal identity. It also only hints at the role of business in the waterfront corruption through a number of references to a mysterious waterfront tycoon. Yet there is much in the portrayal, including the general sense of alienation, that does have roots in the documentary evidence.

Rather like *The Crucible* (1953), Arthur Miller's play about the Salem witch trials of the 1690s, which he wrote having failed to persuade Kazan not to testify, *On the Waterfront* offers a metaphorical commentary on its times. In an age of debate about conformity, with references to grey-flannel minds, anonymous organisation men, and even the 'pod people' of *Invasion of the Body Snatchers*, Brando acted out Kazan's conformity, his coming in from the cold, but created at the same time a powerful and popular image of individual redemption. Kazan's later work – now as producer-director – included *A Face in the Crowd* (1957), a film that was pioneering in terms of its treatment of the use of advertising and marketing in politics, and *Splendor in the Grass* (1961). Perhaps his most personal work was *America America* (1963), which powerfully imagined the myth and reality of the immigrant struggle to reach turn-of-the-century America. Kazan's last film was released in 1976, but the controversy surrounding his honorary Academy Award in 1999 suggests that his reputation is still haunted by the 1952 testimony that provides the subtext of his best remembered film.

12

UN AMERICANO A ROMA

David Ellwood

The years 1954 and 1955 were the most golden of any in the golden era of postwar Italian cinema. Over 800 million tickets were sold in 1954, 819 million in 1955, a peak never to be reached again. Purpose-built picture-houses continued to open in their hundreds each year, and there was a constant stream of new talent and home-grown film sensations. 'If 1954 was Gina Lollobrigida's year, 1955 will be Sophia Loren's', the popular newsweekly *Epoca* predicted in its Christmas edition. Immortal classics of European cinema reached the screen for the first time in these months: Visconti's historical epic *Senso* and Fellini's Oscar-winning *La Strada*, were masterpieces and celebrated as such from the start of their careers.

But it was the extraordinary vitality of film comedy that kept the studios working and the box offices busy. Cheap, snappy, often using hordes of ordinary folk and improvised locations, the *commedia all'italiana* was a genuine new contribution to popular film culture and made the fortunes of actors like Alberto Sordi and Vittorio Gassman, and of directors like Luigi Comencini, Mario Monicelli and Dino Risi. The genre was born casually and spontaneously of a fusion between the postwar, neo-realist tradition of Rossellini and De Sica, and a much older music hall and comic magazine tradition of slapstick. By 1954, neo-realism's sombre tones and socially committed messages were being swept away by an avalanche of Hollywood successes and by the energy of Italy's reconstruction process. The exuberance and vitality of the country's rush towards a new kind of prosperity created audiences who were demanding a lighter, more entertaining attitude to life in their films, who looked likely to choose the American product if nothing better came along. For its part, the neo-realist experience had taught the industry how to get everyday reality on to the screen, how to portray in language, characterisation and imagery the experience of ordinary people up and down the country as they faced life's dramas in good times and bad.

If Hollywood provided the challenge, and social change the occasion, it was the collective genius of a small group of screenwriters, directors and producers, actors and actresses, working together constantly, improvising dialogues, plots and scenes, that produced the extraordinary cinematic *comédie humaine* of the 1950s. Their achievement was such that Italian cinema of the era remains an enduring source of entertainment and the most important historical source of any for seeing and understanding the tumultuous social change Italy experienced in the years of its *miracolo economico*.

Gina Lollobrigida's first year of international stardom in 1954 was also the moment when Alberto Sordi emerged as the dominant male comic talent of the new era. In a career that had begun timidly in 1938, and continues in minor key to this day (embracing over 190 films), Sordi came to be recognised as a supreme icon of Italian national identity, an all-too-perfect representation of a familiar masculine type: vainglorious and obsequious, noisy and self-indulgent, moody and silly, eternally adolescent. But his most famous characters have all the redeeming qualities of youth. Good-hearted and human, ironical and amusing, they are tragi-comics, self-consciously suspended in disbelief at their own merits and defects, above all, astonished at the perversity of fate in its treatment of their well-meaning attentions to other people, especially those closest to them.

Sordi made no fewer than thirteen films in 1954. His offering for Christmas of that year was destined to become a classic of the *commedia* genre and of his career: *Un americano a Roma*, directed by Steno (pseudonym of one of comedy's most typical film-makers, Stefano Vanzina). The story of a Roman working-class youth infatuated with everything American, Nando Mericoni's sole ambition – misunderstood as he is at home – is to get to the land of his dreams, evidently fabricated by Hollywood. After a series of humiliations, Nando threatens to commit suicide from the top of the Colosseum unless he is allowed to emigrate. But he is saved by the American Ambassador himself, whose intervention is prompted by the crowds and the chance to demonstrate America's generosity to its less fortunate allies. Unfortunately, upon his descent, the Ambassador recognises Nando as the youth whose over-enthusiasm had earlier caused the solemn old diplomat and his wife a nasty car crash into a river. The ensuing scuffle lands Nando in hospital, where doctors assure his aged and overwrought parents (the only household objects Nando has been unable to Americanise, a voice-over informs us) that the

Rebel without a clue? A scene from *Un americano a Roma* where the hapless Nando, played by Alberto Sordi, impersonates Marlon Brando in *The Wild One*. (Cineteca Communale, Bologna)

trauma will cure him of his infatuation. But Nando has the last word – literally. Slowly awakening from a coma and encased in plaster, he makes an American salute and reaches out with one finger to write 'The End' – in English – directly on the screen.

The structure of the film is episodic, each sequence revealing a stage in Nando's descent to desperation as his obsession with America is brought up against cruel reality. In a flashback to the bad old days of the Nazi occupation, Nando has organised a jazz welcome for the liberators, but has mistaken his timing and is consequently arrested by the Germans before the Americans arrive. In a forced labour gang, he is bombed from the air by the very men he worships. When the US Army does turn up, it misconstrues his enthusiasm for lunacy, or worse, and almost has him shot. Back in the present, we see Nando leading a chaotic and amateurish 'Broadway'-style dance troupe; it fails ludicrously. When he is taken up by a visiting American heiress and her family,

Nando imagines she wants to marry him; in reality she admires his classical Roman profile and wants only to use him as a model in her art class. Nando's escape across Roman roof-tops dressed as a half-naked satyr thrusts him unwittingly into a live television broadcast. This brings more chaos and allows the film to poke fun at the pomposity of the new rival medium (Italian television had begun regular broadcasting in 1954).

Subsequently, Nando presents himself as an American traffic cop on a huge motorbike, but dressed in the jeans-and-white-T-shirt style of Marlon Brando in *The Wild One* (the film had just appeared amid controversy over its depiction of teenage motorcycle gangs). Coming across the American Ambassador and his wife driving their convertible in the local countryside, Nando is enthralled, and tries in his Romanised, make-believe English to give the Ambassador directions to the best beauty spots, with disastrous consequences. These Nando then tries to exploit, by selling the 'story' to a newspaper from an unlikely rural phone near the scene of the crash: once again he is scoffed at for his efforts.

Although the film is over-long and simply too ridiculous in places, as the critics immediately pointed out, no one doubted the effectiveness of Sordi's characterisation or the meaning of his message. The critic of a specialised weekly wrote: 'Sordi's presence and his acting are absolutely realistic and his most irresistible effects come from the contrast between this most fundamental quality and his efforts to be different, to get from the Testaccio [Nando's working-class, inner-city neighbourhood] to Kansas City.' What *Un americano a Roma* offered, said one of the leading film journals, was

> . . . a review of the last ten years, from the war down to today, listing one by one all the forms of 'Americanism' which have appeared in the Italian way of life. Alberto Sordi, interpreting the kid infatuated with every one of the myths America has sent us (from the soldiers of 1944, to the jazz of 1945, the tourists of 1954, the western, the police film, baseball, the musical, the pin-up, television), offers a series of caricatures which are stupendous in intention.

The film was a homage to the power of the Hollywood myth as much as a satire on its effects. Our first sight of Nando reveals him in the front row of a fleapit cinema entranced by a Hopalong Cassidy Western. The flashback to Nando's wartime misadventures was a parody of Billy Wilder's *Stalag 17* (1953). The Ambassador's car crash fiasco and the attempted 'scoop' make explicit fun of another heavyweight Billy Wilder drama, his *Ace in the Hole* of 1951. Nando's idea of suicide with maximum bathos comes from an intense encounter with a poster advertising Henry Hathaway's 1951 classic *14 Hours*, featuring the ledge of a New York skyscraper and its hapless victim of contemporary life.

The basic comic mechanism at work seems obvious: the poor man's aping of his rich relations, half in self-pity, half in fascinated awe, forever trying to turn their fortune to his own advantage, but in the end always retaining his own hopelessly defective personality. But Sordi's intentions were more complex than this. He told a critic that by pillorying behaviour such as Brando's in *The Wild One* he would save Italian youth from the temptation of imitating him. In this way the film's essentially defensive nature is revealed, showing how the rain of novelties from America could be demystified and dealt with on terms which left the locals much preferring their own traditions. At the same time, Mericoni – like many other Sordi characters of the era – provided an unmatched outlet and source of identification for those lonely individuals disorientated and frustrated by the eruption of the consumer society all around them.

Significantly, Nando's character, invented in a previous Steno triumph (*Un Giorno in pretura*, 1953), did not reappear after *Un americano a Roma*. Had he continued in this vein, Sordi might have become the jester at the court of the American empire. As it was, following the film's success, the actor made his first transatlantic trip, was invited to make a film about a Roman youth in America (never produced) and was given honorary citizenship of Kansas City. Meanwhile, Nando Mericoni lived on in popular memory – and in Sordi's. Thirty years later the great comic declared that after their youthful follies, boys like Nando rolled up their sleeves, got down to work and made the 'economic miracle' what it was.

This comment was typical of Sordi's efforts to give his career its full historical significance; efforts which have been widely shared in books, reviews and television series dedicated to him in recent years. In 1995 Sordi declared that he was happy to have helped Italians reflect on themselves, and especially on their defects. At the same time:

> I always tried to be as topical as possible, to depict changes in the way we live, and I always did what I set out to do – to use my characters to tell the history of Italy from the end of the war down to today.

The topicality of *Un americano a Roma* is announced in a series of vignettes with commentary that opens the film. Each depicts the fixation with

America – with its myths, its fashions and skyscrapers, its stars and its lifestyles – said to be sweeping over Italians in every walk of life in the early 1950s. Children playing cowboys and Indians, matrons demanding health-food menus in restaurants, slinky young ladies in suits emulating the stars, all are declared with mock horror to be caught up in the obsession. Nando, the Roman American, is simply the most extreme case, whose story, the voice-over implies, is a parable showing the pitfalls of such behaviour and the dangers lying in wait for those whose embrace of America is too passionate.

Today no one doubts the central role of American myths and models in forming and directing Italy's tumultuous experience of modernisation in the 1950s. Historians have increasingly used the concept of Americanisation as a key to understanding the processes at work; although this is a tool that explains only some parts of what was happening – much of Italian life remained defiantly resistant to its challenges. Still, the outcome of the 'economic miracle' (so called because it was so unexpected) has led some writers to include Italy as among the most Americanised of all the West European countries in these years.

Italy's need for a strong development model seemed to become more deeply felt as expectations rose and the technological means for fulfilling them became available. Urbanisation (7 to 8 million people moved to the cities in the 1950s), the expansion of welfare, public development projects and the money spent by the government and its American allies persuading ordinary Italians to back the right side in the Cold War were all factors that pushed consumption upwards. It increased on average by 5 to 6 per cent, per year, and for the *dolce vita* classes much more (Fellini's film of that name – first screened in 1960 – was one of the most significant early signs of disenchantment with the results). It was high social mobility – or the prospect of it – that made the American model seem so appropriate and attractive, the economic historian, Vera Zamagni has written, providing 'a common pattern which succeeded in homogenising the Italians and at the same time preserved their localistic traditions'.

In a recent study of the impact of postwar mass culture – especially America's – on the Italian Communist Party (the largest in the West, with nearly 23 per cent of the vote in 1953), Stephen Gundle focuses on the links which emerged between consumption and consumerism under the influence of the American inspiration, and how deeply they upset the traditional outlooks of both the dominant ideological camps, Catholic and Communist:

Only kidding: would-be wild one Nando confronts the law. (BFI Stills, Posters and Designs)

The rapid industrialisation process in a country lacking a true secular culture shared by everyone produced an enormous void, which only the ideas, themes and rules coming from America seemed able to fill. In this sense the desire for America, so evident in the Italy of the 1950s and '60s, was the expression of a real change in attitudes and expectations, as well as reflecting the decline of norms and relationships taken for granted till then.

Commentators at the time struggled to come to terms with what was happening. The film director De Sica denounced the changes as cataclysmic and compared them to the effects of the Bomb: 'We're all terrified of the atom bomb, but that one *might* explode. This one already *has* exploded!' In the summer of 1955 the *New York Times* asked Reuters correspondents across the globe whether or not they thought 'the free world was being Americanized'. The Italian response, datelined Naples, told how:

Delicatessens have ousted many of the old-fashioned salami shops in Naples. Blaring juke-boxes drown the soft notes of the guitar. Hurry and urgency have affected the sleepy Neapolitans. . . . Today teenagers in Naples, Florence, Genoa and some other large Italian cities wear jeans, while American-type sports shirts are on sale in all the big department stores. Bobby-soxers jitterbug in improvised dance-halls.

Everywhere the susceptibility of youth to the new culture was remarked on by the Reuters reports: 'where younger people are concerned popcorn, Coca-Cola and blue jeans, hamburgers, hot dogs, Hollywood, jazz and chewing gum – even dollars – have become part of life in a natural way, [even] without acknowledgement to the source'.

In historical terms, Americanisation appears as a particularly distinctive form of modernisation, superimposed with great political, economic and cultural force, but more or less randomly, on each European country's own variant. Yet these were societies free to resist the projection of American power in all its forms, to take what they wanted from that model and to organise their own means for reconciling what America was offering with their own traditions, customs and priorities. In the Italy of the 1950s the cinema was the most significant of these mechanisms and Sordi's *Un americano a Roma* showed it off with pride.

Early on in the film, in a brilliant scene of improvised visual comedy, Nando returns home late to find the spaghetti and wine his long-suffering mother has left him. He rejects the food with scorn, building up his own dish of bread, milk, yoghurt and mustard, all the while telling himself that this is what Americans eat and what makes them big and strong. But the very first mouthful is disgusting and Nando throws away his imaginary American supper without a second thought. He then turns ferociously back to his spaghetti and his chianti flask – the old certainties – hiding his feeble about-face by swearing that the pasta has 'provoked' him and so has to be destroyed. Pride is saved, but in private; in public the trick will not be so easy.

Yet unlike other postwar European films satirising the Americanisation of gullible natives, such as Jacques Tati's *Jour de Fête* (1949), the Steno/Sordi comedy rejected the grateful return to ancient ways as the solution to the local hero's humiliations. Instead, it showed how the new semi-culture did not destroy, but came to co-exist with local customs, the US component becoming everyone's second culture. *Un americano a Roma* is a prophetic film also, because it pointed to the emergence of a new and distinct section of society: youth, influenced supremely by America; but remaining – through endless conflicts – substantially loyal to its native roots. And so the critics agree: the film can never be considered a milestone in the history of Italian cinema, but it is a milestone in the history of Italian identity, and will always be loved as such.

13

I'M ALL RIGHT JACK

Peter Stead

The suggestion that John Boulting's comedy of industrial relations is a significant film has buzzed around in the minds and writings of British intellectuals ever since it opened in the summer of 1959. Extremely popular, *I'm All Right Jack* was the most commercially successful film from any source released in Britain that year. The production company, British Lion, had been eager to follow up the comparative success of its 1956 release *Private's Progress*, also produced and directed by the Boulting brothers. This film had broadly, and rather farcically, satirised the Army in what were to be the last days of National Service. Adapted from a work by the same author, Alan Hackney, *I'm All Right Jack*, starred largely the same cast. Quite legitimately, the company used 'The *Private's Progress* Shower Are Back' as its chief advertising slogan and this was the theme initially taken up by the more popular national papers and later by the provincial press. In pubs and work places the talk was that this was a very funny comedy that had to be seen, even if it meant missing a few hours of television.

It was the promise of sheer entertainment that created the long queues wherever the new comedy was screened; however, the film's topicality also worked in its favour. The 'Shower' were back, but this time they were 'having a go' at the unions and, in particular, at shop stewards. The Boultings' timing was impeccable: the national press and the increasingly influential television news had been much concerned with reporting strikes, particularly unofficial ones, while a general election was due in which the image of the unions was bound to be a significant factor.

In the event, the film opened in London some seven weeks before the election. Providentially, it went on general release the week after the Conservative Party secured its third consecutive election victory, polling 49.9 per cent of the vote – the most decisive parliamentary majority since 1945: although they had been in office for eight years, the Tories were actually gaining in popularity. In the run-up to the election analysts had noted 'ominous' portents that the links between the Labour Party and the unions had 'helped to tarnish the Party's image'. In the election aftermath, it was thought that the Tories had benefited greatly from the 'blurring' of class differences in the perceptions of both newly affluent workers and young people.

It would be going too far to suggest that anti-unionism was a major factor in Harold Macmillan's election success. However, without doubt, many suburban voters had been irritated by wildcat strikes and by the regular appearance on the television news bulletins of one or two uncompromising union leaders such as Frank Cousins of the Transport and General Workers Union and Sid Greene of the National Union of Railwaymen. The impression formed was that they seemed to care little about the inconvenience caused by their militant members. Certainly suburban film-goers were in the right frame of mind to see a po-faced union leader be taken down a peg or two. Not, of course, that the film was officially marketed in this way – as the *News Chronicle* shrewdly noted at the time, 'the public have a wonderful nose for smelling out what they want'. In the industrial town of Swansea, for example, the local paper restricted itself to talking of the way in which *I'm All Right Jack*, 'rapidly becoming known as "the union film"', takes the mickey out of strikes and their instigators' describing it, all in all, as 'a great satire on the trade unions'. The critic felt no need to spell out the timely relevance of the film, although later that month his paper would splash across its pages editorial headlines such as 'Anarchy in the Unions' and 'Trade Union Treason'. It was quite understandable, argued Derek Hill in *Tribune*, that many critics had 'gleefully seized' on the new comedy; in his view, the film merely repeated 'the editorial policies of nine-tenths of those papers'.

It became increasingly clear that critics like Hill, and readers of socialist publications like *Tribune* and the *Daily Worker* were upset: the *News Chronicle* even reported that in the infamously anti-Tory South Wales coalfield there had been deep resistance to the film. All this only served to boost its popularity in the suburbs. Tory voters were delighted to hear that left-wing intellectuals were angry, on their part disappointed that after years of waiting for a socially relevant film one should come along that had been made by the wrong side. In *Sight and Sound*, Penelope Houston raged against this 'depressingly cynical' and 'malicious' film that appeared to be the work of 'sour' liberals. On reading this, the more balanced New York critic Pauline Kael reflected that, at times, Houston's 'jargon isn't far removed from the shop steward's'.

Rumours that unionists and socialists were angry certainly lengthened the queues, but rumours were all it took. In truth, and certainly by the standards of the tabloids of the Thatcher era, the reporting of the film was fair, honest and totally lacking in sensationalism. *The Times* thought the film 'good-natured' with 'its barbs very fairly divided between Capital and Labour'. The *Daily Herald*'s Anthony Carthew did all he could to keep matters cool by pointing out that what it presented was 'not an attack on trade unions but rather on their abuse', as well as on the generally 'false values that have sustained the fifties'. Such balanced comment should serve to remind us that *I'm All Right Jack* was not a film that suddenly took a whole culture by storm; it occasioned no great polarisation. The film was received primarily as entertainment, not as an important critique. Most serious critics were unimpressed and disappointed at the Boultings' lack of ambition. The most deflating response came from William Whitebait in the *New Statesman*. He wrote of 'mechanical laughs' and the lack of spontaneous wit, but concluded that, after all, the film had not set out with any 'high pretensions'.

Over the years, the reservations of the better critics were forgotten. Historians began to study popular culture, some of them recalling how in 1959 the public had talked a great deal about a 'union' film in which, quite memorably, Peter Sellers had depicted a shop steward. In his fascinating 1970 volume *A Mirror for England* Raymond Durgnat speculated that the film was 'probably a key British movie of the period'. Still the collective memory was slow to crystallise. Then in 1978, Peter Lewis published a popular survey called simply *The Fifties*. In this, Lewis boldly used illustrations and portraits to make the point that this was the decade of James Dean, Marilyn Monroe, Marlon Brando, Brigitte Bardot, Tommy Steele, Fidel Castro, Billy Graham – figures now identified as cultural icons. *I'm All Right Jack* features as early as page 15. The photo is of Peter Sellers as the shop steward, Fred Kite, surrounded by his works committee; the caption simply explains that this was 'the famous film that summed up the philosophy of the late fifties – the Age of Affluence'.

Lewis was breaking new ground, for it was still comparatively rare for any kind of British historian to highlight an individual film as providing clues to an era: only students of cinema would have read Durgnat or the new history of British cinema by Roy Armes. However, disappointingly, Lewis's remarks about *I'm All Right Jack* are confined to a useful explanation of John Boulting's title. In the film, the hero, Stanley Windrush (played by Ian Carmichael), sums up the current state of industrial relations as one in which 'wherever you look, it's

Peter Sellers, besuited as shop steward Fred Kite, confronts 'the management' with a delegation of fellow workers. (Charter/Courtesy Kobal)

blow you Jack, I'm all right!' Lewis explains that the phrase 'I'm all right, Jack' originated with soldiers in the Second World War, but in the 1950s it took on more jocular overtones and 'simply stated a philosophy that was just taken for granted'.

The historian Arthur Marwick, more than any other writer, took the lead in prompting his colleagues and students to let their affection and possible nostalgia for the film develop into an appreciation of its significance. In his 1980 study *Class* he retells the film's jokes before selecting it as the 'one film to represent the outbreak of cultural revolution' at that time. He sums it up as 'a highly deliberate and historically sensitive social satire', which very effectively made its point 'that the two major classes were, in fact, in cahoots to do the nation down'. Professor Marwick did not leave it there. In his 1982 survey *British Society Since 1945* he refers to the 'ruthless gusto' of a film that should be regarded as 'a classic satire'. The influence of this judgement, made in what was to become a widely used textbook, was enhanced by the appearance on the cover of a still of Peter Sellers as the shop steward and Ian Carmichael as his upper-class foil. A year later Marwick returned to the subject in an essay on working-class images published in a prestigious volume *The Working Class in Modern British History*. His considered judgement in this is that *I'm All Right Jack* is a 'social satire of considerable sensitivity and perception'. Given this authoritative enthusiasm, Professor Marwick's students might be surprised that so many other cultural and political historians chose to ignore the film. It does not figure in the important surveys of the period by Sked and Cook, David Childs, Harry Hopkins, Christopher Booker, Bernard Levin, Stuart Laing and Robert Hewison. It was left to film historians like Tony Aldgate and John Hill to sustain the debate. When I published my book *Film and the Working Class* in 1989, the publishers specifically recommended that Peter Sellers' shop steward should adorn the front cover.

For several decades one's only hope of re-examining *I'm All Right Jack* was to look out for a chance television showing, though even then it would be dropped from the schedule if there was a parliamentary contest in the offing, as was the case in 1979. Now with its release on video and the mushrooming of media courses it has re-entered our culture. Viewing the film today, one realises that of those original critics perhaps William Whitebait was nearest the mark in his judgement. Admittedly there are some good jokes and at least one of them is visual (the newsreader's initial information that 'with Victory came a New Age' is immediately followed by Victor Maddern's forceful V-sign), but mostly they are verbal one-liners delivered by a well-cast and well-known squad of comedy actors. For all the chuckles, the film has an insubstantial feel; it has no real body. It is, in effect, just a collection of jokes and sketches. The script is the essence of the whole thing and in this sense it belongs to the same genre as the BBC's thirty-minute radio comedies that were so popular at the time. The inconsequential musical score, veritable kaleidoscope of early scenes and the two-dimensional performance of Ian Carmichael as Stanley Windrush, with his total reliance on exaggerated double-takes, combine to give the film the whimsical slightness of an animated strip cartoon.

The most surprising feature of *I'm All Right Jack* is that it is only in part to do with the unions. The adventures of Windrush, a decent but ineffectual upper-class twit, are used to reveal what is wrong with British industry and, by

'If the TUC wins . . .': this Cummings cartoon from the *Daily Express* of July 1956 sums up a caricature of industrial relations in the period. (*Express* Newspapers)

implication, with British society. The theme of the innocent at large, however, is dissipated by weak scenes such as that in the cartoon mock-up of a cake factory, by the absurdly sinister espionage sub-plot, by the relentless degeneration into farce, and by the gratuitous unpleasantness of the insults thrown at many varied targets, including Arabs, coloured immigrants, stutterers and attractive young women. The film is also preoccupied with satirising television's presentation of current affairs; one suspects that the Boultings and their technicians wanted to settle a few scores with the medium that was now threatening their livelihoods.

Of the many strange phenomena that Windrush encounters in his career as a worker nothing is quite so singular or memorable as his shop steward Fred Kite. In 1959 there were critics who were prepared to forgive all as they gave thanks for what they considered to be Sellers' great performance. *Tribune*'s Derek Hill thought it 'as brilliant as it is contemptible' and Leonard Mosley of the *Daily Express* suggested that, as Kite, Sellers had achieved 'his triumph as a serious artist'. Film critics were obviously following this 34-year-old actor's career closely, fully aware that out in the country Sellers already had a cult following as a radio personality.

As one of the stars and perhaps the main perpetrator of the genuinely original radio comedy *The Goon Show* Sellers had been identified as someone at the cutting edge of zany, surreal and anarchic humour. Following in the footsteps of other radio stars, he was now in the process of finding his feet in a more challenging, more international and lucrative medium. His followers responded by talking up his performances so as to encourage him. Many shared Mosley's view that the creation of Kite was a major turning point. A more balanced analysis was provided by Kenneth Letner who, writing in *Film Quarterly*, appreciated that the actor was in the process of experimenting in styles. Letner could see that Sellers was good, that he combined a 'restraint' that 'smacked of French classicism' with 'the slapstick simplicity' of vaudeville, and yet he also considered the actor's approach 'disembodied', 'not corporeal enough', too dependent on 'outer resources'.

Nevertheless, the cult followers never abandoned their interest in Sellers and, indeed, were given little opportunity to do so. In the new decade he was becoming an international superstar and as such was to be written about and analysed to a far greater extent than any of his individual films. Critics were fascinated by the brilliance of his mimicry and the way in which it seemingly related to a private uncertainty as to his real identity both as an actor and as a person. As early as 1959, Thomas Wiseman suggested that 'there's no such person as Peter Sellers'. Raymond Durgnat explained the art of Sellers, 'a Jewish cosmopolitan', in terms of that 'English obsession with' and gift for 'chameleon impersonations' so understandable and yet so confining in a culture dominated by class judgements and nuances. More often it has been the psychological implications of Wiseman's remark that have been investigated, especially since Sellers' death in 1980. One of his biographers, Alexander Walker, has confirmed that Sellers became preoccupied with the notion that he lacked a personality and that he relied on both acting and spiritualism to provide some kind of foundation. Walker shares Letner's view that for Sellers the externals were basic to the roles he created and yet he often thought of himself as an empty 'medium' actually possessed by the character he was creating.

Increasingly, Sellers' later career has encouraged metaphysical speculation. For the American writer and entertainer Spalding Gray, the actor's confusion of identity was a sure sign that 'he was a kind of holy man'. On the other hand, an exhaustive study of the impact of his psychological problems on his wives and colleagues has led the Welsh scholar Roger Lewis to the view that 'Sellers was evil'. In 1995 further revelations claimed that privately Sellers had been preoccupied with filming himself and maintaining close relations with members of the social elite.

Both Alexander Walker and Pauline Kael have shown their irritation with the wilder theories, reminding us that what was best in Sellers was his professionalism, the way in which he could create and so rapidly develop a real live character. This is why Kite is so memorable. Apparently the character was initially sketched out by the Boultings, who never doubted that Sellers was the man for the part. Sellers himself has explained how all the elements came together: the haircut, the suit, the Hitler moustache, the accent and the deliberate impersonation of a union official at the studio, as well as one or two union chiefs from the television news. The early Kite scenes and lines are very funny; a brilliant satire of the so-called 'Napoleons of the shop floor'. Yet it is a part that leads nowhere. For Roger Lewis, among others, it is wholly plausible that we come to realise that Kite is a hollow figure with no real confidence. But as the film's domestic scenes become maudlin and melodramatic and its public scenes more farcical, Kite not only collapses but becomes depressingly flat, and one senses that the actor is as much responsible for that as the script itself.

I'm All Right Jack still affords a few pleasures and these are largely contributed by the repertory of English character actors, genuine personalities straight out of music hall, provincial rep and Broadcasting House. For me, the tortured genius of Peter Sellers is soon eclipsed by the perky brightness of Victor Maddern, Margaret Rutherford, Irene Handl as the wife who keeps Kite (and Sellers) firmly in place, and above all by Terry-Thomas as the personnel manager (who has most of the best lines). Roger Lewis has explained that there were tensions between Sellers and Thomas especially over one key scene that they shared. A later television producer might well have spotted that this odd partnership could have formed the basis for an ideal sitcom series. But Thomas would have been the star, the perfect expression of how a certain type of Englishman could be stylish, theatrical, sympathetic and at the same time full of 'bull' and pathos. His Major Hargreaves – and how many majors there were in the 1950s – is not a cartoon but a real flesh and blood character, a genuine and quite moving piece of English social history. At the outset he rumbles Kite; the man was 'a real shocker, the kind of chap who sleeps in his vest!' While it is Seller's Kite who has become the movie's dominant image entering the nation's memory as a nostalgically recalled cult figure, it is Terry-Thomas's Major Hargreaves that I most want to see again as I revisit the film.

We should treasure *I'm All Right Jack* as a monument to much that was good and bad in British film in the era of the studios. With gags aplenty and no shortage of fresh-faced music-hall types to deliver them, nobody had the confidence to slow the pace or clear the clutter to permit a concentration on essentials. The factory scenes showing the indolence of the workers and the obstinacy of the unions are the funniest, yet they are not allowed to be the heart of the matter; the silly plot rushes on regardless. The few good anti-union jokes are a useful indication that as early as 1959 a section of middle-class opinion was questioning that favoured place in the life of the nation that unions had enjoyed since 1940.

The anti-union point, however, was only one strand in a film that both wittingly and unwittingly tells us much about the Britain of the 1950s. Certainly, in wanting to indict the selfishness of all sectors of society, the Boultings went for a broad and crowded canvas. Their chosen instrument was farce rather than sustained satire and to that extent the film is childish and disappointing. In their headlong pantomime of non-communicating social types we glimpse a culture apparently incapable of producing either challenging screenplays or more focused politics.

14

LA DOLCE VITA

Stephen Gundle

Although it was made forty years ago, *La Dolce Vita* remains a very contemporary film. Directed by Federico Fellini at the height of his creative powers, it offers an extraordinary panorama of aspects of Roman life at the very moment when Italy was shedding its rural past and becoming a turbulent industrial society. Such is the stylistic appeal of the film that images and scenes from it continue to be copied and re-cycled in magazine articles, fashion spreads and advertisements. The film's louche image, symbolised by the sharply-dressed and sun-glasses-wearing decadents Marcello Mastroianni and Anouk Aimée, is widely used in connection with reportages on nightlife, depictions of clubland, and pop-music promotion. The film brought to light the phenomenon of the unlicensed celebrity photographer (who from then on became known the world over by the name of one of the film's characters, Paparazzo), it gave a commercial boost to Italy's hitherto rather underdeveloped fashion industry and it fuelled a wave of tourism to the Italian capital which continues to this day. At the time of its release, the film gave rise to a fashion for roll-neck sweaters (an item still known in Italy as a *dolcevita*). Regularly, at ten-year intervals after its 1960 release, it is evoked, discussed and its influence assessed. Possibly more than any other single film made in Italy since 1945, it has given rise to memoirs, novels, documentary accounts, television specials and photographic exhibitions.

Part of *La Dolce Vita*'s appeal derives from the film's complex relationship with the new image of life and society that was being communicated to a mass readership through illustrated magazines like *Oggi*, *L'Europeo*, *Lo Specchio* and the news weekly *L'Espresso*. A phenomenon of the 1950s in Italy, these publications did not merely report facts and events; they offered what Daniel Boorstin, in his 1962 book *The Image*, called a 'pseudo-reality', that is to say a parallel world made up of movie stars, images of high society, media events and publicity stunts that bore little obvious relation to everyday life. The film provides a sequence of tenuously-linked set-piece scenes which include the arrival at Ciampino airport of an American movie star, several scenes in night clubs, parties in the palaces of the Roman aristocracy, celebrity-chasing photo-reporters going about their business, night-time rides in open-topped sports cars, encounters with prostitutes and an orgy. These moments are interspersed with others of a somewhat different nature: the journey over Rome of a helicopter from which hangs a large wooden statue of Christ, the media circus surrounding the apparent appearance of the Madonna to two children, meaningful discussion in an intellectual salon, a trip to the seaside. Through all this, the aspirant writer-turned-gossip-columnist Marcello Rubini (Mastroianni) weaves his course, alternating frivolity and debauchery with moments of melancholy and reflection. He escorts the stars, hangs out at night clubs, liaises with the photographers and chases women, but he also argues with a highly-strung lover who waits for him at home and discusses philosophical questions with Steiner (the wealthy intellectual whose pessimism will lead him to commit suicide after killing his two small children). In two moving scenes, Marcello is briefly offered alternatives to his empty life in a meeting with his father, and in a chance encounter with an innocent young girl who waits at tables in a seafront café.

Initially Fellini had planned to make a rather different sort of film. He intended to follow up his darkly humorous analysis of the limitations of provincial life, *I Vitelloni* (1953), by looking at the career in the capital of Moraldo, the one member of the quartet of lower middle-class young men featured in the film who actually manages to up sticks and leave his home town. The director wanted to situate Moraldo in the bohemian milieu of Rome's Via Veneto, which in the early 1950s was the regular evening gathering point of journalists and literati. But Fellini and his collaborators, Ennio Flaiano and Brunello Rondi, soon realised that the Rome they had intended to depict had been replaced by another city, more brash and cosmopolitan. By the later 1950s, the night spots of the Via Veneto were no longer solely the after-hours haunts of writers who had migrated from the provinces; they were the pleasure grounds of Italy's booming film industry and of the many American actors and actresses who came to work and play in Hollywood on the Tiber. Instead of the bicycles that, following Vittorio De Sica's classic neo-realist film *Bicycle Thieves* (1948), symbolised the aspirations of the city's working class, outsize American automobiles signalled the wealth of the

Water nymph: screen goddess Anita Ekberg tempts Mastroianni to join her for a frolic in Rome's Trevi Fountain in one of the film's most famous sexy scenes. (BFI Stills, Posters and Designs)

fortunate few. As Rome became the leading European centre for American location films, so a sizeable movie colony sprang up that included both former stars at the end of their careers like Laurel and Hardy and established names such as Kirk Douglas, Deborah Kerr and Ava Gardner. Thanks to the stars, Rome became once again an outpost of international café society, a gathering point of exiled foreign royalty, speculators, playboys, socialites and artists.

During this period Italy entered a new phase of growth and change. No longer the predominantly agricultural and only primitively industrial country that had emerged from the Second World War, it was rapidly developing into an industrial society with a profile of its own. Although few Italians could yet afford cars, Vespa and Lambretta scooters began to be seen on the streets, radios entered working-class homes and television broadcasts spread elements of what would become a new common culture. In increasing numbers, peasants abandoned rural areas to seek a better life in the cities, young people gave rise to a culture fashioned by foreign-inspired sounds and fashions, and the values of consumerism came to be widely accepted. Although it would only be in the mid-1970s that the vast majority of households would possess a television set, a washing machine and a refrigerator, aspirations for these goods were forged earlier. The economic dynamism of the 1950s was evident in many ways, in the extraordinary boom of the building industry, in the investment in mass production, in the expansion of the mass media, in the transformations in family life.

Unprotected by the studios that in their heyday had been able to control completely the flow of news about their properties, foreign stars found themselves at the mercy of opportunist photographers who snapped them off-duty and sold the results to the scandal sheets. Their antics were a source of endless fascination to Italians who read about them and watched them in magazines and newsreels. Celebrities offered a larger-than-life version of the consumer lifestyle. Their hedonism, conspicuous consumption, leisure, mobility and child-like freedom from everyday constraints made them a focus for the dreams and aspirations of ordinary people. The implications of this were never fully grasped by Italy's elites. While religious spokesmen and the political left expressed grave concern about the consequences of the rapid decline of the countryside and the development of an American-style neo-capitalism, the ruling Christian Democrats complacently assumed that new values and cultures would dovetail easily with traditional ones to reinforce the existing social hierarchy. In a series of ways, *La Dolce Vita* demonstrated that this was a vain hope.

Fellini always claimed that he was not a moralist, that he had no intention of judging the new society that was emerging in Italy or even the particular fauna that he depicted. This is plausible in that the film does portray the seductive fascination of the café society as well as its intrinsic vacuity. Indeed, the long-term impact of the film has mainly been in the area of style. But there seems little doubt that he wanted to say something critical about the change of culture that was occurring. If Fellini was not moralistic then he was at least satirical. As in previous films, such as his first work *Luci del Varietà* (Variety Lights, 1950), which dealt with the decline of travelling theatre companies displaced by cinema, or *Lo Sceicco bianco* (*The White Sheik*, 1952), which explored the artificial world of the photo-romance magazines, he viewed the big city as an outsider. Like his character Moraldo, Fellini was a provincial who had migrated from the seaside town of Rimini to Rome. Despite his international successes (he had won an Oscar for *La Strada* in 1955), Fellini frequently returned for his inspiration to the experiences of his youth and the particular mentality and atmospheres of his hometown. *La Dolce Vita* presented a stark contrast between figures, behaviour models and values that belonged to an old world, and which generally were endowed with a positive connotation, and those which were representative of a new world that had lost its soul. The use of black and white photography, several years after the first Italian colour film, underscored this dichotomy.

Within Italy, the film was a watershed; it marked a shift in what could be represented on the screen and it also heralded the replacement of the austere neo-realist aesthetic by a focus on the ephemeral and the superficial. For perhaps the first time in postwar Italian cinema, style triumphed over substance. For this reason the film was deplored by Roberto Rossellini, the father of Italy's postwar cinema and the director of *Rome Open City*, the influential 1945 wartime film on which the young Fellini had collaborated.

Although Fellini had successfully lobbied to avoid any censorship of his film, *La Dolce Vita* was intensely controversial from the moment of its release in February 1960. While some welcomed its exploration of the negative side of economic boom, others, including conservative opinion leaders and the Catholic Church, denounced it as the work of a Communist. The Rome premiere on 4 February passed off peacefully but the Milan opening the following day was marked by a very different atmosphere. One irate spectator spat in the director's face; others accused him of being a clown and of having dragged Italy's good name through the mud. The depiction of a picturesque whirlwind of decadence and frivolity which implied that society was on the point of irredeemable degeneration led to questions in parliament and to calls for the film's immediate withdrawal. *La Dolce Vita* was attacked as immoral and subversive, and branded as a mock-trial that aimed to condemn Italian society as a whole and the capital in particular. Aristocrats who had taken part in the film found themselves ostracised by their peers, while those clerics who had initially seen it as a useful moral reflection were swiftly brought into line. The establishment was not united but a majority closed ranks against the film.

The controversy raged for weeks in the press and turned *La Dolce Vita* into a social and cultural event. Although uncommonly high ticket prices were charged to see the nearly three-hour-long film, it proved a huge success. It broke all box-office records, easily outclassing its main rival, Billy Wilder's *Some Like It Hot* (1959). It not only did exceptional business in the period immediately after its release but it was still making money five years later. The film scandalised well-to-do conservative audiences but intrigued people in the provinces and the South. An amusing example of this occurs in Pietro Germi's *Divorce Italian Style* (1961), a comedy of manners set in Sicily that also starred Mastroianni. In one scene a group of men is seen in church looking up at the priest who is delivering a tirade against the immorality of *La Dolce Vita*. In the next they are all seen gawping at a screen on which the film is being shown.

The film held up a mirror to the nation, offering a rare opportunity for a collective reflection on the state of society. But it was also a spectacle that appealed as entertainment, and employed a theme new to Italian cinema: eroticism. The film used many fewer well-known stars than Fellini had intended. Originally, Maurice Chevalier, Henry Fonda and veteran Oscar winner Luise Rainer were given roles, but the difficulty in securing adequate finance delayed the start of shooting and made the participation of the former two impossible. Dino De Laurentiis, a prospective producer before the role finally fell to the Milan publisher Angelo Rizzoli, wanted the lead role to be offered to Paul Newman but Fellini insisted on Mastroianni. Although the film turned him into an international sex symbol, Mastroianni was in fact chosen because he was familiar and reliable, a respectable and unexciting everyman with whom spectators could easily identify. His cordial and unexceptional features were the ideal vehicle for transporting audiences on a journey through a world of temptation and corruption. He was supported by a varied female cast including the Swedish actress Anita Ekberg, Anouk Aimée, Yvonne Furneaux and Nadia Gray.

Much of the film is permeated with sexual tension but two scenes in particular came to symbolise its daring novelty. The first of these comes early in the film when the voluptuous Ekberg, who plays the part of a visiting Hollywood star, decides to take a night-time dip in the Trevi fountain. Mastroianni, the press agent who is detailed to follow her, simply watches in amazement as he witnesses the statuesque actress parade through the waters like a goddess. When he finally responds to an invitation to join her, he does not touch her but holds himself back, fearful that he will be lost if he succumbs fully to the fascination of a woman who symbolises a new world of consumption, ease and uninhibited behaviour. With her child-like curiosity, irrepressible spirit and extraordinary physical presence, Ekberg transfixed Italians and added an important fantasy element to the film.

The film's second signature scene was less influential in the long term, but it contributed more than any other single factor to its *succès de scandale*. This was

The birth of cool? Aimée (in glasses) and Mastroianni provided ambiguous models of sophistication for the Italy of 1960. (BFI Stills, Posters and Designs)

the 'orgy scene' that occurs towards the end of Mastroianni's progressive absorption into a decadent and inauthentic way of living. In the company of a heterogeneous band of aristocrats, foreign exiles, entertainers and homosexuals looking for something new to awaken their jaded appetites at the conclusion of a night of revelry, he breaks into a villa where the party continues. The proceedings are enlivened by the impromptu striptease of an exhibitionist American, played by Nadia Gray. The scene is mild indeed by today's standards, but in 1960 it carried a powerful charge of transgression. It was also seen as central to the alleged denunciation by Fellini of the corrupt indolence of the rich and the powerful. In the film's subsequent and final scene, the motley gathering, now transferred to the nearby beach, watch in amazement as a dead sea monster is hauled ashore. Many observers saw the rotting flesh of this creature as a metaphor for the putrefaction of a society that was on the point of collapse. At the end of the film, Mastroianni is seen dismissing with a careless wave the innocent girl from the seafront café. Despite a shouted invitation to join her, he cannot hear her words above the sound of the waves. Finally corrupted beyond redemption, he prefers the company of the debauched and the damned.

Both the Trevi fountain scene and the 'orgy' provide examples of the way Fellini and his collaborators wove reinterpretations of real events into the narrative of *La Dolce Vita*. Ekberg was required merely to act as herself. She had arrived in Rome in 1958 to make *War and Peace* and had immediately become a favourite of the illustrated weeklies. Her wedding to the British actor Anthony Steel in Florence received almost as much coverage as the marriage of Tyrone Power and Linda Christian in 1949. Ekberg had also been photographed in the Trevi fountain. The orgy was modelled on the strip performed by the Turkish dancer Aiche Nana at Rome's Rugantino nightclub in November 1958. What had originally been a rather sedate party had suddenly taken a bohemian turn when the ubiquitous Ekberg had cast off her shoes to dance. Nana took things several steps further and, as the women present mostly withdrew, she contorted to the jazz rhythms of the band in front of an audience that included several well-known young members of the aristocracy. Before the police intervened, Tazio Secchiaroli, the photographer on whom the character of Paparazzo was based, recorded the event in a series of images that appeared – complete with strategic black strips to obscure the identity of those present and partially conceal Nana's nudity – in the political weekly *l'Espresso*. The publication of these pictures caused an outcry and the magazine was impounded as an obscene publication.

Although both of these key episodes in the film actually occurred, they were in fact examples of what Boorstin called 'pseudo-events'. From his office on the Via Veneto, the press agent Enrico Lucherini devised a whole series of stunts that served to publicise new films. These included Ekberg's dip in the fountain and events that mimicked aspects of the Rugantino scandal. Between them, Lucherini and photographers like Secchiaroli created the sensational image of Roman life that formed the basis of Fellini's inspiration and fuelled Rome's reputation as a centre for style, sex and scandal to which the film greatly contributed.

Perhaps the most salient aspect of the film's triumph as image was the utter disjunction of this from any critical judgement, moral or otherwise. In the promotional materials prepared for distribution in the United States, exhibitors were encouraged to persuade local stores to use the idea of 'the sweet life' to sell chocolates, air-fresheners or Italian products. Any satirical element completely disappeared.

Long before the term 'Fellini-esque' entered the English language, *La Dolce Vita* became a seductive cliché. Among the foreign authors who set their work in a Rome reminiscent of Fellini's film was Tennessee Williams, whose *The Roman Spring of Mrs Stone* was made into a film starring Warren Beatty in 1961. Irwin Shaw's *Two Weeks in Another Town* was also filmed (released in 1962), with Kirk Douglas as an American film star in decline, while Muriel Spark wrote of a British actress on the ascendant in *The Public Image*, which for good measure included an orgy. Among the many original films which traded on Italy's appeal to film audiences after *La Dolce Vita* was John Schlesinger's *Darling* (1965), in which Julie Christie abandons a comfortable existence in London with Dirk Bogarde for an ultimately unhappy life in Italy that includes a brief marriage to an ageing aristocrat.

The success of *La Dolce Vita* at home and abroad heralded the end of the Via Veneto's popularity with movie stars, the aristocracy and the international rich. The celebrities fled as tourists flocked to the road hoping to catch a glimpse of the famous and perhaps even receive an invitation to an orgy. But the city's reputation was perpetuated by occasional events such as the affair between Elizabeth Taylor and Richard Burton during the filming of *Cleopatra* in 1962. As the 1960s began to swing and youth emerged as a distinct cultural category, Rome was replaced as the leading centre of fashion by London. Yet its appeal was never entirely eclipsed. Vespas, sharp suits and sunglasses all became a part of the British Mod look.

For two centuries, Italy had offered well-off foreign travellers a taste of excitement, mixing wonderment at the glory of its ancient civilisation and artistic heritage with the ambiguous attractions of its more primitive passions. After *La Dolce Vita* the country was seen as a forerunner of the permissive society. In reality, Italian society continued to be closed and intolerant. Prior to the divorce referendum of 1974, which signalled a historic defeat for clerical conservatism, films were frequently censored and magazines seized. Artists and journalists were regularly sent for trial on charges of outraging public decency. But the country had acquired a sexy new image that refurbished its old glamour in the eyes of outsiders, and definitively replaced both the residual memories of Fascism, and the social and political concerns of the postwar years.

15

ALFIE

Anthony Aldgate

> England swings like a pendulum do
> Bobbies on bicycles, two by two,
> Westminster Abbey, the Tower and Big Ben,
> The rosy red cheeks of the little children.

Despite the banal lyrics, crass rhymes and trite tourist imagery of its chorus, Roger Miller's 45 rpm record, 'England Swings', made the Top 10 in the American pop charts in November 1965 and the British Top 20 by late January 1966. It was further, albeit modest, recognition of the country's new-found cultural role as the harbinger of everything that was exciting and dynamic in the 'Swinging Sixties'.

Following the considerable success on both sides of the Atlantic during the previous two years of beat groups like The Beatles and The Rolling Stones, and of films like *Dr No*, *Tom Jones* and *A Hard Day's Night*, British popular culture was riding the crest of a wave. Little wonder, perhaps, that show business personalities sought to jump on the triumphalist bandwagon with yet more novelty discs such as Dora Bryan's 'We Love You Beatles' (soon adopted with variations as a football crowd chant) or Bruce Forsyth's 'I'm Backing Britain'(soon consigned to oblivion).

Lewis Gilbert's film of Bill Naughton's *Alfie*, given its premiere on 24 March 1966, also proved an enormous transatlantic hit. Its origins lay in Naughton's radio play, *Alfie Elkins and His Little Life*, which was first presented on the BBC Third Programme on 7 January 1962. BBC Audience Research reported that some people found the play offensive. 'Not so much kitchen sink as kitchen garbage tin', was one comment. 'Time was', another listener maintained, 'when the BBC would not have considered broadcasting anything so revolting.'

But a majority of listeners claimed to have formed a high opinion of the programme. They had been 'completely absorbed, even fascinated'; it was a memorable piece, some said, which still haunted them. Bill Owen's performance as Alfie, in particular, was warmly praised.

The play scored an appreciation index rating of 73, well above the then current average (63) for Third Programme features. The BBC consequently repeated it twice more in 1962. And when a forum of radio critics – including Stephen Potter, Dilys Powell and Edward Lucie-Smith – gave it their stamp of approval, Naughton, much pleased, was prompted to adapt it for stage production. Considerably expanded, and re-titled *Alfie*, the play was quickly snapped up by Bernard Miles for performance at his Mermaid Theatre in June 1963, as part of a short Naughton season that included *All in Good Time* (also later transposed to film as the Boulting Brothers' *The Family Way* in 1966, starring Hayley Mills and Hywel Bennett). *Alfie* transferred to the Duchess Theatre on 22 July with John Neville in the lead role (and Glenda Jackson and Gemma Jones in supporting parts) where it ran for over a year.

Terence Stamp took over the part of Alfie for the American production at Broadway's Morosco Theatre on 17 December 1964, but the show closed after just twenty-one performances. Stamp attributed the failure to 'A devout Catholic critic who was reputedly offended by the abortion scene but, too smart to mention the fact, found other ways of making the play seem unwatchable.' The fashion model, Jean Shrimpton, was probably as close to the truth when she pointed out that 'the audience did not understand the Cockney rhyming slang; in fact they did not understand the play at all'. 'Terry was dynamic enough', she added, 'but this near-monologue from him in an East End accent was baffling to the audience.'

In the light of the play's short-lived New York run, however, Stamp declined Lewis Gilbert's offer to make a screen version, much to Michael Caine's relief. The 1966 film finally settled Caine's star status, after earlier acclaim for his roles in *Zulu* (1963) and *The Ipcress File* (1965) – 'Michael Caine is Alfie', the publicity billing declared.

Naughton then proceeded to turn his work into a novel published to coincide with the film's release. An instant best-seller, the book was reprinted four times in paperback during May 1966 alone. Cilla Black entered the British Top 10 on 9 April, with Burt Bacharach and Hal David's spin-off song of the same name, while Cher covered it for the American market, making the US charts on 20 August. The dubbing of her version onto the film's soundtrack

Michael Caine and friends in a publicity photograph for *Alfie* (1966). The film's depiction of a cheerfully cynical womaniser was recognition that the austere 1950s had now given way to the growing permissiveness of the 'Swinging Sixties'. (Paramount/Courtesy Kobal)

over the final credits to tailor it for exhibition in the States also helped secure *Alfie* an Oscar nomination for 'Best Song' at the 1967 Academy Awards.

Except for its solitary Broadway failure, *Alfie* progressed with ever-increasing success from radio to stage play, from film to tie-in novel, with both UK and US spin-off pop records thrown in for good measure. As a marketing opportunity, it was only bettered at the time by exploitation of The Beatles' products. As well as reaping huge rewards in international box-office returns, moreover, the screen version was critically acclaimed with even the scholarly Berkeley journal, *Film Quarterly*, maintaining that 'its wit and its stubborn humanity make it seem a giant of a film today'.

Few would agree with that judgement now. In fact, the film's reputation was soon revised. 'Had *Alfie* come out in the 1970s when Women's Lib was digging its spurs into male flanks', the British critic Alexander Walker argued in 1974, 'it

would have been dubbed a crude propaganda tract for chauvinist male pigs' –
doubtless, and with good reason. Alfie is interested in scoring with the 'birds' and
little else besides. His story is one long litany of sexual conquests in which he
pays scant regard for the emotional hurt he causes his many partners (a veritable
Who's Who of sixties British acting talent including Jane Asher, Shirley Anne
Field, Julia Foster, Millicent Martin and Vivien Merchant). Gone, even, is any
trace of John Osborne's Jimmy Porter from *Look Back in Anger* whose vitriolic
yearning and heartfelt lament over the loss of 'good brave causes' to fight in
1950s Britain thereby explains, without ever excusing, his misogynous character.

What Naughton's Alfie shares initially with Alan Sillitoe's Arthur Seaton in
Saturday Night and Sunday Morning (1960) by way of selfish hedonistic instinct,
furthermore, differs markedly in its evolution and resolution. Where Arthur
regrets being the cause of a girlfriend's attempt at abortion and appears
resigned finally to his domestic lot, Alfie is but momentarily diverted by a
lover's desperate need for an abortion and returns to his customary routine of
'chatting up the birds'. Though prompted to consider settling down with the
American Ruby (Shelley Winters) – 'a good sort' and 'great big lust-box' –
when he is jilted for once, by her, he renounces all notions of domesticity in
favour of a renewed affair with a married woman. Alfie, as presented on the
screen with his knowing looks, arch asides and cocky comments to camera, is
the amoral and promiscuous sixties cockney 'wide boy'. The film says much
about the changing image of masculinity in British cinema between the
moment of the 'Angry Young Men' and the advent of 'swinging London'.

Alfie is often cited as an example of progressive liberalisation on the part of
the film censors – following in the wake of the 1960 trial for *Lady Chatterley's
Lover* (which proved 'the great liberation for printed literature'), and in keeping
with the 1960s movement towards wider 'de-censorship' in the arts (which
culminated in the 1968 Theatres Act and removal of the Lord Chamberlain's
powers of censorship). The case, however, is hardly watertight. By the time the
script for *Alfie* landed on the film censor's desk in 1965, it had already been
shorn of several controversial aspects, not least in regard to its abortion scene.

When first presented as a play to the Lord Chamberlain's office in 1963, for
instance, it was the subject of long negotiations to ensure that potentially
offensive and objectionable items would be removed or rewritten. In particular,
the abortion scene was carefully considered, and face-to-face discussion ensued
between the Lord Chamberlain's men, the playwright and the producer,
resulting in extensive revision before all parties declared themselves relatively
happy with proceedings. Even then the stage censors found it necessary to send

along both 'incognito' and 'open' inspectors to early public performances of the play, to ensure the Lord Chamberlain's strictures had been followed. One or two points of concern were observed and further amendments required, though nothing like as many as the Public Morality Council (PMC) would have wished.

The PMC sent its own 'reporter' along to view *Alfie*, certain the producer had slipped things in after submission for a licence. The organisation's stage plays sub-committee complained to the Lord Chamberlain's office that it considered the play 'deplorable'. The change in moral standards and the new permissive climate were as unpopular with the Public Morality Council as they were with Mrs Mary Whitehouse. In 1964 she embarked upon her 'Clean-up TV' campaign and, as Arthur Marwick notes, 'a running battle between the advocates of permissiveness and tolerance and those of purity and censorship was joined'. 'That battle in itself', he continues, 'served to publicise the fact that change was indeed taking place.'

One such change was the 1967 Abortion Act. Marwick cites *Alfie* as precisely the sort of film that highlighted the 'attendant horror and danger' of backstreet abortions, thereby contributing to the tide of public opinion in favour of 'liberal legislation in the sphere of sexual mores' evident in 1967, especially, with the passage also of the National Health Service (Family Planning Act) and the Sexual Offences Act. Perhaps so. But, noticeably, when a film script of *Alfie* was tendered for pre-production scrutiny to the British Board of Film Censors in 1965, the film-makers stayed pretty much within the bounds of what the censors had already allowed and chose not to overstep the mark in their depiction of contentious issues such as abortion.

Naughton and Gilbert opened up the scenes of the play to accommodate its interpretation on film, with new characters and outside locations added to flesh out the story and lend variety. The abortion scene was rendered more obvious, moved into the foreground with the protagonists and the abortionist plainly on show (the latter deftly played by Denholm Elliott). But it was not graphically done – the act itself taking place behind a curtain in the manner originally intended for the stage play. Its overall and cumulative effect still depended largely upon dialogue and characterisation (enhanced by some excellent acting from Vivien Merchant and Michael Caine, as well as Elliott).

Crucially, Alfie's key speech of contrition about the aborted foetus of his child remained precisely as Naughton had fashioned it to meet the Lord Chamberlain's requirements. The film-makers stayed essentially within the confines of what had already been permitted. The finished film would still have to be given an X-rated certificate, of course, because of 'the grossness of some of the sex talk' and because it highlighted a successful abortion. (Here, however, it scored something of a victory considering that only a few years earlier, in 1959, Woodfall Films and Alan Sillitoe had been told quite categorically that they would not be allowed the cinematic depiction of a successful termination of pregnancy in the film version of *Saturday Night and Sunday Morning*.) But despite the continued reservations of the British Board of Film Censors (BBFC), the screenplay for *Alfie* was deemed 'the most moral "X" I have met for some time', by its script-reader. 'We really do not feel that the sex is dragged in to titillate the idle mind', was the considered opinion among film censors, and it was 'a basically moral theme'. Thus, there was 'a case for being as lenient as possible', the BBFC's secretary wrote to the film-makers on 4 May 1965: '. . . it should not give us too much trouble'.

Certain incidents proposed by the script were not exactly welcome, however, such as Alfie taking a pair of women's panties from his pocket and tossing them back with the line '. . . 'ere, mind you don't catch cold'. This was considered 'more suggestive' than the censors would have liked. There was to be no business with a banana if it was meant to have any 'visual significance' – 'substitute an apple or something of this kind', was the instruction. 'Discretion' should be used when Alfie 'adjusts his trousers and generally makes himself less uncomfortable'. The same would apply when Siddie is seen 'hitching up her skirt and tidying herself up'. There should be no nudity in one scene. 'This kind of thing' had become 'a cliché', and 'at most, only a back view would be accepted'.

'Ruby's costume should be adequate and not transparent', was a further stricture, and the censors were 'not happy' about the phrase 'lust-box', which really ought to be dropped for preference. But if the film-makers persisted in using it in production, then 'you should have an alternative available'. It made sense, after all, to have another voice-over take readily to hand. When it came to the phrase 'having if off', the censors reckoned it would 'probably be acceptable', yet 'here again, you might have an alternative for post-synching if it should not be' when it came to viewing the completed film for final certification.

The abortion scene, though 'strong . . . will probably be accepted in the context, since [it does] make a valid point against abortion'. But 'we would not want any really harrowing moans and screams' and 'obviously we shall not see what Alfie sees in the bathroom' following the termination. The BBFC secretary even tendered some helpful advice that had nothing whatever to do with censorship concerns – 'I am doubtful whether you can get a train from Waterloo Station to Forest Hill Station. I would have thought that Victoria was more likely.'

So it went on. A bit of give and take as usual along carefully laid down and well formulated, if ever-evolving, lines. It is no wonder that the BBFC secretary, John Trevelyan, once described film censorship in terms of 'a curious arrangement' and, as he aptly added, 'rather typically British in some ways'. When it finally reached the screen on 24 March 1966, *Alfie* had been through a lengthy and arduous, if sometimes fruitful, process of censorship at the hands of both the theatre and film examiners, all of whom contributed substantially – along with the film-makers themselves – to its emergence as a 'basically moral' film. Some things were permitted anew in the British cinema of the 'Swinging Sixties', to be sure, but permissiveness was still bound and circumscribed in its depiction.

Alfie has since been issued several times on video and is now widely available, though not in the version released in Britain during 1966. The video copy, like the one often shown on British television, is the American version with Cher singing the title song over the end credits. Bacharach and David's composition did not appear on the original British release which had a musical score from the tenor sax player, Sonny Rollins, and that alone. In addition, Michael Caine did some post-synching of the dialogue soundtrack for the American edition – comprising 125 new sound loops – so as to render his character's 'very thick cockney accent' into 'clearer English' for American consumption. Clearly, lessons had been learned from the play's decided lack of success on Broadway. To see *Alfie* today, however, is to see an altogether different film to the one released in Britain in 1966.

Part Four
FILMS OF ROMANCE AND FANTASY

16

MADONNA OF THE SEVEN MOONS

Sue Harper

When *Madonna of the Seven Moons* was released in December 1944, it was an immediate smash hit; cinema audiences in London and, later, in the provinces flocked to see it. The trade magazine *Kinematograph Weekly* soon listed it as a box-office success. But the 'quality' critics – those writing for highbrow readers – panned the movie and tried to persuade their readers not to attend. In *The Sunday Times*, Dilys Powell derided the film's preoccupation with sex: 'it is a highly osculatory piece, comprising the kiss filched, the kiss rejected, the kiss paternal, the kiss devout, the kiss marital, the kiss passionate'. From the far right of the cultural politics spectrum, husband-and-wife team E.W. and M.M. Robson objected to the film's 'marital double-crossings, venal murder, and split-minded lunacies'.

Such widespread ill-temper was a sure sign that something important was afoot. In the 1940s, critical opinion could set a seal of status on a film (for example, Olivier's 1944 *Henry V*) and encourage audiences to attend. Violently negative reviews, on the other hand, could lead to box-office demise (as in the case of Leslie Arliss's and R.J. Minney's 1948 flop, *The Idol of Paris*). However, in general, a clutch of bad reviews did not ensure a film's failure. 'Quality' critics had their own agenda, and rarely praised films which aimed at a mass, female or low-status market. But such films had an important social function: they provided images of pleasure and liberation, and they assisted their audiences to resolve, albeit on a symbolic level, real problems in their own lives. Works like *Madonna* and its successor, the phenomenally successful *The Wicked Lady* (1945), provided a sense of optimism for their audiences. Their visual style required creativity and ingenuity in the act of viewing.

Even today, the representation of women in film is a thorny issue. Some feminist critics have argued in favour of a 'politically correct' position, in which

Phyllis Calvert as Maddalena. She begins going back to the personality of her alter ego, the gypsy Rosanna, heroine of *Madonna of the Seven Moons*. (Gainsborough/Courtesy Kobal)

films are judged according to the degree of autonomy accorded to their female protagonists. Others have deployed a reflectionist approach, in which fidelity to real events is the standard by which films are assessed. Neither of these responses is particularly helpful. To berate texts from the past for their political incorrectness is pointless and shows a lack of historical understanding. Films are artistically and financially successful not because they are realistic, but because they provide a coherent symbolism for their audiences. Like all works of art, films give us access not to a historical period, but to some of its imaginative habits.

So it is not the job of films to tell us, for instance, how women really lived or felt. Even the most cursory glance at (say) the film output of the 1940s shows how varied screen culture could be; women appear in many different guises and with a wide range of narrative functions. Initially, we can categorise images of women in a linear fashion; we establish whether a film is innovative by contrasting it with those which preceded it. Truly ground-breaking representations do have their progenitors, but they are often unexpected.

Madonna of the Seven Moons was one such 'ground-breaker'. It was made at Gainsborough Studios, produced by R.J. Minney and directed by Arthur Crabtree; the art direction was by Andrew Mazzei and the costumes were designed by Elizabeth Haffenden. The script was adapted by Roland Pertwee and Brock Williams from the best-selling novel by Margery Lawrence. Its stars were Phyllis Calvert, Stewart Granger and Patricia Roc. The Italian setting is used (as it has habitually been deployed in English novels) to provide vibrant local colour and a sensual alternative to northern European puritanism. The heroine of the film is Maddalena (Phyllis Calvert), a rich and frigid bourgeoise who suffers from a split personality; in her other life, she is Rosanna, the wild gypsy/peasant mistress of a Florentine low-life gangster. At the beginning of the film, the adolescent Maddalena is raped by a vagabond. After she is married to aristocratic wine merchant Giuseppe Labardi, her neuroses manifest themselves and she has difficulty in coming to terms, some years later, with her daughter Angela (Patricia Roc), who represents a more liberated femininity. At a key moment, while she is playing the piano, Maddalena's split personality is glimpsed for the first time. Initially, her whole body held rigidly tense, she plays a tinkling, classic piece. Then the tune changes to a sweeping romantic one, and her impassioned self emerges, full of confidence, expressivity and desire. The whole narrative takes off from that moment.

When her daughter becomes engaged, Maddalena is urgently forced to confront her own neglected sexuality. At various crises in her life, she has run away to her repressed self; but now, in a swoon, she is transformed from 'good' to 'bad' woman, a moment signalled (*à la* Cinderella) by the chiming of a clock. The new woman emerging from the pupa of the old moves sinuously; she shakes loose her hair, converts the private garment of a nightdress into the public one of a blouse and dons gypsyish clothes. Her final act before leaving the marital home is to scrawl on to the mirror the sign of seven moons. This is the name of the local district from whence her alter ego hails; it is also the pattern on a pair of earrings given to her by Angela. These both fascinate and repel Maddalena, since, as she remarks, they are 'like the peasant woman used to wear'. The moon symbol usually signifies a mysterious femininity: here multiplied by the magic number of seven, that femininity is represented as excessive, dangerous and unratified.

The new Rosanna finds her old lover, a gangster called Nino Barucci (Stewart Granger), and engages in some uninhibited love-making in scenes unusually explicit for the period. Rosanna's amorous propensities are matched by her appetite for food, wine, cigarettes and money; she aids and abets Nino and his brother Sandro in their robberies. Meanwhile, as Angela seeks her lost mother, Sandro arranges a subterfuge whereby, during the carnival, he can drug and rape her. In the twilight zone between her two selves, Rosanna recognises her daughter and blocks Sandro by killing him. But in saving Angela, Rosanna is fatally injured and thus sacrifices herself. She dies at home with two parting gifts resting on her bosom: her husband's crucifix, and a rose tossed there by Nino.

Madonna of the Seven Moons avoids realism in every way. The rites and symbols of Catholicism figure prominently at almost every turning-point in its narrative. Music consistently heightens the emotional temperature. The decor is sumptuous and floridly detailed. The Labardi courtyard and the ruined Florentine garden are designed to stimulate the eye in a manner that suggests that the world of visual pleasure does not require naturalistic perspective. The film is curiously imprecise in its handling of historical period. A brief shot of Maddalena's prayer book informs us that her daughter was born in 1918; as we see Angela later, leaving finishing school, we must assume that the main action takes place in about 1937. However, none of the clothes worn by characters in the film are anchored in the 1930s; the gypsy/peasant styles are resolutely timeless, and the modern dresses (in the fashion show, for example) are similar to those of the 1940s New Look. Moreover, there is a studied avoidance of any contemporary social or political reference. The costumes evoke a world of desire which transcends common sense. This alternative world is open to men as well as women. In a key scene during the carnival, all the males don Pierrot disguises. Thus, to the drugged eyes of Angela, all men become masked, and split between white and black; but to the eyes of the audience this confused double state and fuzzy sense of self is presented to the as a necessary part of a generalised human condition.

The film, then, deals in a rich and complex way with the themes of sexual desire, religious taboos, female power and the symbolic excision of elements 'dangerous' to society. In its range and type of representation, only one other British film had preceded *Madonna*. This was *The Man in Grey*, released in July 1943 by the same studio. All other British films which profile self-willed and passionate females (*The Seventh Veil*, 1945, *Black·Narcissus*, 1946) post-date it.

So who was really responsible for *Madonna*? Films are different from books in that their authorship is plural. It is often fashionable to present the director of a film as its 'onlie begetter', yet it is only in certain cases that he or she should be seen as the sole progenitor. Rather, a film should be interpreted as a work of art which is also an industrial product. The film text is a place where the labours of different personnel are on display. The decor, costume, camerawork, lighting, editing, music, script and body language of the actors can all be analysed as separate discourses. But the way in which these languages are orchestrated depends entirely upon the way the studio is managed. The person responsible for that is the producer.

Although Gainsborough was owned by J. Arthur Rank, he interfered little in the day-to-day work of the studio until 1946. Maurice Ostrer was Head of Production, and he appointed veteran cost-cutter Harold Huth and writer R.J. Minney as joint producers. They insisted on careful costing and budgeting, so that every penny spent on the sets, costumes and stars, appeared on screen. The different sections of the workforce were kept apart. But once film-workers had accepted the financial controls, there was considerable artistic freedom. Art director Maurice Carter recalled that 'provided you could perform money-wise, and get the sets there on time, the executive producers were reasonably happy. They didn't have much to say on the artistic side.'

During the period in which *Madonna* was made, Gainsborough was one of the few British studios to offer congenial employment to those designers and film artisans who were interested in expressionist work. Significantly, all the films produced there in this period were flamboyant in style, and on closer examination it is clear that the various languages (decor, costume, etc., as described above) functioned with a relative autonomy: each had different things to say, and their messages sometimes conflicted. However, this lack of overall consonance was no bar to the success of these films at the box office.

Madonna of the Seven Moons is the film in which R.J. Minney's influence is most evident. An intellectual of liberal politics and tolerant sexual attitudes, Minney had written and co-scripted the 1934 Hollywood success, *Clive of India*. He was the author of a range of novels and biographies, had an unerring sense of popular taste, and believed that 'the commodity must be what the public wants, and what the public at present is educated enough to like'. Melodrama, not realism, was the mode best suited to pleasing mass audiences. For film adaptation, Minney preferred texts 'with blood and thunder'. Producers should aim for 'a full-blooded story, such as may be found in the pages of the Bible'. Minney's preference was for a sort of primitive *urtext*, which could echo and evoke the audience's repressed fears and desires.

Minney set about the production of *Madonna* with enthusiasm, costing and casting it and intervening in the scripting process. He was also responsible for the publicity material, and suggested to cinema managers that the film be exclusively targeted at women, by emphasising its fashion and hairstyles. More crucially, the studio wanted schizophrenia to be redefined as a female ailment, with local papers paid to carry the headline 'Split-Mind Disorder Gives Idea for Year's Finest Romance!' Minney used his contacts to prompt a psychiatrist to write an article in the influential *Picturegoer*. The piece argued that cases like Rosanna/Maddalena were evidence that sometimes in women 'the normal personality is blanked out and the dark forces of the libido are released'. Of course, women's situation had changed radically in Britain during the Second World War because of conscription, evacuation and some liberalisation of sexual behaviour. Minney was nuancing the marketing of *Madonna* to take account of the latter, albeit indirectly.

It is tempting to suggest that the box-office success of *Madonna* was merely proof that some entrepreneurs were canny enough to dupe unsuspecting audiences. But such an explanation is mistaken, because it proposes that popular films represent a kind of 'false consciousness' from which the fantasy-ridden audience should be awakened. It is more sensible to acknowledge that some films contain elements which evoke residual, forgotten or repressed aspects of culture. The individual consciousness contains such aspects too. When there is a match between an audience's secret mind and a film's inner landscape, popular success is almost guaranteed to result.

So what does it mean that Nino's gypsy mother insists on equal sexual licence, commenting 'Fair's fair, my son. You had other women'? What does it mean when the impassioned Rosanna declares to Nino, 'I only live when we're together'? What does it mean when she implores 'Don't let me kneel!' as the Catholic procession passes by? How did it feel to the film's first audiences to watch erotic scenes that only take place in exotic settings? How did it feel to see the carnival surging past?

To answer these questions, the cultural historian needs to consider the roles of marginal groups in popular cultural forms in Britain. Such groups have always played a volatile role in popular literature, social fractions on the periphery of social power or 'common sense'. They provide a way of exploring the limits of social pollution; that is, of negotiating the boundary between the pure and the impure, the safe and the dangerous. In a range of popular texts of different types, the powerful groups are gypsies, harlots, Catholics and taboo-breaking aristocrats. These groups exhibit enormous energy because they are

The deathbed scene from the film – with the harlequinned Nino looking on, symbolically offstage. (Gainsborough/Courtesy Kobal)

poised ambiguously on the margin between the sacred and the profane. Many popular films of the 1940s display a continuity from the novels of Bulwer-Lytton, Rider Haggard, George Borrow and Maria Corelli. In *Madonna*, 'gypsyness' is a space where the pleasures of the forbidden can be rehearsed, and a balance struck between special occult knowledge and dangerous excess. Catholicism, too, simultaneously evokes forbidden rituals and is a siren of the senses. Rational creatures can only withstand its charms if they are deaf, or strapped to the mast.

How did audiences respond to *Madonna?* Minney and the studio clearly wanted the film to emphasise the dangerous aspects of schizophrenia, and the positive qualities of the new femininity as represented by Angela, the daughter. But there is evidence to suggest that female audiences took pleasure in other elements of the film. Women who replied to the enquiries of sociologist J.P. Mayer of the London School of Economics (author of *Sociology of Film*, 1946, and *British Cinemas and their Audiences*, 1948) revealed that they experienced strong sexual arousal from the love scenes with Granger. They also derived enormous visual pleasure from the costumes and sets, caring little whether they were realistic or not. When asked by Mayer whether their dreams had ever been triggered by films, two respondents cited *Madonna*. One woman had a vivid dream of the sign of the seven moons being written on the mirror again and again: 'it got bigger each time'. Another kept hearing a line repeated from the film, but this time it was applied to herself: 'it isn't possible, no one could be so lovely'. In their dreams, the women selected from the film those elements which celebrated female sexuality and self-confidence.

Another interesting response was made to a Mass-Observation questionnaire in the 1950s. This asked respondents which films had moved them deeply, and one woman remembered *Madonna* thus:

> I was very affected. It is the one film I can remember clearly, that made me cry more than any other. At the very end, when the heroine realised her dual-personality as she was dying – I was suffering too. And when she died and the husband of one side of her life and her lover of another, stood together, and placed, respectively, a crucifix and a wild rose on her breast, I'm ashamed to say I wept unashamedly.

What is significant here is that the writer has dramatised the original scene; she has also rendered it more permissive. In the film, the lover and the husband are crucially separated. The be-suited husband is indoors, ratified and speaking aloud; the lover, in carnival costume, is excluded from the home and has to stand outside the window. He speaks *sotto voce* and throws, rather than places, the symbolic rose on Maddalena's bosom. In her memory, this respondent has restructured the film so as to draw its moral boundaries less strictly. In effect, she has argued that the 'good' and the 'bad' woman can ultimately be reconciled. A film like David Lean's classic of frustrated emotion, *Brief Encounter* (1945), of course, could not carry such an interpretation, since the sexual and respectable elements in the heroine's personality are differently arranged; the narrative structure privileges the respectable side. In *Madonna* they are equally weighted.

There was a rash of 1940s films with strong and self-willed heroines, from Gainsborough and other studios (*The Wicked Lady*, 1945, *Caravan*, 1946, *Blanche Fury* and *So Evil My Love*, 1948) which were all well received by female viewers. One woman wrote to *Picturegoer* that 'these naughty wenches have their female fans. Men want to meet them and women to be like them. Women of doubtful character hold a fascination for the average person because their lives are never dull.' The editor of the magazine noted glumly that, after she took on vicious roles, Margaret Lockwood's fan letters went up by thousands. But it is interesting to note how short-lived the phenomenon was. After 1949, there were few films containing wild and self-willed women.

This was for two reasons. Firstly, key personnel in the melodrama genre had declined artistically, died or left the country. Secondly, and more importantly, times – and the audience – had changed. The postwar 'baby boom' and shifts in employment patterns meant that there were far fewer women going to the cinema, and the sexual politics of such films as *The Wicked Lady* were no longer appropriate. Memories of wartime sexual adventures were fading, helped on their way by a general sense that the 'good-time girls' ought to be roped back into the social corral.

But for a short period, *Madonna of the Seven Moons*, and films like it, had contributed to the female audience's sense of sexual potential. The roots of these films were hidden deep in popular subcultures, from which they had emerged and to which they eventually returned.

17

LA BELLE ET LA BÊTE

Susan Hayward

Jean Cocteau's *La Belle et la Bête* (1946) was only his second film, completed sixteen years after his first foray into the medium with *Le Sang d'un poète* (1930), an anti-realist, semi-surrealist film. Although public memory might more readily associate him with film-making due to the lasting success of *La Belle et la Bête* and *Orphée* (1949-50), Cocteau never wished to define himself as a *cineaste* because he did not want to feel under obligation to make films. He did, however, see film as a way of reaching a greater audience with his 'message-as-poet' of the importance of the unconscious. Indeed, Cocteau always saw himself as a poet. In his lifetime, he made only six films over a period of thirty years: all were intensely personal and, to a degree, self-referential.

Nonetheless, in the early 1950s, thanks to his film-making practices in *La Belle et la Bête* and *Orphée*, Cocteau was given *auteur* status by the influential critics writing for the *Cahiers du cinéma* – the journal primarily responsible for initiating the *auteur* debate (*auteur* status was granted to those film-makers who scripted, directed and edited their films or whose works had specific personal hallmarks that re-occurred from film to film). These critics decried contemporary French cinema, labelling it the *cinéma de papa* and *cinéma de qualité* – both negative epithets used to denounce what they considered unimaginative, script-led work, produced according to reliable formulas and stultifying film practices. But in Cocteau (who wrote the scenario, scripted, directed and edited his films) – as in only a few other French film-makers, like Jean Renoir and Robert Bresson – they recognised the hand of the *auteur* and praised him for being a 'film-maker's film-maker'.

Undoubtedly, his eclecticism as a poet working in so many media (including theatre, poetry, the novel, drawing, music, sculpture and decor), enabled

Cocteau to bring something new to the cinema screen. His influence on a new generation of film-makers known as *la nouvelle vague* (the French New Wave of 1958–64), some of whom were former critics of the *Cahiers du cinéma*, is duly acknowledged by them. Jean-Luc Godard cites Cocteau's *La Belle et la Bête* as a source of inspiration for his thriller *Alphaville* (1965) – in its use of lighting and camera angles in particular. Alain Resnais used *Orphée* to explain the effects he wanted the Japanese cameraman to produce in *Hiroshima mon amour* (1959). François Truffaut so regarded Cocteau's work that he helped produce his last film *Le Testament d' Orphée* (1959), while in that year, the hundredth volume of *Cahiers du Cinéma* was dedicated to Cocteau (entitled *Le Cent d'un Pòete*).

La Belle et la Bête was two years in the making, with the discussions and preparations dating back still earlier, to 1943. The idea to make a film of this famous fairy tale was first suggested to Cocteau by his partner, the actor Jean Marais, who, until then had only played one other major film role: that of a modern-day Tristan in Delannoy's *L'Eternel retour* (1942). Marais's portrayal of the Beast would effectively launch his film career, leading to a string of starring roles.

Conditions for film production were extremely difficult in post-Liberation France, not simply in terms of obtaining funding, but also in terms of obtaining film stock – and usable stock at that – and in gaining access to studios. Cocteau would be successful on all counts, but he had to make many complicated negotiations along the way.

In order to obtain funds, Cocteau first took his project to Gaumont in Paris who rejected it. Contemporary taste for films tended towards realism – a knock-on effect of the impact of Italian neo-realism. Although a small number of costume dramas were being produced (including *Boule de suif* in 1945 and, more famously, *Les Enfants du Paradis* in 1944), realism was the order of the day. More particularly, if film was to have any function at all during the uncertain days that followed Liberation, it was to help redeem the nation's shattered sense of identity. Of the seventy-six films made between August 1944 and December 1945, eleven were about the war or the Occupation, and, of those, eight were about the Resistance.

In this climate, Cocteau's scenario seemed an irrelevance. His films, like other aspects of his life, were totally disengaged from the socio-political climate of the time. His activities during the Occupation make this abundantly clear. His theatre work was produced despite the fact that it was vilified as 'abject, perverted and judaic' in the pro-Nazi paper *Je suis partout*. The journalists Francois Vinneuil and Alain Laubreaux were among the most vituperative (incidentally, the latter gets short shrift in Truffaut's 1980 film, *Le Dernier métro*). And Cocteau consorted both with Resistants, in the person of Paul Eluard, and Occupiers, in particular the German author and francophile Ernst Jünger – a German officer at the time. He also wrote a pamphlet favourably acclaiming the Parisian exhibition of the work of Arno Breker, the Third Reich's official sculptor.

Undeterred by Gaumont's rejection, Cocteau approached an independent producer, André Paulvé, who had previously financed Delannoy's *L'Eternel retour* (itself scripted and commissioned by Cocteau). Paulvé, at first sold on the project by the extraordinary mask Marais would wear, initially agreed to finance the film. But he subsequently got cold feet and withdrew his assistance, deciding that no one would want to watch an actor disguised as a beast (how

Dreams and desire: Jean Marais as the Beast looks longingly at the sleeping Beauty (Josette Day). (BFI Stills, Posters and Designs)

wrong he proved to be). However, persuaded by Marais, he agreed at least to watch some pre-production rushes. Marais suggested to Cocteau that he select the most moving scene of the script and film it; Cocteau chose to shoot Beauty's arrival at the Beast's castle, and the now-famous scene where she appears to glide along a corridor lined with billowing, white evanescent curtains. The trick here was to pull Beauty (played by Josette Day) along on a trolley, thus giving the impression that she was floating into her subconscious. The illusion was also greatly assisted by Josette Day, a former dancer, who convincingly used her arms and body to convey the idea that she was floating.

According to Marais, Paulvé brought his wife to the screening, and she was moved to tears by what she saw. Paulvé, too, was so moved as to agree once again to finance the film. Despite the apparent irrelevance of its subject matter, Cocteau believed that *La Belle et la Bête* was making an important statement in terms of its political-cultural resonance. But if his choice of subject was not influenced by the times, the same cannot be said of his production practices. In his film-making methods, which were based on the fast-disappearing French tradition of artisanal teamwork, Cocteau took up a stance against the homogenising effect of Hollywood on French films. This effect would eventually have a severe impact on French cinema. By the mid-1950s, in response to American competition, the French film industry found itself obliged to adopt a standardisation of technology and production techniques that enabled it to make films that were as pleasing to its audiences as those of Hollywood.

In a sense, then, Cocteau was very forward-looking, even though evidence of Americanisation was already in place by 1946. By this time, France was inundated with Hollywood productions which, during the Occupation, had been proscribed. Economically, the French film industry was in such a parlous state that it was in no real position to resist this plethora of imports, which represented 70 per cent of films screened in France over a three-year period – at least not until negotiations in 1948 reinstated an import quota of 120 American films per year. Cocteau's stance, therefore, at least in his own mind, was anti-Hollywood and, in this respect, protective of France's cultural heritage, a position acknowledged, albeit post-facto, by the *Cahiers* group.

In terms of genre, too, a certain form of nationalism was at play. Cocteau's film, based on a fairy tale by a French *woman*, using human beings and a human disguised as a beast, and shot in black and white (always his preferred medium), countered any number of Disney's coloured animations. Again, a sense of nationalism can be attached to the film, albeit perversely, in that it was chosen alongside five others to represent France at the International Cannes Film Festival in 1946. This was the very first postwar Cannes festival – held in abeyance since 1939 when the idea was first mooted to counter the nationalistic, cultural tub-thumping of the Italians and the Germans at the earlier-instituted Berlin and Venice film festivals. However, if producing the film had been a 'nightmare' – as Cocteau put it in his diary – the critical reception of *La Belle et la Bête* at Cannes would prove even more distressing. The film was panned by the critics, and was a resounding failure with the jury who awarded Best Film Prize to René Clément's *La Bataille du rail*, a film about the heroic resistance of the railway workers during the Occupation.

This was ironic. Clément had worked as Cocteau's technical adviser on *La Belle et la Bête*. Of the three other films nominated, one was clearly a Resistance film in disguise: Louis Danquin's *Patrie*, set in the sixteenth century, was about patriotic Belgians resisting the Spanish invaders; another, Delannoy's film of André Gide's *La Symphonie pastorale*, celebrated the oeuvre of one of France's 'great' authors, for which Michèle Morgan won the prize for Best Female Role. The final film in the French selection was Christian-Jaque's *Un Revenant*, a strongly realist and anti-bourgeois film about provincial mentalities of greed and bitterness. *La Belle et la Bête* was literally squeezed out because it was so against the current, both visually and in terms of content. The film was criticised for its stylised, expressionistic and, therefore, *arrièriste* look. It was considered static, artificial, obsessed with objects and unmoving.

In the end, the film took only one prize. This went to Georges Auric for Best Musical Score. Auric was a member of a disparate group of musicians labelled *Les Six* in the early 1920s by Cocteau who had no time for Wagnerianism or impressionism (as in Debussy's music). This award would have particularly rubbed salt into Cocteau's already wounded pride at Cannes, because at the film's final editing stage, he had cut up the post-produced version (i.e., the film with its music track already synchronised) and inverted fragments, thus destabilising and disjointing Auric's score and creating what Cocteau termed a *synchronise de hasard* (an accidental synchronicity). As a result, the score was almost as much Cocteau's as Auric's. This was consonant with Cocteau's whole approach to this very personal film. Although *La Belle et la Bête* was certainly the result of the work of many different artists, crafts-people and technicians, and despite the fact that it is densely inter-textual, Cocteau left it in no doubt that, ultimately, he was its *auteur*.

At the time of its general release in late October 1946, critics continued, on the whole, to voice their dislike of the film. They accused it of being cold,

Cocteau on set directing his two 'stars', Marais and Day. (BFI Stills, Posters and Designs)

painterly and – worst of all – Picturesque. The Picturesque was a genre loathed by Cocteau and he hated to see the term applied to his own work. Numerous critics also accused the film of being expressionistic and even of verging on academicism. However, what perturbed them so deeply about this film is revealed in their accusations that it possessed Germanic aesthetics (most of which Cocteau rejected, bar the German cult of the body – as in Breker's sculptures) and that certain images displayed the 'affected simperings of an old queen'.

La Belle et la Bête is, indeed, a film made by a man who never denied his homosexuality and who had an openness that braved the morality of the times. Cocteau was also highly assertive in his sexuality and imposed his lovers onto the literary and artistic scene: he first 'imposed' Marais (his lover of ten years) on the screen in 1942, with *L'Eternel retour*. Undoubtedly, *La Belle et la Bête* is a film about homoerotic love. But it is also about attempting to discover a different, non-phallic perception of human relationships. Why, otherwise, is Belle so terribly disappointed at the end of the film when the Beast – *la Bête*, whom she now realises she loves – transforms into Prince Charming? Why is the audience equally disappointed? As Cocteau takes care to make plain, Belle does not wish to go and live happily ever after and have lots of children. She wants more from life than a marriage of reason – the underlying message from Mme Leprince de Beaumont's eighteenth-century fairy tale – Belle wants to be 'frightened' ('*J'aime avoir peur*', she declares).

The psychology of the unconscious, sexual awakening and the female expression of desire were images that had not been seen on screen since the avant-garde cinéma of the 1920s. The advocacy of a female subjectivity (the story is told from Belle's point of view) and the notion of equality, so present in this film, ran contrary to prevailing messages about sexual relations in films of the late-1940s and early-1950s. Women either died or had their dreams of independence firmly quashed. In France, as in America, the wider purpose was to get women back into the domestic sphere. Cocteau's message, then, was a radical one, and audiences at the time (at least female ones) appear to have understood it better than the critics. Cocteau once said that 'it is not up to us to obey the public that does not know what it wants, but to oblige it to follow us'. He also said that he did not seek to please, but to be understood. For 'public', he should have substituted 'critics'. Not until the late 1960s, with the advent, in French film theory, of psycho-criticism, was *La Belle et la Bête* fully understood by critics. It took them twenty years to come to grips with what the public had already discovered.

Cocteau, the poet of the past and the future, was not of his time. What is significant is that it is precisely those aspects for which the film was originally reviled or misunderstood that have made it such an important one today in terms of film history. *La Belle et la Bête* represented a radical break with the regressive, inward-looking and 'safe' narratives of the time. It also countered dominant production practices. The soundtrack was disliked because of its lack of dialogue; however, it was Cocteau's use of asynchronicity that would have such an impact on the use of soundtrack by Godard and Resnais. The painterly emphasis irritated some because there were so many references. But by weaving music, painting and literature into the fabric of his film, in such depth and with such measure, Cocteau would, in fact, show the way for French cinema to be reborn. The effect became clear some twelve to fifteen years later, primarily in the films of Godard, who readily acknowledges Cocteau as one of his mentors, but also in those of Resnais and Agnes Varda.

Cocteau's influence continues. Luc Besson quotes him as having a major bearing on his film work, while the contemporary New Queer Cinema acknowledges its debt to him, also. Finally, in counterpointing realist images in terms of their look with a fairy tale he created what he called a *sublimation du style documentaire* – an oxymoronic tension between documentary and fantasy, which has had an impact on the working styles of Resnais, Godard and Jacques Demy in France, and Pier Paolo Pasolini in Italy. In *La Belle et la Bête*, Cocteau drew attention to film practices to reveal the ideological operations in mainstream cinema that seek to conceal the fact that what we are watching is pure illusion. In this respect, he was anti-Hollywood. He was also ahead of the *nouvelle vague*, which is more readily credited with resisting these Hollywood practices.

Unlike *La Bataille du rail*, *Patrie* and *La Symphonie pastorale*, *La Belle et la Bête* did not get widely released in Paris. It only appeared in two cinemas on the Champs-Elysées: the Colysée and La Royale. This would explain why its success was rather slow in coming. In terms of provincial venues, so far as can be determined, it was in the eastern part of France, particularly Lyon, that it met with greatest approval. Few critics at the time were bold enough to predict that the film would become the classic it now is, nor that, in 1985, it would be revived in a new 35mm copy – the highest accolade to be paid to a film from the past, and one that will guarantee its survival. But the audiences of 1946 knew its value as spectacle. They fell in love with the Beast and in the process made Marais into a star.

18

THE LEOPARD

Pierre Sorlin

What do art critics do? Usually, they produce knowledge. By exploring the social and political, aesthetic and technical issues of concern to artists and by knitting these matters into critical readings, they provide their readers with new interpretations. However, in some instances, critics have to 'clean' the work they study of the comments surrounding it which prevent amateurs from seeing it as it is. Such a cleaning is, I believe, necessary in the case of *The Leopard*.

Luchino Visconti, the descendant of an aristocratic Milanese family, was already a well-known theatre director and journalist when he began, at the age of thirty-six, to make films. With the two exceptions (*The Earth Quakes*, 1948, which was never distributed, and *The Stranger*, 1967, a too literal adaptation of a novel) all his films were big hits, but the most successful by far was his sixth picture, *The Leopard* (in Italian, *Il gattopardo*). First released on 28 March 1963, this was awarded the Golden Palm at the Cannes film festival and went on to win many other prizes. The quality of the work is outstanding but its long-lasting fame rests on themes which are not necessarily linked to its artistic achievement.

When the film was shot, many of the most famous Italian film-makers, namely De Sica, Antonioni and Fellini, were reluctant to use colour film stock arguing that it was artificial, vulgar, fit for popular comedies, but artistically less rewarding than black and white. In this respect Visconti had been a precursor since, as early as 1954, he had made his fourth picture, *Senso* in colour. But he had then come back to black and white for *Rocco and his Brothers* (1960). Spectators noted that the shift to colour, far from being casual, had a precise purpose. The four black and white films dealt with contemporary problems and featured poor people, vagrants (*Ossessione*), fishermen (*The Earth Quakes*), slum dwellers (*Bellissima*) and factory workers (*Rocco and his Brothers*). The two colour pictures, on the other hand, told the stories of aristocrats living in the mid-nineteenth century, during the Risorgimento, the period in which the House of Savoy founded a new nation, the Kingdom of Italy.

After *The Leopard*, Visconti was considered a neo-realist, intent on exploring social matters, and a maker of historical films. But many critics felt uneasy with the obvious differences they could see between his Risorgimento movies. *Senso* depicts a world which once existed and has been ruined by the course of events. It opens with the voice of Countess Livia Serpieri, narrating not 'things as they really happened', as is often promised at the outset of history films, but the destruction of her own life. The film is about how a lady remembers her past and how she tells it to herself and to others. It takes place within a traditional framework of beginning (Countess Serpieri, who lives in Austrian-occupied Venice, encounters Lieutenant Franz Mahler, an Austrian officer), middle (their love affair) and end (their mutual betrayal which results in the execution of Mahler).

While history and story coincide in *Senso*, they seem to be only loosely connected in *The Leopard*. The film is built around a central character, Prince Salina, but very little happens. The title might be *Chronicle of an Empty Season*. As they have long been used to doing, Salina and his family pass the spring on their estate near Palermo, leave the torrid plain during the summer for another palace somewhere in the hills, and return to Palermo in winter.

However, the historical background to these timeless rituals is the early 1860s, a climactic period between Garibaldi's disembarkation in Sicily and the defeat of the great leader by the royal army, the months during which the Bourbons lost their kingdom and Sicily became Italian. The film provides us with a few glimpses of the fights in Palermo, the name of Garibaldi surfaces every now and then, and we observe the referendum on whether Sicilians want to become Italians. But these facts seem of little relevance to a family more preoccupied with society life, than with the making of a new state.

Commentators who had appreciated *Senso*'s ability to represent the relationship between individual wills and a social, historical situation, were disconcerted by the separation of great events from everyday concerns in *The Leopard*. Fascinated by such a discrepancy, they tended to focus exclusively on the historical aspect of the film and its significance for an interpretation of the Risorgimento. The period of the Risorgimento has long been problematic in Italian political evolution. A war of liberation is always shrouded in myth – the

The family gathers around the patriarch, Prince Salina, as he reads out news of the imminent revolution. (Titanus/SNPC/Courtesy Kobal)

heroic legend of a country that has created itself. But Italian unity was imposed from above, by a dynasty that was never accepted, that submitted in the face of the rise of Fascism, and was eventually dismissed by a popular vote. To this day, Italians have argued about the significance of their Risorgimento.

The interpretation offered in *Senso* is violently critical. Livia is an ardent Italian patriot, possibly because she is a misfit, unhappy with an older husband who has not given her children. But once she has fallen for Mahler, she gives him the funds that the Italian insurgents have saved to buy guns and hidden in her castle. Paradoxically, Livia's husband, a loyal subject of Austria, comes to the aid of the Italians when he understands that the Austrians will withdraw. What is more, the historical climax of the film is the battle of Custozza, lost by Italians in 1866; although defeated, Italy gains Venice and its province, whereas the Austrians, who have won, leave the Peninsula for all time. In his films,

Visconti suggests that confusion, lies, betrayals and, above all, the diplomatic interests of the Great Powers were the basic ingredients of unification.

The Leopard is less polemical and attempts to interpret rather than condemn. Salina has quickly understood that a long-distance monarch would be far less dangerous than a king based in Palermo – for a Sicily which has developed a civilisation of its own, unlike that of any other region. Officials sent from the North do not care much for the burning Sicilian countryside and are anxious to go back to the capital as soon as possible. Salina tells his chaplain: 'Do you know what is happening in our island? Nothing. Nothing but a trifling switch of class almost on the spot. In the end, everything is going to remain in the same place.' But, for that purpose, he has to ally with other Sicilians against the North and he chooses, cleverly, one of the men he hates most, a *nouveau riche* 'countryman', Don Calogero Sedara, who has become a big landowner by exploiting farm workers.

The political part of the film is about the confrontation of apparently incompatible societies, and of how an aristocrat uses an upstart, the very sort of man who is less understanding of Sicily and its history, to keep the past alive. Tancredo (Alain Delon), Salina's beloved nephew, becomes an officer in the Italian army and marries the only daughter of the *nouveau riche*. Tomorrow Tancredo will be an ambassador, his sons will inherit his name, together with the fortune of their mother.

As the film has generally been interpreted in this vein, this reading of it cannot be totally disregarded. But we must not forget that Visconti was a master of making films that operate on different levels. The clear narration and political analysis would appeal to those interested in history, while less erudite or more sensitive spectators would appreciate his interest in artistic work, dreams and contemplation. However exciting it is, a purely ideological reading of the movie is too limited and does not take into account its cinematic qualities.

When Visconti looked for a vehicle to express his understanding of mid-nineteenth-century Sicilian history he fixed on *The Leopard*, the fictitious biography of a Sicilian prince, written by a Sicilian aristocrat, Giuseppe Tomasi di Lampedusa. Visconti had the advantage of a gripping story out of which he fashioned a film that does justice to the complexities of the central character and his situation. However, he took certain liberties with the novel. Lampedusa had made his book testament to a retired existence lived across the historic divide of the Risorgimento. He was extremely pessimistic, and if his Salina succeeded in keeping the monarchy out of the island, the price was high. In the book, Tancredo's money match was a dramatic failure; the protection of Sicily's past became a very part of Italy's arduous, strangely tentative and partially failed engagement with the modern world. In Visconti's version, the affair between Tancredo and his fiancée, Angelica, is an important part of the film, a kind of sub-plot that turns out to be a touching relationship of love. Everything ends well, and Salina, realising that he might soon die, can boast that, instead of marrying a degenerate aristocrat (a 'female monkey', as he says) who would have given him weak heirs, Tancredo will produce an entirely new, healthy breed. The happy outcome is all the more strange, given that a sad conclusion would have been more in tune with Visconti's previous analysis of the Risorgimento; his earlier films all finished either with a tragic event or a personal defeat.

Part of the appeal of *The Leopard*, and one of the reasons for its universal success, I believe, lies in its capacity to emphasise a man's worries and ambitions within the confines of his culture and traditions. The famous American actor, Burt Lancaster, was cast as the Sicilian prince; he was hired because he was the only big name available at the time, though Visconti, while admitting that Lancaster was a performer of outstanding gifts, did not like the choice. Lancaster was, in fact, perfectly fit for the part. He portrayed Salina as a hard man, handsome, aristocratic to the tip of his fingers, shrewd and perceptive, respected by relatives, servants and countrymen, but not very intelligent, extremely rude with most people and not much liked. The father of seven children, Salina's marriage seems to have dwindled into nothing and he clearly feels suffocated. He loathes his frigid wife, who starts crying whenever she is annoyed, and he seldom talks to his children. With his mixture of haughty cleverness and moral superiority, he acts the gentleman and is a perfect egoist, determined to save the historical inheritance of his family at any cost.

What redeems Salina and makes him acceptable, is that he is lonely and is governed by his own personal rules which have always restrained his desires and enabled him to go on through an empty life. He has no friends; the society in which he moves and the people with whom he mixes are absolutely decadent; he hates the etiquette and conventions of an outworn civilisation. At the beginning of the film, Salina gets a letter from a neighbour who has heard of Garibaldi's arrival on Sicily and emigrates. 'What cowards they are' says Salina who knows that, if he wants to guard something, he must stay. But he has no desire to return to the past, to some form of quieter relationship with his peers and inferiors. The Prince epitomises the ideal of aristocracy. His faith in the principle of heredity is heroic because, paradoxically, he is utterly deprived of illusions, does not trust his family and merely wants to maintain what he has received from his father.

There is another enticing aspect to this fictional personality, and that is Salina's fear of death. We are not given any hint that he is seriously ill, his anxiety is purely internal. It may derive from his consciousness that, as he points out, 'we have to change something in order to leave things as they stand'. What will move if institutions remain untouched? Only men. Two themes, or rather two unbearable burdens, conflict in the film: Salina's apprehension and final acceptance of death, and his endeavour to preserve a state of affairs he does not really like. In the last sequence of the film, after a bright night-time ball, everybody leaves joyfully – Tancredo and Angelica lovingly entwined, but Salina, alone in a cold street, kneels while a funeral procession passes in the background. We see him then vulnerable, exposed, naked of everything, moving helplessly towards his end. Yet we are not crushed because the man, after all, has been able to accomplish what mattered to him.

Garibaldi's redshirts take Palermo by storm. A shot from one of the fine battle scenes of the film. (Titanus/SNPC/Courtesy Kobal)

Salina's fate is gripping, but not very original. What prevents the film from collapsing into sentimentality is that his struggle is filtered through an exceptional command of visual material. This, I believe, is the most seductive aspect of the film. Visconti was inspired by places to an unusual degree. His films, instead of being distributed into themes, or chronological order, could be divided into locations. *Senso* depicted Venice and its surroundings, *The Leopard* paints Sicily. In *Senso*, wealth is openly displayed. When at home, Livia is shown against the most luxurious of settings among opulent accessories in a closed atmosphere, often clothed in dark colours and filmed against a dark background. Nothing of the external world, not even the sun, should trouble her privacy so that Franz's every intrusion is experienced as a delicious rape. The Salinas, meanwhile, are not poor but they do not display their riches, their furniture is simple, women wear plain, white clothes and are photographed against pale colours, with white flowers in their hands. One day, Tancredo and Angelica decide to explore the palace in the hills; they end up in a huge, empty attic, a palace in itself, where only useless objects can be found. Such a scene represents, in the most tangible way, the past power of the landed aristocracy before the arrival of well-off countrymen like Angelica's father. Salina's two mansions, immense, never inspected, never re-furnished, are the perfect images of the forgotten splendour and immobility of Sicily, an island of silence.

While trying to recreate an atmosphere in *Senso*, Visconti took up another challenge. During the mid-nineteenth century, Northern Italian cities, especially Florence, witnessed the development of an important school of painters who were called with derision, *I Macchiaioli* – those who paint with large patches of pure colours – a nickname that they adopted as their own, since it fitted them perfectly. These artists supported the cause of unity and enlisted in the various campaigns against Austria; one of them, Sernesi, was even killed in 1866. They illustrated some famous battles, but above all they were the artists of the gentry and the middle class, of peaceful landscapes and animated street scenes. Countess Serpieri could have bought one of their canvases: at least, she lived in the very atmosphere they had tried to recreate.

Visconti built up many scenes of *Senso* as moving developments of motionless pictures. This is particularly clear with the battle of Custozza. The film-maker has closely scrutinised a huge painting by Giovanni Fattori and has re-ordered in sequences what was shown simultaneously on the canvas. Other scenes, Livia and Franz strolling at dawn through the popular districts of

Venice, Livia in her country garden, or in her home, reproduce not only the clothes and locations chosen by the painters, but also the sharp contrast between patches of primary colours.

Senso was a curious experiment in the translation of one sort of visual art into another. *The Leopard* went much further. Carlo Levi's novel published in 1945 is entitled: *Christ Stopped at Eboli*. Eboli is a small town, not far from Naples and the title means that nobody, not even Christ, went farther than Naples. We could also write: *I Macchiaioli Stopped at Eboli*; they made views of Naples but never visited Calabria, Sicily or Sardegna. Visconti decided that he would be the first 'painter' of Sicily. Whereas pictorial influences are easily spotted in *Senso*, there are none in the following colour film. One of *The Leopard*'s delights, however, is the rich visual poetry of the dusty, the earthly and the sun-burnt – making palpable the shimmering heat, blinding light and stifling powder of the island. Visconti does not seek to explain anything: the incandescence of the day is not a painful metaphor for the immobility of Sicily, it is merely an impression that the brightness of the screen is able to translate. The delicately lit interiors are occasionally offset by explosions of sunny radiance in outdoor scenes where the wonderful, silent palaces stand surrounded by an expanse of summer fields, or in vistas of beautiful gardens. If a film in which so little happens is rather long, it is because many shots were taken uniquely to celebrate, capture and enhance the beauty of nature – in other words, to give pleasure.

However, Visconti was not merely interested in landscapes. On the morning of the second day in the film, Salina is shaving and then getting dressed in his bathroom while Tancredo talks about recent events. Instead of alternating shots of the two characters, the camera makes an inventory of the room in which, at times, it crosses one of the men on whom it lingers. By mixing up scenery and conversation, the film creates a world of complicity based as much on the shape and tint of the objects as on the words. Interior sequences, which sound a bit verbose if we only listen to the dialogues, allow the camera to cut to and from the protagonists. Exploration triggers curiosity, thus producing a light tension between the content of the conversation and the quality, the agility of the shooting.

This might be the reason why *The Leopard* is still Visconti's most appreciated film, among movie buffs as well as lay spectators. The shift from putting idle images into motion, to searching new types of spectacle, new ways of colouring the screen, announced another cinema, less intent on telling than on showing. However, Visconti was never tempted by formalism. The innovations ventured in *The Leopard* were celebratory both of the pleasure of colours and of the interest in narrative content. The film chronicled an interesting period, it featured an impressive, provoking character, and it was beautifully filmed. It is a very rare achievement – to say the least.

19

SOUTH PACIFIC

Michael Sturma

When the musical-comedy South Pacific was released by Twentieth Century Fox in March 1958, *Variety* predicted the film would 'mop up'. After all, the movie had had almost a decade of pre-publicity in the form of the highly successful Broadway production which first opened in April 1949. Apart from its entertainment value, though, *South Pacific* provides a useful window on some of the issues that preoccupied America in the mid-twentieth century. It reflected on the American presence in the Pacific during the Second World War, while its underlying themes of racial and cultural tolerance also came at a crucial juncture in American race relations.

American interests (economic, strategic and cultural) in the Pacific were long-standing. By the end of the nineteenth century, the United States held territory stretching from the Hawaiian islands to the Philippines. In Hawaii, it acquired exclusive rights to Pearl Harbor as a naval base from 1887, followed by annexation of the islands in 1898. America's imperial involvement, however, tended to be overshadowed in the popular mind by exotic and romantic images of the Pacific islands. Although tourism did not replace sugar as Hawaii's main industry until after the Second World War, the islands were marketed as a tourist destination long before this. Postcards of Hawaiian hula dancers were in wide circulation by the 1890s. From the 1930s, America experienced a Hawaiian music craze with songs such as 'My Little Grass Shack'. The Hawaiians were typically represented as a happy-go-lucky people – despite their loss of sovereignty and integration into the economy as wage labourers.

In particular, a succession of Hollywood films of the 1930s represented the South Pacific as a sensual paradise. Perhaps more than anything else, the tropical setting allowed a level of voyeurism not normally permissible at the time. The actress Dorothy Lamour made famous the scanty and gracefully

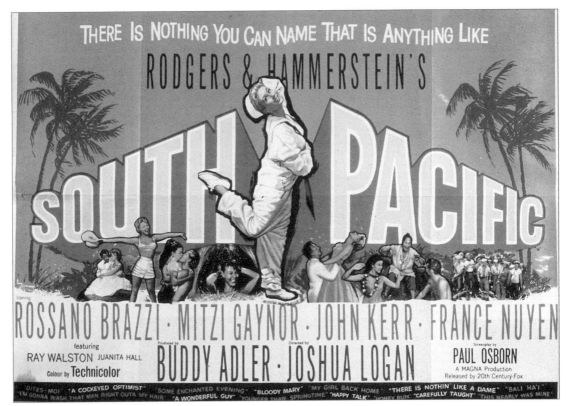

South Pacific given the big screen treatment in its 1958 publicity poster – but its themes had a depth that the image hardly hints at. (20th Century Fox/Courtesy Kobal)

draped 'sarong' in her roles as an island maiden. A former New Orleans beauty queen, Lamour appeared in films such as *The Hurricane* (1937) and *Aloma of the South Seas* (1941). A similar formula was adopted in other movies. Maria Montez, for example, portrayed the sarong-clad, island girl Melahi in *South of Tahiti* released in 1941. While genuine Hawaiians often found work as extras in such films, the stars were typically European or Mexican.

Once the Japanese attacked Pearl Harbor in December 1941, popular images of the Pacific islands as a tropical paradise seemed incongruous. American forces suffered subsequent defeats in the Philippines at Bataan and Corregidor, on Guam and at Wake Island. The islands became the site of a bitter war of attrition. Nevertheless, South Pacific stereotypes were tenacious. *Song of the Islands* (1942) starring Betty Grable, for example, continued to portray Hawaii as a romantic paradise. In some ways the perpetuation of the South Seas myth was believed good for morale.

From one perspective, *South Pacific* may be viewed as an attempt to reconcile the role of the islands as a war zone, with their traditional romantic mystique. The idea for the film came originally from James Michener's Pulitzer Prize-winning novel *Tales of the South Pacific* published in 1947. Having studied at Swarthmore College and at the Colorado State College of Education, Michener worked as an educator and later as an editor with Macmillan publishers. During 1944 and 1945 he had served with the US Navy in the South Pacific. It was his wartime experiences, especially in the New Hebrides and New Caledonia, that provided material for his book. Michener wrote most of *Tales of the South Pacific* while stationed on the Vanuatu island of Espiritu Santo.

Hollywood executive Kenneth McKenna showed some initial interest in Michener's book, but his studio rejected it as unsuitable for a film. Through McKenna's stage designer brother, however, the book came to the attention of composer Richard Rodgers and lyricist Oscar Hammerstein. The pair already had a highly successful Broadway musical collaboration with *Oklahoma!*. Together with director Joshua Logan (who would later direct the film version), they adapted Michener's story to the stage.

Those reading Michener's book may be surprised at how little of it was actually translated on to the stage and screen. As a loosely connected collection of vignettes, Michener admitted that *Tales of the South Pacific* lacked an obvious dramatic storyline. The musical version basically interweaves two of the eighteen chapters into parallel love stories set on a South Seas island during the Second World War. In one story an American nurse, Nellie Forbush, becomes romantically involved with a French planter, Emile De Becque, who lives on the island where she is stationed. In the film's parallel love story, US marine Joe Cable becomes involved with a local 'Tonkinese' girl named Liat.

In part, Michener's tales reflect the disillusionment of many US servicemen whose expectations of the South Pacific had been shaped largely by Hollywood films. Such disappointment was popularly referred to as the 'Dorothy Lamour Syndrome' by American service personnel. In one scene in the book, a group of marines discuss the discrepancy between film versions of the Pacific and their own experience. A character called Eddie quotes a letter from his girlfriend back in Minneapolis: 'I certainly hope you are not dating one of those luscious South Sea beauties we see so much in the movies.' The marine plans to send an unflattering photo of a Melanesian woman back to Minneapolis, and questions 'how Hollywood dares to cook up the tripe it does'.

In the film *South Pacific*, the gap between the expectations of American servicemen and reality is satirised. A group of American sailors and seabees bide their time while waiting to go into combat against the Japanese. The Dorothy Lamour type 'native' is conspicuous by her absence on the island where the Americans are based. All the young women have been sent to the neighbouring island of Bali Ha'i for fear that they might fall prey to the lust of US troops. The only local woman is the shrewd, but sexually unappealing, Bloody Mary (Juanita Hall), who is more interested in making money than love. Like many of the real islanders at the time, Mary is happy to supply the Americans with the souvenir grass skirts, which had themselves become an icon of the South Seas mainly through Hollywood images.

The film manages to juggle the conflicting images of the Pacific as both theatre of war and sensual paradise. It does this mostly by juxtaposing the neighbouring islands of Bali Ha'i and Maria-Louise. The lush and mystical Bali Ha'i promises all the sensual delights of the mythical South Seas. Brimming with young women, it is here that Joe Cable has his romantic rendezvous with Liat. Maria-Louise, on the other hand, offers danger and the prospect of death. It is infested with Japanese, and the reality of war is forcefully brought home when, later, Cable is killed during a reconnaissance mission on the island.

The historical significance of *South Pacific*, however, relates not so much to war as to civil rights. Embedded in the plot are themes of bigotry and racial intolerance, issues developed still more explicitly in the original book. (Indeed, the need to overcome racial prejudice might be identified as the common theme in all James Michener's writings.)

The Second World War brought some dramatic changes to the American home front in many areas, and especially in terms of race relations. During the war there was a mass migration of African-Americans from the South to northern and western cities. Along with generally improved working conditions and pay came rising expectations about quality of life and greater political power. The war also highlighted racial inequalities in other ways. While American rhetoric vigorously attacked the racial policies of Nazism, African-Americans were openly discriminated against in the US armed forces. In 1942 the Congress on Racial Equality (CORE) was founded to fight against segregation, and civil rights leaders called on the government to promote at home the democracy it advocated overseas. *South Pacific*, at least indirectly, puts forward a similar challenge.

The central character in the film is naval nurse Nellie Forbush (played by Mary Martin on Broadway, and in the film by Mitzi Gaynor. Ironically, Gaynor began her show business career performing in USO shows for the armed forces.) Coming from Little Rock, Arkansas, Nellie is a woman of limited worldly experience. In spite of her attraction to the French planter De Becque (Rossano Brazzi), she is troubled by their different cultural backgrounds. What most complicates her feelings, however, is the fact that De Becque has two children by a Polynesian woman. Although the children's mother has since died, Nellie finds it hard to accept De Becque's past liaison with a woman of colour. In fact, in Michener's original story De Becque had eight daughters by four different women of varied ethnicity. The musical abbreviates his sexual history, as well as Nellie's, who in Michener's tale was previously involved with a married man.

A similar racial dilemma is depicted in the film's other love story. Bloody Mary, on her first meeting with the US marine lieutenant, decides Joe Cable is the perfect mate for her daughter Liat (France Nuyen). Cable seems to agree, falling instantly in love with Liat after meeting her on Bali Ha'i. In a later scene he offers Liat his grandfather's watch as a token of his affection. But he

'Bloody Mary' (Juanita Hall) playing carousing matchmaker to her daughter Liat and the clean-cut WASP lieutenant Joe Cable. (20th Century Fox/Kobal)

quickly turns sullen when Mary tells him, 'You have special good babies.' Cable leaves protesting that he cannot marry Liat. Although he comes from the northern city of Philadelphia and is an Ivy League graduate, Cable holds some of the same prejudices as small-town Nellie.

The tensions involved in crossing racial and cultural barriers are, in a sense, reflected in the musical's show within a show. Nellie is responsible for organising the 'Thanksgiving Follies' in order to raise troop morale on the island. The American holiday of Thanksgiving itself conjures up inter-cultural images, given that the original celebration involved both Europeans and American Indians. In the Follies, boundaries are further challenged. Nellie appears on stage wearing an over-sized, male sailor's uniform, while another character, Luther Billis, appears in drag with mop-like hair and coconut husk breasts. As Marjorie Garber persuasively argues in her book *Vested Interests: Cross-Dressing and Cultural Anxiety* (Routledge, 1992), gender cross-dressing frequently serves to displace anxieties about transgressing racial boundaries. The exchange of sexual identity in the Thanksgiving Follies both mimics and distracts from the more profound challenge to categories posed by the film.

The theme of racial intolerance in *South Pacific* is crystallised in the musical number 'You've Got to be Carefully Taught'. The song is performed by the Joe Cable character (played by John Kerr in the film, with vocals performed by Bill Lee). In the preceding scene, Nellie has told Emile De Becque that she cannot marry him because of his children's Polynesian mother. She explains that her decision is not so much based on reason, as something born in her. But Emile rejects the idea that such prejudice is inborn. Having witnessed this exchange, Joe Cable sings the song which begins 'You've got to be taught to hate and fear'. The lyrics challenge the notion that racism is something innate, but argue that it is learned from an early age.

When the stage version of *South Pacific* was originally produced in 1949, a number of experienced theatrical people pressured Rodgers and Hammerstein to leave out 'You've Got to be Carefully Taught'. Some felt its sensitive content might prevent the musical from achieving the success it deserved. However, the duo remained adamant that the song be included in the play. Several early reviewers did criticise its inclusion, but as time went on the song received more praise than criticism. It continued to elicit comment in the film. *Variety* believed the song would 'raise discussion', describing it as 'a punchy Hammerstein lyric that frankly propagandizes against racial bigotry'. Another critic, writing for *Films in Review* in April 1958, praised the number as a 'commendable plea for racial tolerance'. In fact, recent events in America lent the theme of racial intolerance, and the song in particular, a special poignancy.

It was with some prescience that Michener had his Nellie Forbush character originating from Little Rock, Arkansas. The city was to explode on to the American consciousness only a short time before the screen version of *South Pacific* was released. From the late 1940s, lawyers, including Thurgood Marshall (destined to become the first African-American justice of the Supreme Court), increasingly challenged segregation through the courts. Following a Supreme Court decision in 1954, that racial segregation in public schools was unconstitutional, federal attempts to desegregate schools were actively resisted in many localities. It was at Little Rock, however, where the issue reached flashpoint. When nine African-American students tried to enrol at Little Rock Central High School in September 1957, the Arkansas governor, Orval Faubus, ordered the state's national guard to bar their entry. In a dramatic move, President Eisenhower responded by sending regular army paratroopers to Little Rock, and placing the Arkansas national guard under federal control. The black students were escorted into the school under army protection. The media gave the whole episode wide coverage, including the ugly taunting of the black children by some local residents. Little Rock became a potent symbol of racial bigotry.

In the years between the first production of *South Pacific* on Broadway and the subsequent film, other changes also made for a more receptive atmosphere. Hollywood was no longer subjected to Senator McCarthy's anti-Communist congressional investigations, which in the early 1950s discouraged explicit critiques of social issues. In 1956 Hollywood's self-managed censorship system, the Motion Picture Production Code, underwent its first major modification since the 1930s. Henceforth, topics such as 'miscegenation' were no longer considered taboo. By the late 1950s, with the emergence of leaders including Martin Luther King Jr, and campaigns against racial segregation, the civil rights movement was also having an impact. In 1957, Congress passed its first civil rights legislation in over eighty years.

Despite all these changes, *South Pacific* still handles the subject of inter-racial romance gingerly. After singing 'You've Got to be Carefully Taught', Cable tells De Becque that he will stay in the islands with Liat if he survives the war. But he does not survive. Cable is killed while he and Emile carry out an intelligence mission on Maria-Louise. The dilemma of inter-racial marriage and children is thus resolved, as indeed it was in other films of the period such as westerns, which depicted romantic relations between white men and American-Indian or Chinese women.

It may be that at the time he wrote his stories in the 1940s, Michener doubted that inter-racial marriages were tenable, considering prevailing social attitudes. In an interview of 1993, the author is quoted as saying that during the Second World War he would have found the prospect of falling in love with an island woman 'unthinkable'. However, it was not long after the publication of his 1954 novel *Sayonara* (which also deals with the theme of inter-racial romance and ends with the deaths of the lovers) that Michener first met a Japanese-American woman, Mari Yoriko Sabusawa. Sabusawa told him she did not like the book's conclusion, insisting that inter-racial liaisons did not necessarily have to end tragically. The following year, she and Michener were married in what proved to be an enduring union.

In *South Pacific*, the relationship of Emile and Nellie fares better than that of Joe and Liat, but the barriers crossed are more cultural than racial. Once Nellie learns of the Frenchman's dangerous mission with Cable, she decides she can overcome her prejudices and marry De Becque if he survives. When Emile returns, he is reunited not only with his children but also with Nellie, forming a new, blended family unit as the film ends.

Some critics were sceptical of Nellie's conversion to a more liberal viewpoint. Her motivation appeared under-developed. Nevertheless, she emerges as a more sympathetic character than in Michener's original story. In *Tales of the South Pacific* Nellie's decision to marry De Becque comes after he rescues her from a group of American soldiers intent on raping her. Nellie's racial bias does not appear so greatly changed, as she declares in the book, 'I don't care who he lived with, I got me a man!' In the film, her behaviour is full of unselfconscious irony. She tells Emile she left Little Rock partly to meet different kinds of people, but she frets about his foreign background. She is reassured when he tells her he believes, along with the American Declaration of Independence, that 'all men are created equal'. Yet, while she can accept with relative equanimity that he left France because he killed a man, she is unable to cope with the idea that he has fathered children with a woman of different race.

Although often sensitive to racial matters, it is probably not surprising that the film does not touch on more profound issues, such as the right of De Becque to carve out his plantation on islanders' land. To do so might have reflected uncomfortably on the role of American planters in Hawaii, and on US claims to other territory in the Pacific. As it happens, most of the location shots for *South Pacific* were filmed on Kauai, site of the first successful sugar plantation in the Hawaiian islands.

In many ways, too, the film perpetuates racial stereotypes. When Bloody Mary is introduced, for example, she is standing next to a human skull. The first time she meets Joe Cable she tries to give him a shrunken head. When Cable later visits the island of Bali Ha'i, the locals perform a dance sequence described by one reviewer as 'Hollywood-primitive of the most obvious kind'. Meanwhile, apart from some brief exchanges in French when she first meets Joe, Liat remains effectively mute throughout the rest of the picture. She epitomises the exotic woman as passive and pliant.

In spite of this, *South Pacific* did represent something of a bold step forward. Especially considering that a film like Stanley Kramer's *Guess Who's Coming to Dinner* (1967) could still inspire intense controversy a decade later. Although ostensibly about Americans in a far-away place, *South Pacific* served as commentary on domestic politics which were difficult to approach directly. It rearranged American anxieties in a less threatening form. In the context of the late 1950s, the film assumed a relevance which was, in some ways, distanced from its audience, yet was nevertheless still recognisable to them.

20

INDOCHINE

David Nicholls

In the early 1990s two inter-related phenomena became visible in French culture. On the one hand, a number of films and rather more books indicated a renewed fascination with the epoque of French colonialism in Indochina, principally in Vietnam. Renewed interest in a largely forgotten colonial conflict was pushed into the public domain by controversial revelations about captured French soldiers who had joined the Viet Minh during the war of 1946–54. Old wounds were re-opened and revealed to be festering.

Popular memory of the Indochinese war had been overlaid for many years by the far greater national trauma of the Algerian war of independence (1954–62). The domestic repercussions of the Algerian conflict had been immeasurably wider: Indochina had over-turned no domestic governments, let alone a Republic; no conscript soldiers had been sent there; there was no massive number of Europeans to be repatriated; and the conflict had had no violent side effects in France itself. Opposition to the American war in Vietnam had pushed France's role in the 'Thirty Years' War' in Indochina into the background.

The renewed interest, then, was in part a mere catching up with the passage of time, a belated acknowledgement of its significance in modern French history and for France's postwar pretensions to remain a world power, an aspect of national identity that the 1996 furore about nuclear testing in the Pacific showed to be very much alive. However, it may also be linked with European concern about the 'new economies' of the Pacific rim and the Far East, an attempt to come to terms with France's historical role in an increasingly significant and vigorous area of the globe.

At the same time, French cinema's search for domestic audiences and international prestige induced producers to invest in what has become loosely

Catherine Deneuve as the French colonial matriarch Eliane Devries, standing out from the crowd in the film's portrayal of 1930s Indochina. (The Ronald Grant Archive)

known as the 'heritage film', films asserting or re-assessing French national history and identity in an era when the political integration of Europe has been one of the main topics of political debate. In fact, 'heritage films', which include adaptations of Marcel Pagnol by Claude Berri and Yves Robert, Berri's version of Emile Zola's *Germinal* (1993), and Patrice Chereau's *La Reine Margot* (1996), have little in common, apart from being (mostly) literary adaptations set in the past. But they have been a success story for a French film industry that likes to portray itself melodramatically as engaged in a life-and-death struggle against the cultural imperialism of Hollywood. They have enjoyed considerable popularity at home and abroad and have helped to refurbish the image of a national cinema often seen as being too intellectual, low key, depressing or pretentious.

Régis Wargnier's *Indochine*, released in 1991, is one of the successes of 'heritage' cinema, a hit at the French box office and winner of an Oscar for Best Foreign Language Film. It also represents the most lucrative fruit of a

Franco-Vietnamese agreement allowing French film-makers to shoot films in Vietnam, unlike the Americans whose movies about the Vietnam war have had to be shot in the Philippines or Thailand. France, it is asserted, may co-operate culturally with countries where her cultural influence is strong and (of course) beneficent. History may be confronted honestly in a new era of post-colonial collaboration, while on the domestic front, Wargnier's film allows France to come to terms with her colonial past in an age of economic recession and what French politicians call the 'construction of Europe'.

The very title *Indochine* is nostalgic, conjuring up a lost world from which the affix 'French' is inseparable. Indeed, it is a film about the end of Indochina, told in flashback from the vantage point of Geneva in 1954 at the time of the negotiations which marked the final French withdrawal from Vietnam. But in a flashback to 1936, already, *Indochine*'s Vietnamese 'Red Princess' declares that 'Indochina no longer exists. It is dead.' It is, then, an evocation of a past that, even within the film, is diffused with the light of remembrance. Yet in the context of the 'heritage film' *Indochine* is closer to historical 'reality' (that is history as written by historians) than is, say, *La Reine Margot*, which is largely based on romantic and entertaining, but discredited and at times wildly inaccurate, portrayals of real historical characters. Dealing with still-resonant events, contemporary sensibilities – both French and Vietnamese – have to be taken into account, and a form of 'political correctness' married to popular appeal.

The road to popular success lies in telling a good story. *Indochine* is a melodrama, a lengthy, complex and highly unlikely tale, interweaving the personal and political in such a way that the historian and critic Jean-Pierre Jeancolas was moved to liken it to a 'left-wing *Gone With the Wind*'. The central character, Eliane Devries, played by Catherine Deneuve, is remotely based on a real-life rubber planter in Cochin-China (southern Vietnam), a certain Madame de la Souchère. But for the most part, the leading players are types who would be mere clichés or even caricatures in a shorter and less skilfully made and performed film.

The precise historical period of the story is not made explicit until near the end, when the release of political prisoners is ordered by the Popular Front government, thereby signalling to French audiences that we are in 1936 or 1937. In fact, the bulk of the action takes place between about 1928 and 1932. These were crucial years in the development of Vietnamese nationalism, with the foundation in 1930 of the Indochinese Communist Party led by Ho Chi

Minh, the economy badly hit by the consequences of global depression, and peasant uprisings in Annam and Tonkin (central and northern Vietnam) in 1930–1.

Despite the complexity of the story, it all revolves around the figure of Eliane Devries. The casting of Deneuve in the central role necessarily bestows a symbolic status on Eliane: the actress is not only the leading French female star of the day, but also quite literally the iconic representation of the French Republic, having replaced Brigitte Bardot as the model for Marianne, the female personification of the Republic displayed in town halls and other public places throughout the country. The key relationship in the film is that between Eliane and her adoptive Vietnamese daughter, Camille (Linh Dan Pham), whose rich parents have died in an air crash. Colonial and 'native' elites are fused, but Camille will reject her inheritance – turn her back on her wealth and background – in favour of the independence struggle.

Eliane represents colonial paternalism (or maternalism), but the 'native' daughter rebels and rejects her colonial and privileged inheritance, an action paralleled by her fiancé, Tanh (Eric Nguyen), the scion of a rich merchant house who becomes a cadre of the Communist Party. Both partners in this arranged marriage abandon their mothers, and the colonial world they represent, for a life of clandestine political activism. The educated 'Annamite' elite, the film suggests, become transformed into the leaders of the people.

The social world of the French revolves around the plush hotels of Saigon and regattas on the Mekong, while the Annamite elite is represented by the old and desiccated notables of the Confucian mandarin class and by the imperial court at Hue, a haven of tradition, but illusory and anachronistic, an old power structure theoretically left intact by the French, but reduced to an empty shell. Poorer Vietnamese, meanwhile, have to come crawling for help to the rich. But the worm is in the bud. Reference is made to the killing of French officers by their Vietnamese troops in an abortive uprising at the army garrison of Yen Bai in the Red River valley in Tonkin in February 1930. Tanh, expelled from France for demonstrating in solidarity with the soldiers, is the archetypal 'native' intellectual, whose anti-colonialism is fuelled by Western education and its humanist ideals of liberty and equality.

But Camille is the true Vietnamese heart of the film. She falls romantically in love with a young naval officer, Jean-Baptiste Le Guen (Vincent Pérez), unaware that he has previously had a brief but intense affair with Eliane. When he is transferred to the north as a punishment for his unruly behaviour, Camille sets forth to find him, and her journey becomes a voyage of discovery, of her country and herself. Swapping her elegant European clothes for the black pyjamas familiar to viewers of Vietnam war films as the uniform of the Viet Cong, she experiences the realities of life in Annam and Tonkin: famine, epidemic disease and forced labour, far removed from the refined colonial society in which she has been brought up.

The revelation of sordid reality continues when Camille finds Jean-Baptiste at a transit camp in the Red River delta where 'volunteers' from the starving north are recruited for the plantations of the south through a system which amounts to slave labour. After escaping from the camp and recuperating in a hidden valley, the lovers are sheltered by a travelling theatrical troupe, who in turn are Communists involved in stirring up the peasant revolts of 1930–1, directed against the mandarins and pro-French village notables and landlords. Historians are divided about the extent of the Communist Party's role in the uprisings: the Party was only founded in 1930, but it was formed by a fusion of various groups, some of which possessed considerable organisation in the countryside. The Party did set up village committees which took control in some areas, the so-called Nghe-Tinh Soviet Movement, and village self-defence forces which official Vietnamese histories, published in 1974 and 1981, transmuted into the first units of the People's Army of Vietnam. But there is no doubt that the roots of the revolts were economic, lying in the appalling burden of taxation imposed upon the peasantry and the dreadful hardship of rural Annam and Tonkin. The film, realistically or not, goes along with the official version as the fires of rebellion flare up along the track of the subversive theatrical company.

After their capture by the French, the story of the two lovers, who now have a son, becomes a legend, enacted on travelling stages throughout the country, but it ends with Camille's imprisonment and the death of Jean-Baptiste, officially through suicide but, in fact, he has obviously been killed by the secret police. The story now jumps forward five years to 1936. The Popular Front government in France orders the release of political prisoners and dismisses the head of the secret police, the Sûreté Générale de l'Indochine, Guy Asselin (Jean Yanne). Camille, now known as the 'Red Princess', emerges from prison camp, but refuses to return to the plantation with Eliane: she will devote her life to the cause of Vietnamese independence. Eliane sells her plantation and 'returns' to France, a country she has never seen. In the course of the film it has gradually been revealed that Eliane is narrating the story to Camille's now adult son in Geneva in 1954, where his mother is part of the Vietnamese delegation to the peace talks.

The film, therefore, has a peculiar time scale: the crucial action takes place in 1930–1 and is then placed in context by leaps forward to 1936 and 1954. This is convenient for all concerned. Concentrating on 1930–1 allows a heroic portrayal of Vietnamese nationalists without upsetting any but the most absurdly hidebound of French sensibilities. The first painful birth-pangs of Communist Vietnam are shown in an acceptable but not sanitised manner. The years after 1931 are skipped over, and the whole period between 1936 and 1954, any allusion to which would be very embarrassing for the French and not entirely comfortable for the Vietnamese, is ignored. Jeancolas calls *Indochine* 'the first pro-Communist film in the history of French cinema', a sign that Communism belongs to the past. The end of the Cold War, in this interpretation, allows France to come to terms with her colonial heritage, but, it must be added, only up to a point and in a selective and idiosyncratic manner.

Making the figure of Eliane, elegant, attractive and ageless, the emotional centre of the film clearly tempers and even distracts attention from the pro-Communist politics. She is, in more ways than one, an attractive figure, sympathetic but flawed. 'Unfulfilled as a woman' in a quite conventional sense, she is a romantic heroine in the grand tradition of such figures in French and American cinema, as capable of courage and self-sacrifice as she is of self-delusion. Her illusions are those of colonialism: she thinks she can pass on her inheritance to Camille and that a new pro-French elite will gradually take over the running of the country. In her admiration for Vietnamese culture and her attempt to cement the two races, French and Vietnamese, she may represent the most sympathetic type of settler, but certainly not the most typical.

Around her, France is represented by the police and the armed forces: the rest of settler society is barely glimpsed. And here some old taboos are still at work. The film shows the peasant uprisings, but not the savage repression that followed. The worst aspects of colonial rule, the forced labour system and migration of starving 'volunteers', are portrayed vividly, with no punches pulled, but nevertheless selectively. The repression of the revolts was mainly the work of the Foreign Legion and French-led Annamite troops. To show Vietnamese soldiers massacring their own people would clearly be unacceptable to the Vietnamese, while the Legion is of course an eternally fascinating subject, and one granted almost untouchable status in French military legend. Since the end of the acknowledged colonial wars, the Legion has continued to play a major part in French military action in the world, from Chad to Bosnia, and at the time of *Indochine*'s release in France, had just fought, under the fascinated gaze of the media, in the Gulf War.

La haute: an array of planter society on the terrace of the Grand Hotel de la Rotonde in Saigon. (Agence Roger-Viollet)

In the tradition of French colonial cinema, the army is not denounced, least of all the Legion. To this day French films about the colonial wars prefer to show defeats rather than criticise the armed forces: the other 'big' film to result from Franco-Vietnamese agreements on film-making was Pierre Schoendoerffer's reconstruction of the fall of Dien Bien Phu in 1954 (*Dien Bien Phu*, 1992). Films showed the heroism and stoicism of ordinary soldiers doomed to die fighting a faceless and ruthless enemy in a harsh and alien environment. It is significant that the only major movie showing a French victory in colonial warfare, Gillo Pontecorvo's *Battle of Algiers* (1966), though remarkably objective in its presentation of the conflict, was made in Algeria after independence and banned in France for several years. Politicians may be vilified for selling out the army, but French soldiers are above criticism. *Indochine* remains, if largely by default, in the French colonial tradition.

The role of villain is assumed by the police, specifically by the Sûreté Générale de l'Indochine. Guy Asselin is the archetypal colonial policeman, aware that brutal methods are necessary if the empire is to survive and

En bas: conditions in a rubber factory in Anloc, Indochina, 1926. (Agence Roger-Viollet)

personally supervising or taking part in the torture of suspects. His ruthless realism will not allow him to release Camille from prison, even to please Eliane, the woman he loves. If Asselin is cynical but realistic, his subordinate, Castellani, is downright psychotic, humiliated by Jean-Baptiste and filled with hatred and contempt for the Vietnamese. But whether inspired by realism – 'just doing the job' – or by personal hatred, harsh and brutal policing is seen as the essence of colonial rule, the necessary protection for the privileged world of the settler elite.

The armed forces in *Indochine* means not so much the soldiers, who are only seen as guards for prisoners, as the navy. The higher echelons, represented by Jean-Baptiste's commanding officers, are punctilious and correct. In an exchange with Asselin towards the end of the film, the admiral in command refuses to let Jean-Baptiste be interrogated by the police because he disapproves of Asselin's methods, an example of the squeamishness which Asselin believes will lose France her colonies. Jean-Baptiste is more enigmatic. He is the only leading character who expresses no viewpoint about the colony and its future, and his actions and reactions throughout are all emotional rather than rational, let alone political. His name, 'John the Baptist' suggests a particular forerunner, and he is captured while baptising his son in a river, a coincidence too obvious to be accidental. But of what exactly is he himself a forerunner? A new Franco-Vietnamese relationship? French anti-colonialism? His death precludes the need for any answer.

As for the Vietnamese, the elites are either blind, like Tanh's mother who believes that she and her kind are destined to rule forever because they are rich, or ossified and decadent, like the mandarins who are the prime target of nationalist attacks. 'Native' traditions, apart from the theatre, are portrayed as negative: the cult of ancestors is shown as a kind of moral blackmail of the living by the dead, used by Asselin to try and force a prisoner to turn informer and by Tanh's mother to dissuade her son from going underground as a revolutionary cadre – in other words to preserve the social hierarchy and colonial rule.

The people are resentful, but passive. Only the Communist Party, the film implies, will allow them to become historical actors in their own right, and this in turn means the adoption of progressive Western ideas, the 'liberty' and 'equality' that Tanh has learned about in France. In a sense, by its destruction of 'feudal' structures by rendering them meaningless, imperialism is (as Karl Marx thought) a progressive force. The idea that Vietnam was liberated as a result of absorbing French ideas is clearly a comforting one for French audiences – 'we taught the Vietnamese to be free' – but a distorted one, ignoring the blend of traditional and modern elements in Vietnamese nationalism, its association with Marxist-Leninist internationalism, and the role of Moscow and the Comintern in the formation of Vietnamese Communists. To this limited extent, *Indochine* is a vindication of French imperialism as a transitory historical phenomenon. In this context Eliane/France is akin to Brecht's Mother Courage, trying to hold on to her children, Camille and Indochina, but foiled by social and political reality.

Indochine, then, allows French audiences to look back on their colonial heritage with what might be termed an 'acceptable degree of contrition', while leaving aspects of it, notably the role of the army, unquestioned. The final shot shows Eliane, dressed in a chic Parisian version of the Vietnamese 'black pyjamas' gazing out on a sunset over Lake Geneva. It is a beautiful but enigmatic image which makes a suitable close to the film. The sun sets on French Indochina, now safely confined to the past with a mixture of regret and acceptance of inevitability. It still lives as dream and nightmare, beautiful but ignoble like the human traffic which provided the labourers for Eliane's estate. France and Indochina, inseparable at the beginning of the film, are now estranged.

Early in the film Eliane's voice-over tells us that youth is perhaps a belief that 'the world is made up of things that cannot be separated: men and women, mountains and plains, humans and gods, Indochina and France'. By implication, the film suggests that the end of empire means national adulthood for France as well as Vietnam. This seems to be an idea easier to accept in theory than in practice.

21

THE EXORCIST

Nicholas Cull

It all began on the day after Christmas 1973. An unearthly screeching followed by the sound of the Islamic call to prayer pitched America headlong into the first screening of William Friedkin's film: *The Exorcist*. During an atmospheric prologue a Jesuit priest and archaeologist, Lankaster Merrin (Max von Sydow), digging in Northern Iraq, uncovers the carved head of a demon, made to ward off the forces of darkness as 'evil against evil'. But Merrin is troubled by a premonition of horror. The scene switches to Georgetown in the United States, where a twelve-year-old girl, Regan (Linda Blair), the daughter of an actress, Chris MacNiel (Ellen Burstyn), is wracked by bizarre convulsions. Doctors, who are powerless to treat her, speculate that the girl may be demonically possessed. After Regan has apparently committed murder, a Jesuit priest, Damien Karras (Jason Miller), is summoned to help. Convinced that he is facing an authentic demonic possession he asks the church to arrange an exorcism. The church sends Merrin to officiate and together the two priests struggle to free the child. Merrin dies of heart failure. Karras prevails, but only by forcing the demon into his own body and throwing himself to his death from the girl's bedroom window. The manifestations of the demon hit hard. In a guttural voice the girl barked a stream of obscenity such as had never before been heard in a Hollywood film; she vomited; she levitated; she twisted her head through a hundred and eighty degrees and she masturbated with a crucifix.

Critics from the *Wall Street Journal* to Moscow's *Isvestia* were appalled, but audiences were overwhelmed by the result. As newspapers reported viewers fainting, Americans lined up to see what all the fuss was about, and then queued to see it all again. In San Francisco a deranged patron charged the screen in an attempt to kill the demon; in Harlem a priest attempted to exorcise drugs from his neighbourhood; in Boston a woman was carried

Dealing with an evil beyond comprehension: the arrival of the Exorcist. (The Ronald Grant Archive)

from the theatre murmuring: 'it cost me four dollars but I only lasted twenty minutes'.

By March 1974, the film had sold 6 million tickets in the United States and was poised to sweep the world. At one level *The Exorcist* phenomenon was just a skilfully mounted spectacle, stretching the limits of a newly liberal Hollywood. Yet the scale of the reaction suggests that the film – like William Peter Blatty's 1971 novel of the same name, and on which it was based – had hit a nerve. *The Exorcist* touched on issues that were all too alive for the world of 1973. This was not a coincidence. It was more than a product of its time; it actively sought to shape that time. Like the carved demon's head unearthed in the prologue, *The Exorcist* was an image of 'evil against evil', or such evils as were identified by its conservatively inclined and deeply Catholic creator, William Blatty.

As the Warner Brother's publicity department reminded the press in 1973, *The Exorcist* was based on a historical case. In August 1949, the Washington newspapers reported that a boy in Mount Rainier, Maryland, had been freed from demonic possession by the rite of exorcism. It was an unusual step. The rite, as codified in 1614, was usually regarded as a relic of the dark ages before a modern understanding of mental illness. But this was also an unusual case. The tormented boy had spoken in languages he had never studied and strange symbols and letters had appeared spontaneously on his body. The story broke at a time of crisis. America was terrified of the mounting power of Communism overseas. Spy scandals and labour disputes raised the spectre of a Communist enemy within. With such discord abroad, one reader, at least, saw the Mount Rainier exorcism as a ray of hope. William Blatty, a young student at Georgetown University, saw the possession as evidence that supernatural evil existed, and that, therefore, supernatural good must also exist. Twenty years later, with the mood of crisis again in the air, Blatty sought to communicate this conclusion to others. Although a successful writer of comedies, he felt confined by this genre. He wrote *The Exorcist* and produced it as a motion picture to scare a new generation of Americans back into church. Blatty was quite open about this aim. He called his novel 'an apostolic work'. Thirty years after its publication he even claimed that the book's best-selling status was a direct result of divine intervention, which opened a slot for him on the Dick Cavett chat show.

Blatty's novel is explicit about the manifestations of evil in the modern world. On its opening page he juxtaposed an epigram from the gospel of Luke in which Jesus confronts a demon with a succession of quotations showing contemporary evil at work: an extract from an FBI wire tap in which a gangster jokes about torture and murder; a graphic account of Communist atrocities against priests, teachers and children from the writings of Dr Tom Dooley, an American doctor who worked in Vietnam in the 1950s; names that evoked the Nazi extermination of European Jews: Dachau, Auschwitz and Buchenwald, a subject that was at last being addressed by American thinkers. Within the body of the book, Blatty selected an epigram that alluded to a further topical manifestation of evil: American conduct in the Vietnam War. In late 1969 the world learned that American troops had massacred some 200 Vietnamese civilians at My Lai. The war in Vietnam had become a perverse pseudo-industrial enterprise in which units were rewarded for their 'body count' like insurance salesmen reaching their target. It was this aspect of the war that attracted Blatty's attention. His epigram for part three of his novel came from a 1969 edition of *Newsweek*: 'a [Vietnam] brigade commander once ran a contest to rack up his unit's 10,000th kill; the prize was a week of luxury in the colonel's own quarters'. The novel also alludes to what many Americans still regarded as the 'original sin' of the era: the murder of President John F. Kennedy in 1963. In an early chapter the child Regan visits Kennedy's grave, and a Georgetown church, introduced as the site of JFK's marriage, is the scene of revolting desecrations (apparently perpetrated by Regan under demonic control). Blatty sought to draw these disparate manifestations of evil – crime, Communism, genocide, war and assassination – together into a cohesive presence. The demon of *The Exorcist* was the result.

Blatty's bid to revive the idea of a personal devil flew in the face of the academic theology of the time. The Warner press pack pointed interested journalists to the German theologian Herbert Haag, who had just published a multi-volume work entitled *Farewell to the Devil*. Yet others shared Blatty's desire to revive the notion of a personal evil. As Mark Kermode has pointed out, in November 1972, Pope Paul VI urged Catholics to return to the study of the Devil: 'Evil is not merely a lack of something, but an effective agent, a living spiritual being, perverted and perverting. A terrible reality. . . .' The project was sufficiently plausible for three Jesuits to give their services as technical advisors to the film; two of whom, William O'Malley SJ and Thomas Bermingham SJ, even acted in it (playing Father Dyer, a friend of Karras, and the president of Georgetown University respectively).

On its release *The Exorcist* received a mixed reception from those who concerned themselves with public morals. Many took exception to the depiction of blasphemous acts, child sexuality and the vivid representation of evil. Media alarm ranged from criticism of the relaxed 'R' certificate attached to the American release, to lurid accounts of viewers being driven to breakdowns and suicide. As a result, the film was picketed by some clerics and condemned by the Protestant evangelist, Billy Graham. But the *Catholic News*, at least, suggested that the theme of evil was apposite for the age, and urged viewers to look beyond the excesses of language and style under the headline: 'Exorcist needs careful attention'.

The screen adaptation of *The Exorcist* avoided the novel's epigrams and allusions to the spectacular evils of the age. The film revolves around 'social evils' the foremost of these being inter-generational conflict. *The Exorcist* found the US divided as never before along generational lines. The world of the young, whose language and culture openly defied the past, was increasingly a closed book to older Americans. College campuses across the country had erupted in protests against the war in Vietnam, culminating in the shooting of protesters at Kent State University, Ohio, in May 1970. This background is evoked in early scenes of *The Exorcist* in which we learn that Regan's mother is an actress in a film portraying campus dissent. She is seen begging an angry crowd of students to 'work within the system'. The theme of a young girl's transformation into a demon-possessed beast played with America's growing fear of its youth. The girl is named Regan in an allusion to one of literature's original 'thankless children' in Shakespeare's *King Lear*. Yet the film also touches a second nerve: the guilt of the middle aged over the neglect of their parents. The priest, Father Karras, is wracked by guilt after seeing his mother committed to a mental hospital. His guilt becomes a principal avenue of attack for the demon during their climactic confrontation.

The action of *The Exorcist* takes place within a realm that had been uniquely privileged in American postwar culture: the home. The evil is doubly disturbing for erupting in so familiar a setting. The poster for the film traded on this. A man with a suitcase stands on a street, silhouetted in the light from a bedroom window over the caption: 'Something almost beyond comprehension is happening to a girl on this street, in this house and a man has been sent for as a last resort. This man is The Exorcist.' The sacred sphere of the home is at risk. The family context is no less eloquent. Blatty's story clearly reflects contemporary fears over the breakdown of the family. Regan is the child of a 'broken marriage'. Her mother is caught up in her career and alternates neglect with cloying overcompensation. The early manifestations of the demon as an 'imaginary friend' seem like a substitute for the girl's absent father. A different sort of Father restores the situation. Beyond this *The Exorcist* plays on the guilt of women moving into the work place and 'usurping the masculine role'. To this end, the mother is given a male name: Chris. The events that follow beg to be read as a punishment for nothing more than being a woman of her time.

In re-working the Mount Rainier case for 1970s America, Blatty altered the gender of the possessed child. In so doing he moved his story into the typical territory of the horror genre: the female body. From Regan's body flows a stream of obscene words, actions, deeds and copious fluids of various hues and textures. Is this the male fear of the castrating female re-animated for the era of Women's Liberation? *The Exorcist* also played on concerns over reproduction that had surfaced during the preceding decade. The 1960s had seen shocking images of birth defects resulting from the drug Thalidomide, sharpening fears of giving birth to the 'monstrous'; it had also seen an intense debate over the issue of abortion, which reached its climax in January 1973 with the Supreme Court's ruling in the case of Roe *v.* Wade. The murderous, possessed child Regan can be read as a projection of the guilt of a generation that had conceded that legal abortion was a necessity. The abortion debate had turned on the issue of a woman's right to control her own body. In *The Exorcist* both bodies and children are out of control. However, the gender politics of the film did not excite much comment at the time. Critics were more concerned by the violence of the images, and there were many more tangible subjects demanding the attention of the women's movement.

Blatty also transformed the class and geographical background of the original story. The ordinary Mount Rainier household of 1949 became the Georgetown home of an actress modelled on Blatty's Hollywood neighbour Shirley MacLaine. The use of Georgetown was significant. The district, close to the heart of Washington DC, was inseparable from American political power: a senator is among the guests at Chris's ritzy party. Chris and her circle add a cultural dimension to this power: her life is shown splashed on the cover of *Photoplay* magazine. The murder of film star Sharon Tate by Charles Manson in 1969 gave the 'evil hits Hollywood star' scenario a chilling topicality. Beyond this, an 'enemy within' the American movie industry was a favourite theme of isolationists before the Second World War and of anti-Communists after it. Blatty's story flirts with this same notion. Indeed, Father Merrin's warning to beware of the demon's voice as it mixes lies with truth is exactly the sort of thing President Nixon had begun to say about the American media as it probed the breaking story of Watergate.

The Exorcist touched other themes of its era. In the 1950s, American horror films had displayed concern over the capabilities of science; by 1973 it seemed appropriate to ponder its limits. In one of the early manifestations of Regan's possession, the ancient world of the demon comes face to face with modern science. Regan confronts an astronaut at her mother's party and predicts his death. Her symptoms defy scientific explanation. Like the church, medical science has its costumes, dogmas and ceremonies (the numerous tests on Regan are shown in gut-wrenching detail). Unlike the church, it cannot help. The audience is offered a choice of world views: the assumption of the doctors that human thought is nothing more than a collection of electrical impulses, and the assumption of the priests that human beings are pawns in a cosmic struggle between good and evil. Both have unsettling implications.

Although Blatty's screenplay for *The Exorcist* followed his novel faithfully, the film added a new level of social comment. In the novel the principal characters

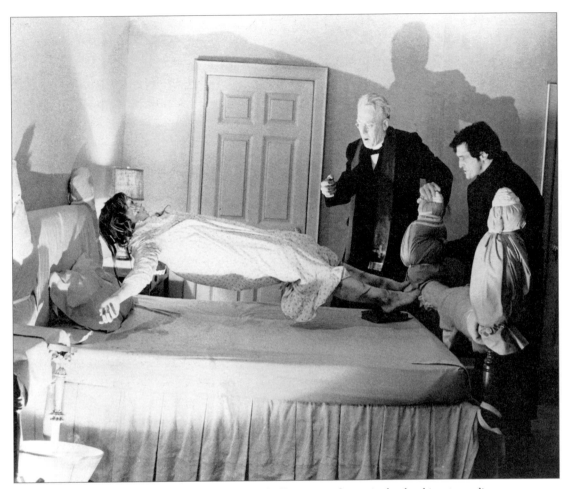

The heavy make-up and visual and aural effects proved genuinely shocking to audiences. Linda Blair as Regan and Max von Sydow as Merrin with Jason Miller as Damien Karras, a Jesuit priest. (Warner Bros/Courtesy Kobal)

are straining to be warm and supportive. In an unfilmed sub-plot a kindly Jewish police officer, helps the servant, Karl, by arranging rehabilitation for his drug addict daughter. The novel is resolved with the cop, Kinderman, and a surviving priest, Dyer, becoming friends. They go off into the sunset chatting about films and quoting the end of *Casablanca*. It is 'the start of a beautiful friendship' between church and state. The film is bleaker. The characters all live and remain in a state of mutual alienation. By failing to deliver emotional resolution, the film successfully keeps viewers ill at ease. The city in which the characters live is introduced as an emotional desert: the camera first cuts to Georgetown from the prologue amid desert ruins in Iraq, as sounds of dogs fighting and an evil screeching blend into what is clearly meant to be their modern equivalent, the traffic noise of a contemporary American city.

The visual realisation of the Iraqi prologue also carried political implications, with multiple allusions to an established lexicon of American filmic and news images. At the climax of the Iraqi sequence, Merrin confronts a statue of the demon like a western gun-slinger amid the ruins of Nineveh. The demon, identified in the novel as Pazuzu, was a genuine character in Mesopotamian mythology; a demon associated with the wind. As the enemy of the bringer of sickness, Lamashtu, the image of Pazuzu was a popular protective amulet for childbirth, but the choice of the image in the 1970s had other resonance. The demon's fist is raised in something that looks oddly reminiscent of the Black Power salute, the era's abiding symbol of African-American rage, made world famous when used by two Black American athletes on a medal rostrum at the Mexico Olympics of 1968. The Iraqi prologue was already firmly rooted in the tradition of American horror movies. The archaeological dig recalls stories of Egyptian curses from the 1920s and the films they inspired. Meanwhile, the trenches cut by the archaeologists suggest the battlefields of the First World War and hence an enduring struggle. Yet, above all, the prologue anticipates a phobia that would become a fixed part of American popular culture from the 1970s onwards: fear of the Arab world.

It was in keeping with the American isolationist mistrust of things foreign, that the inner evil in *The Exorcist* has a foreign source. It is doubly significant that the origin of this evil is located in the Arab world. The film heightens this. Iraq is represented as a place in which time has stood still. This is made explicit when the clock in an official's office stops. Iraqi sights and sounds (frenetic digging and hammering, dark passages, the alien glances of Iraqi people, the Islamic call to prayer) are used to unnerve the audience. Such attitudes did not auger well for Arab-American understanding. The release of *The Exorcist* coincided with a new low in US relations with that region. With Middle Eastern oil producers doubling prices overnight on 23 December 1973, it was already clear that more than one demon could be released from the sands of Arabia.

Although Blatty's name appeared in three places on the poster, the film's success owed much to the artistry of its director, William Friedkin. *The Exorcist* is an astonishing piece of cinematic manipulation. Friedkin's camera technique, restrained by the structure of the house, and borrowing from documentary, builds the sense that we are in a real space, surrounded by real sound. In this context, the eruption of the demonic voice is all the more terrifying. The film is more subtle than the novel. Friedkin allows its message to form in the mind of the viewer, paring down his dialogue to such an extent that only the audience is aware of the full narrative. Yet Friedkin's accomplishment undermined Blatty's political project. The shock of the visceral experience of viewing *The Exorcist* obscured all else. Vincent Canby of the *New York Times* reported that large sections of the youth audience talked and smoked during the establishing sequences and only tuned in to the movie during the possession. Such audiences could hardly be identifying with the forces of order in the film. Despite Blatty's intent, it would seem that for many who watched *The Exorcist*, this was horror functioning in exactly the same way as it had in the era of Boris Karloff, recycling the fears of the age as escapist entertainment and captivating audiences with the anarchic license given to the monster.

The Exorcist did not drive America back to the church, but it did drive America back to the horror film. Its success ushered in a new golden age of American 'A Movie' horror: directors like John Carpenter and Wes Craven came forward to revitalise the genre, and were glad to use the license won for them by the excesses of Blatty's film. The legacy of *The Exorcist* was a rich and frequently subversive vein of horror cinema. Themes like social fragmentation and the questioning of family relationships, which had surfaced in earlier films like *Rosemary's Baby* (1968) or *Night of the Living Dead* (1968) and bloomed in *The Exorcist*, remained current. Evil children did especially well. In Richard Donner's *The Omen* (1976), Satan's son reeks havoc in the life of his adopted father, an unsuspecting American diplomat. In the wake of Watergate it was not that surprising that by the end of the movie the evil child had moved in to the White House.

Some directors used the genre for social satire. In George Romero's *Dawn of the Dead* (1979), Americans resurrected as flesh-eating zombies still feel compelled to congregate at the shopping mall and go through the motions of consumerism. Others like David Cronenberg in *Videodrome* (1982) suggested new ways of thinking about the human body and its relationship with technology. The genre continued to trade on fears of the female body, and frequently punished characters who indulged in such things as pre-marital sex or who smoked dope, yet it also opened up the imagination. The most formulaic horror films became a branch of American camp, showing audiences how personal identity could be constructed and a range of possibilities for alternative behaviour.

As a key player in the evolution of the genre, *The Exorcist* retains cult status. Warner's marked its twenty-fifth anniversary in 1998 by releasing a new version with a digitally re-mastered sound track. Given this legacy, Blatty's original political intent for his story now seems as curious a relic as the stone head of Pazuzu. Rather than exposing or even exorcising the 'enemy within', *The Exorcist* and the films it inspired became 'enemies within' in their own right. There was clearly more mileage to be derived by American conservatives in denouncing such films than in making them. 'Evil against evil' might have worked in ancient Iraq, but it did not work in 1970s America.

FURTHER READING

PART ONE

Wings

Brownlow, Kevin, *The Parade's Gone By . . .*, Columbus Books, 1989
Farmer, James, *Celluloid Wings*, Blue Ridge Books, 1984
Paris, Michael, *From the Wright Brothers to 'Top Gun': Aviation, Nationalism and Popular Cinema*, Manchester University Press, 1995
—— (ed.), *The First World War and Popular Cinema, 1914 to the Present*, Edinburgh University Press, 2000
Pendo, Stephen, *Aviation in Cinema*, Scarecrow Press, 1985.
Pisano, Dominick, *Thomas Dietz, Legend, Memory and the Great War in the Air*, The Smithsonian Institution, 1992

All Quiet on the Western Front

Cecil, Hugh, and Peter H. Liddle (eds), *Film and the First World War Experienced*, Leo Cooper, 1996
Chambers, John, 'All Quiet on the Western Front (US, 1930): The Anti-war Film and the Images of Modern War', pp. 13–30, in John Whiteclay Chambers II and David Culbert (eds), *World War II, Film and History*, Oxford University Press, 1996
Dibbets, Karel, and Bert Hogenkamp (eds), *Film and the First World War*, Amsterdam University Press, 1995
Eksteins, Modris, *Rites of Spring: The Great War and the Birth of the Modern Age*, Anchor Books, 1990
Fussell, Paul, *The Great War and Modern Memory*, Oxford University Press, 1975
Kelly, Andrew, *Filming* All Quiet on the Western Front: *'brutal cutting, stupid censors, bigoted politicos'*, I.B. Tauris, 1998
Wohl, Robert, *The Generation of 1914*, Harvard University Press, 1979

Fires Were Started

Aldgate, Anthony, and Jeffrey Richards (eds), *Britain Can Take It: The British Cinema in the Second World War*, Edinburgh University Press, second edition 1994
Calder, Angus, *The Myth of the Blitz*, Jonathan Cape, 1991
Hodgkinson, Anthony W., and Rodney E. Sheratsky, *Humphrey Jennings: More than a Maker of Films*, University Press of New England, 1982
Jackson, Kevin (ed.), *The Humphrey Jennings Film Reader*, Carcanet, 1993

Jennings, Mary-Lou, (ed), *Humphrey Jennings: Film-maker, Painter, Poet*, British Film Institute, 1981
Sansom, William, *Westminster at War*, Faber & Faber, 1947
Wassey, Michael, *Ordeal by Fire*, Secker & Warburg, 1941

The Green Berets

Adair, Gilbert, *Hollywood's Vietnam: From the Green Berets to Full Metal Jacket*, Heineman, 1987
Anderegg, Michael A. (ed.), *Inventing Vietnam: The War in Film and Television (Culture and the Moving Image)*, Temple University Press, 1991
Corrigan, Timothy, *A Cinema Without Walls: Movies and Culture After Vietnam*, Rutgers University Press, 1991
Dittmar, Linda, and Gene Michaud (eds), *From Hanoi to Hollywood: The Vietnam War in American Film*, Rutgers University Press, 1991
Karnow, Stanley, *Vietnam: A History*, Penguin Books, 1991

Star Wars

Baucom, Donald, *The Origins of SDI, 1944–1983*, University Press of Kansas, 1992
Erickson, Paul D., *Reagan Speaks: The Making of an American Myth*, New York University Press, 1985
Linenthal, Edward Tabor, *Symbolic Defence: The Cultural Significance of the Strategic Defence Initiative*, University of Illinois Press, 1989
Payne, Keith B., *Strategic Defence: 'Star Wars' in Perspective*, Hamilton, 1986
Pollock, Dale, *Sky Walking: The Life and Times of George Lucas*, Samuel French, 1990
Rogin, Michael, *Ronald Reagan, the Movie and Other Episodes in Political Demonology*, University of California Press, 1987
Ryan, Michael, and Douglas Kellner, *Camera Politica: The Politics and Ideology of Contemporary Hollywood Film*, Indiana University Press, 1988

PART TWO

The Great Way

Hosking, G., *A History of the Soviet Union*, Fontana, 1992
Roberts, Graham, *Forward Soviet, History and Non-fiction Film in the USSR*, I.B. Tauris, 1999
Shub, Esfir, *Zhizn moya kinematograf [My Life – the Cinema]*, Moscow, 1972
Taylor, R., *Film Propaganda*, I.B. Tauris, 1998
Taylor, R., and I. Christie (eds), *The Film Factory*, Routledge, 1992
Youngblood, D., *Soviet Cinema in the Silent Era*, University of Texas, 1991

Triumph of the Will

Grunberger, Richard, *The Twelve Year Reich: A Social History of Nazi Germany*, Penguin Books, 1984
Kershaw, Ian, *Hitler: 1889–1936, Hubris*, Allen Lane, 1998
Loiperdinger, Martin, and David Culbert, 'Leni Riefenstahl, the SA, and the Nazi Party Rally Films, Nuremberg 1933–34: Sieg des Glaubens and Triumph des Willens', *Historical Journal of Film, Radio and Television* 8 (1) 1988, pp. 3–38

Peukert, Detlev, *Inside Nazi Germany: Conformity, Opposition and Racism in Everyday Life*, Penguin Books, 1989

Riefenstahl, Leni, *A Memoir*, St Martin's Press, 1993

This Is the Army

Barrett, Mary Ellin, *Irving Berlin: A Daughter's Memoir*, Limelight, 1996

Bergreen, Laurence, *Thousands Cheer: The Life of Irving Berlin*, Viking, 1990

Doherty, Thomas, *Projections of War: Hollywood, American Culture, and World War II*, Columbia University Press, 1993

Furia, Philip, *Irving Berlin: A Life in Song*, Schirmer Books, 1998

Glancy, H. Mark, 'Warner Bros Film Grosses, 1921–51: the William Schaefer ledger', *Historical Journal of Film, Radio and Television* 15 (1) 1995, pp. 55–73, plus microfiche supplement

Koppes, Clayton R., and Gregory D. Black, *Hollywood Goes to War: How Politics, Profits and Propaganda Shaped World War II Movies*, University of California Press, 1994

Rubins, Josh, 'Genius without Tears', *New York Review of Books*, 16 June 1988, pp. 30–3

Shattuck, Kathryn, 'Veteran Broadway Troupe Celebrates "This is the Army"', *New York Times*, 9 June 1997, p. B2

Thomas, Tony, *The Films of Ronald Reagan*, Citadel Press, 1980

I Was a Communist for the FBI

Caute, David, *The Great Fear: The Anti Communist Purge under Truman and Eisenhower*, Secker & Warburg, 1978

Fried, Richard, *Nightmare in Red: the McCarthy Era in Perspective*, Oxford University Press, 1990

Haynes, John Earl, *Red Scare vs. Red Menace: American Communism and Anti-Communism in the Cold War Era*, Ivan R. Dee, 1996

——, and Harvey Klehr, *Venona: Decoding Soviet Espionage in America*, Yale University Press, 1999

Herman, Arthur, *Joseph McCarthy: Re-examining the Life and Legacy of America's Most Hated Senator*, Free Press, 2000

Inglis, Fred, *The Cruel Peace: Everyday Life and the Cold War*, Basic Books, 1991

Jenkins, Philip, *Cold War at Home: The Red Scare in Pennsylvania, 1945–1960*, University of North Carolina Press, 1999

Sawatsky, John, *Gouzenko: the Untold Story*, Macmillan of Canada, 1984

Whitfield, Stephen J., *The Culture of the Cold War*, Johns Hopkins University Press, second edition 1996

PART THREE

Citizen Kane

Bordwell, David, and Kirsten Thompson, *Film Art: an Introduction*, McGraw-Hill, third edition 1990

Carringer, Robert, *The Making of Citizen Kane*, John Murray, 1985

Gottestman, Ronald, (ed.), *Focus on Citizen Kane*, Prentice Hall, 1971

Kael, Pauline, Herman J. Mankiewicz and Orson Welles, *The Citizen Kane Book*, (includes 'Raising Kane' by Pauline Kael and 'The Shooting Script' by Mankiewicz and Welles), Limelight Editions, Books on the Performing Arts, 1984

On the Waterfront

Anderson, Lindsay, 'The Last Sequence of On the Waterfront', *Sight & Sound*, 24, 3, 1995, pp. 127–30

Kazan, Elia, *A Life*, Da Capo Press, 1997

Michaels, Lloyd, *Elia Kazan, a Guide to References and Resources*, G.K. Hall & Co, 1985

Navasky, Victor, *Naming Names*, Viking, 1980

Neve, Brian, *Film and Politics in America, A Social Tradition*, Routledge, 1992

Rapf, Joanna E., (ed.), *Cambridge University Handbook on On the Waterfront*, Cambridge University Press, forthcoming 2001

Schulberg, Budd, *On the Waterfront, a Screenplay*, Southern Illinois University Press, 1980

Young, Jeff (ed.), *Kazan on Kazan*, Faber & Faber, 1999

Un americano a Roma

Bonandella, Peter, *Italian Cinema*, Roundhouse Publishing, 1999

Ginsborg, Paul, *A History of Contemporary Italy*, Penguin, 1990

Gundle, Stephen, *Between Hollywood and Moscow. The Italian Communists and the Challenge of Mass Culture*, University of North Carolina Press, 2000

Liehm, Mire, *Passion and Defiance. Film in Italy from 1942 to the Present*, University of California Press, 1984

I'm All Right Jack

Burton, Alan, et al, *The Family Way, The Boulting Brothers and British Film Culture*, Flick Books, 2000

Gray, Spalding, *Swimming to Cambodia*, Pan 1987

Lewis, Roger, *The Life and Death of Peter Sellers*, Century, 1994

Richards, Jeffrey, and Anthony Aldgate, *Best of British, Cinema and Society from 1930 to the Present*, I.B. Tauris, 1999

Stead, Peter, *Film and the Working Class: The Feature Film in British and American Society*, Routledge, 1989

Walker, Alexander, *Peter Sellers, The Authorised Biography*, Weidenfeld & Nicolson, 1981

La Dolce Vita

Baxter, John, *Fellini*, Fourth Estate, 1993

Boorstin, Daniel, *The Image: A Guide to Pseudo-Events in America*, Penguin, 1962

Buss, Robin, *Italian Films*, Batsford, 1989

Kezich, Tullion, *Il dolce cinema: Fellini e glialtri*, Bompiani, 1960

Liehm, Mira, *Passion and Defiance: Film in Italy from 1942 to the Present*, University of California Press, 1984

Alfie

Aldgate, Anthony, *Censorship and the Permissive Society. British Cinema and Theatre 1955–1965*, Clarendon Press, 1995

——, and Jeffrey Richards, *Best of British, Cinema and Society from 1930 to the Present*, I.B. Tauris, 1999

Haste, Cate, *The Rules of Desire: Sex in Britain, World War I to the Present*, Pimlico, 1992

Marwick, Arthur, *The Sixties*, Oxford University Press, 1999

Phelps, Guy, *Film Censorship*, Victor Gollancz, 1975
Robertson, James C., *The Hidden Cinema: British Film Censorship in Action, 1913–72*, Routledge, 1989
Trevelyan, John, *What the Censor Saw*, Michael Joseph, 1973

Part Four

Madonna of the Seven Moons

Cook, P. (ed.), *Gainsborough Pictures*, Cassell, 1997
Gledhill, C., and G. Swanson (eds), *Nationalising Femininity: Culture, Sexuality and British Cinema in the Second World War*, Manchester University Press, 1996
Harper, Sue, *Picturing the Past: the Rise and Fall of the British Costume Film*, British Film Institute, 1994
——, *Mad, Bad and Dangerous to Know: Women in British Cinema*, Cassell, 2000
Murphy, R., (ed.), *The British Cinema Book*, British Film Institute, 1997

La Belle et la Bête

Cocteau, Jean, *'La Belle et la Bête'/'Beauty and the Beast', Scenario and Dialogues*, edited and annotated by Robert M. Hammond, New York University Press, 1970
Hayward, Susan, 'Cocteau's Belle is not that Bête', in Susan Hayward and Ginette Vincendeau, *French Film: Texts and Contexts*, Routledge, 1990
Rearick, Charles, *The French in Love and War*, Yale University Press, 1997
Rigby, Brian, *Popular Culture in Modern France: A Study of Cultural Discourse*, Routledge, 1991

The Leopard

Bacon, Henry, *Visconti: Explorations of Beauty and Decay*, Cambridge University Press, 1998
Bondanella, Peter, *Italian Cinema: From Neorealism to the Present*, Ungar, 1990
De Giusti, Luciano, *I filmi di Luchino Visconti*, Gremose, 1985
Lagny, Maurice (ed.), *Visconti: classicisime e subversion*, Sorbonne Nouvelle, 1990

South Pacific

Garber, Marjorie, *Vested Interests: Cross-Dressing and Cultural Anxiety*, Routledge, 1992
Green, Stanley, *Encyclopedia of the Musical Film*, Oxford University Press, 1981
Grove Day, A., *James A. Michener*, Twayne Publications, 1964
Leibman, Nina C., *Living Room Lectures: The Fifties Family in Film and Television*, University of Texas Press, 1995
Michener, James, *Tales of the South Pacific*, Fawcett Publications, 1947
Vallance, Tom, *The American Musical*, A.S. Barnes, 1970

Indochine

Bernal, Martin, 'The Nghe-Tinh Soviet Movement 1930–1931', *Past & Present*, 92, August 1981, pp. 148–68
Duiker, William, *The Rise of Nationalism in Vietnam*, Cornell University Press, 1976
Jeancolas, Jean-Pierre, review of *Indochine*, in *Positif*, no. 375–6, May 1992, pp. 89–91

Smith, Ralph, 'The Development of Opposition to French Rule in Southern Vietnam, 1880–1940', *Past & Present*, 54, February 1972, pp. 94–129

The Exorcist

Jancovich, Mark, *American Horror from 1951 to the Present*, Keele University Press/ British Association for American Studies, 1994
Kermode, Mark, *The Exorcist*, British Film Institute, second edition 1999
Skal, David J., *The Monster Show: A Cultural History of Horror*, Plexus, 1993

GENERAL TEXTS

Aldgate, Anthony, and Jeffrey Richards (eds), *Britain Can Take It*, Edinburgh University Press, second edition 1994
Carnes, Mark (ed.), *Past Imperfect: History According to the Movies*, Henry Holt, 1995
Ellwood, David, and Rob Croes (eds), *Hollywood in Europe: Experiences of a Cultural Hegemony*, Amsterdam University Press, 1994
Elsaesser, Thomas, *New German Cinema*, London, 1986
Hayward, Susan, *French National Cinema*, Routledge, 1993
Marwick, Arthur, *Class: Image and Reality in Britain, France and the USA since 1930*, Collins, 1980
Puttnam, David, *The Undeclared War: The Struggle for the Control of the World's Film Industry*, HarperCollins, 1997
Reeves, Nicholas, *The Power of Film Propaganda: Myth or Reality*, Cassell, 1999
Rosenstone, Robert (ed.), *Revisioning History: Film and the Construction of a New Past*, Princeton University Press, 1995
Sklar, Robert, *Movie Made America*, New York, second edition 1996
Sorlin, Pierre, *European Cinemas, European Societies 1939–1990*, Routledge, 1991
Stead, Peter, *Film and the Working Class*, Routledge, 1989
Street, Sarah, *British National Cinema*, Routledge, 1997
Taylor, Philip, *British Propaganda in the 20th Century: Selling Democracy*, Edinburgh University Press, 1999
Whiteclay Chambers II, John, and David Culbert (eds), *World War I, Film and History*, Oxford University Press, 1996

INDEX